Mike Oakley was born and brought up in Dorset before moving to Bristol in the mid 1960s, where he worked in town and country planning until retiring in 1996. In recent years he has developed a keen interest in the history and role of railway stations and halts, particularly in the West Country. As a result, he has built up a substantial library of photographs of Wiltshire's stations, a selection of which are reproduced in this book. He is also the author of *Bristol Suburban* (1990), an illustrated account of the city's stations and halts, 'Discover Dorset' *Railway Stations* (2001), *Somerset Railway Stations* (2002) and *Gloucestershire Railway Stations* (2003).

Following page
Devizes. A fine interior view in the early 1890s of staff posing for the camera beneath the overall roof. Note the display of enamel advertisements on the station walls.

INTERNATIONAL TEA
GARTON'S
ALES
& STOUTS
LONDON

WILTSHIRE RAILWAY STATIONS

Mike Oakley

THE DOVECOTE PRESS

Calne. GWR engine No. 853 outside Calne signal box in about 1900.

First published in 2004 by The Dovecote Press Ltd
Stanbridge, Wimborne, Dorset BH21 4JD

ISBN 1 904349 33 1

Printed and bound by KHL Printing, Singapore

All papers used by The Dovecote Press are natural, recyclable products made
from wood grown in sustainable, well-managed forests.

A CIP catalogue record for this book is available
from the British Library

1 3 5 7 9 8 6 4 2

CONTENTS

Swindon GWR. An engraving of the station looking west in 1852. Parts of the building on the right on the island platform are still in use today.

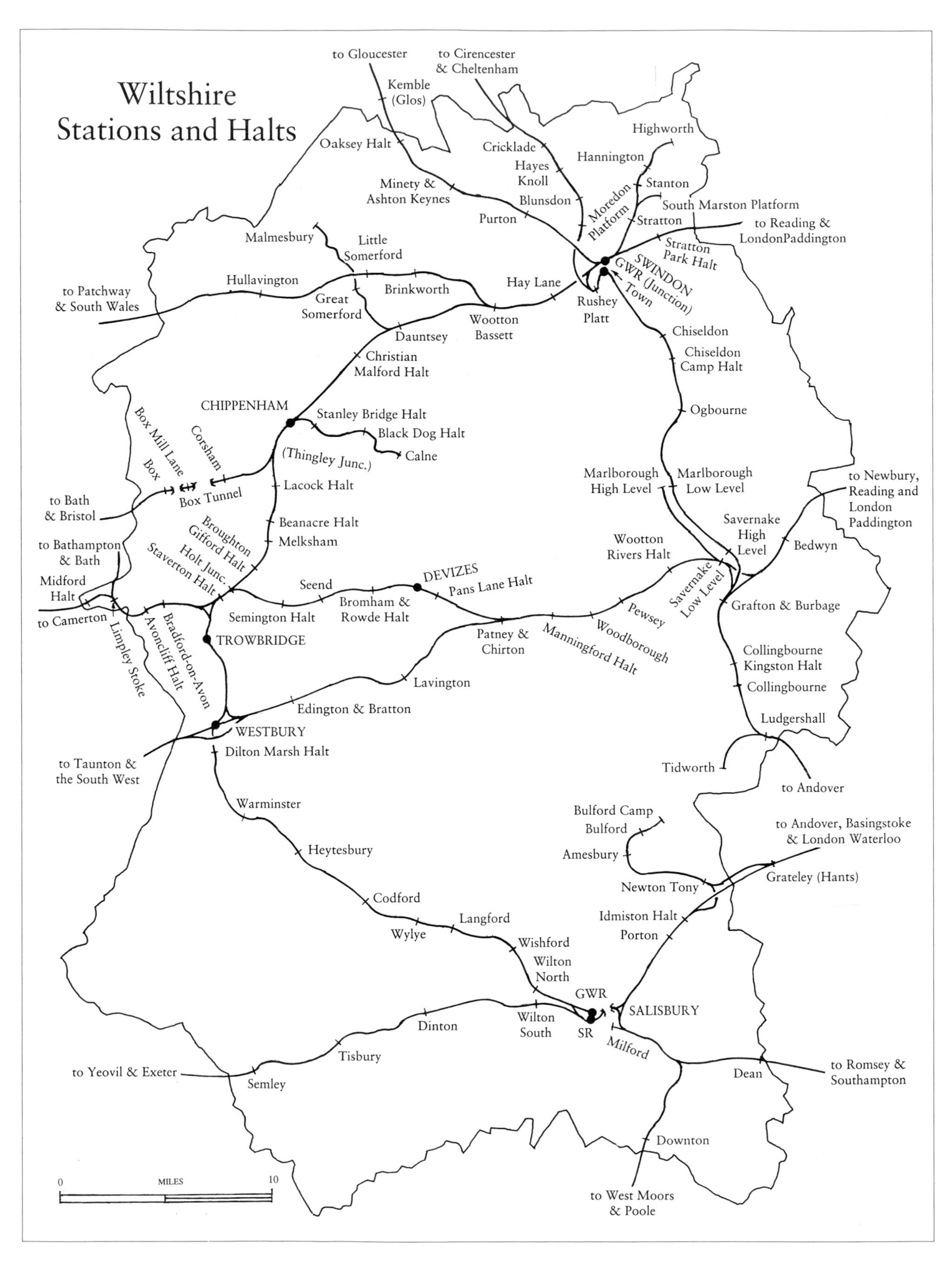
Wiltshire
Stations and Halts
to Gloucester
to Cirencester
& Cheltenham
Kemble
(Glos)
Oaksey Halt
Cricklade
Hayes
Knoll
Highworth
Hannington
Stanton
Minety &
Ashton Keynes
Blunsdon
Moredon
Platform
South Marston Platform
Purton
Stratton
to Reading &
LondonPaddington
Malmesbury
Little
Somerford
Stratton
Park Halt
SWINDON
GWR (Junction)
Town
Hullavington
Brinkworth
Hay Lane
Rushey
Platt
to Patchway
& South Wales
Great
Somerford
Wootton
Bassett
Dauntsey
Chiseldon
Christian
Malford Halt
Chiseldon
Camp Halt
CHIPPENHAM
Ogbourne
Stanley Bridge Halt
Black Dog Halt
Box Mill Lane
Corsham
Calne
(Thingley Junc.)
Box
Marlborough
High Level
Marlborough
Low Level
to Newbury,
Reading and
London
Paddington
Lacock Halt
to Bath
& Bristol
Box Tunnel
Beanacre Halt
Savernake
High
Level
Broughton
Gifford Halt
Wootton
Rivers Halt
Melksham
Bedwyn
to Bathampton
& Bath
Holt Junc.
Staverton Halt
DEVIZES
Midford
Halt
Seend
Pans Lane Halt
Savernake
Low Level
Bromham &
Rowde Halt
Grafton & Burbage
to Camerton
Semington Halt
Pewsey
Bradford-on-Avon
Avoncliff Halt
Limpley Stoke
TROWBRIDGE
Patney &
Chirton
Manningford Halt
Woodborough
Collingbourne
Kingston Halt
Lavington
Collingbourne
Edington & Bratton
Ludgershall
WESTBURY
Dilton Marsh Halt
to Taunton &
the South West
Tidworth
to Andover
Warminster
Bulford Camp
Bulford
to Andover, Basingstoke
& London Waterloo
Heytesbury
Amesbury
Newton Tony
Grateley (Hants)
Codford
Idmiston Halt
Langford
Porton
Wylye
Wishford
Wilton
North
GWR
SALISBURY
Dinton
Wilton
South
SR
Milford
Tisbury
to Romsey &
Southampton
Dean
to Yeovil & Exeter
Semley
Downton
0
MILES
10
to West Moors
& Poole

INTRODUCTION

Wiltshire is a county rich in railway history. Brunel's broad gauge Great Western Railway – known affectionately as God's Wonderful Railway – traversed the county on route from London to the West Country. The broad gauge tracks are long gone, but the bridges and tunnels still bear testimony to his engineering skills. The 'railway town' of Swindon gave employment (and housing and welfare benefits) to thousands as huge workshops manufactured and serviced an ever increasing rolling stock. To the south of the county the cathedral city of Salisbury became a railway hub as the London & South Western Railway developed its rival route to the west.

These topics and many more are well documented elsewhere, but scant attention has been given to the stations and halts – the departure points and destinations of the passengers and goods transported by the railways. This book seeks to chronicle the development and architectural style of these stations. Was the site, for instance, chosen for proximity to the town or village which it served, at the junction of two railway lines, or was it at the whim of a local landowner who gave consent for a railway to pass through his land providing he had his own personal facilities at the station?

Wiltshire is largely an agricultural county and many stations were important not only for passenger traffic, but also for the export of milk and livestock, as well as the import of animal feeds, building materials, coal etc. However, in contrast with many rural counties, in Wiltshire there was another factor which greatly influenced the development of the railway network, gave impetus to the development of new lines and significantly increased the usage by passengers and goods. This factor was the establishment of military camps on Salisbury Plain from the early 1900s and the construction of branch lines to transport personnel and equipment, especially during the First and Second World Wars.

All ninety two stations or halts that at some time existed in Wiltshire are included. Every station has been researched, mainly from previously published sources, and the site personally visited within the period October 2003 to April 2004. The current situation is described. The accounts of the stations and halts are in alphabetical order; in a few instances an introduction is given where the local railway history is particularly complicated (eg Salisbury). Where the term 'Halt' is included in the title it can be assumed that no facilities for the handling of goods were ever provided. Where the terms 'up' and 'down' platform are used they normally refer to the platform used for travel towards, or away, from London respectively. Where this is not clear further indication is provided by reference to the nearest town along the line.

The photographs reproduced are drawn from a collection assembled over recent years. They have been selected primarily to illustrate significant and interesting features of the station or halt; thus only a few include engines or trains as their presence can obscure details of the station buildings!

THE RAIL NETWORK
1840-2004

The railway era came to Wiltshire when, on 17th December 1840, the Great Western Railway (GWR) opened a section of its London to Bristol line from Faringdon Road in Oxfordshire to Hay Lane, west of Swindon. (No station was provided at Swindon itself at this time, this opened in July 1842.) Six months later on 31st May 1841 the line was extended as far as Chippenham. The final section through Box tunnel to Bath opened a month later on 30th June when it joined the already operating Bath to Bristol line.

Simultaneous with the commencement of services on the Hay Lane to Chippenham line, the Swindon Junction to Kemble section of the Cheltenham & Great Western Union Railway opened together with a short branch to Cirencester. Further developments followed in the west of the county, initially under the auspices of the Wilts, Somerset & Weymouth

Railway (WS&WR), and then the GWR after it absorbed the WS&WR in March 1850. In 1845 the WS&WR received parliamentary approval for the construction of a line south from Thingley Junction, on the GWR west of Chippenham, to Westbury with branches in Wiltshire to Bradford-on-Avon, Devizes and Salisbury. The Thingley Junction to Westbury line opened on 5th September 1848; an extension on to Frome in Somerset followed on 7th October 1850. The line to Salisbury opened in two stages: as far as Warminster on 9th September 1851 and on to Salisbury (Fisherton) on 30th June 1856, the second railway to reach the cathedral city.

Problems arose in the provision of the proposed branch to Bradford-on-Avon but this town eventually joined the county's rail network with the opening of a through line from Bathampton Junction on the GWR Chippenham to Bath line to Bradford South Junction on the Chippenham to Westbury line on 2nd February 1857. The third branch, originally authorised in 1845, was opened twelve years later on 1st July 1857 from Holt Junction on the Chippenham to Westbury line to the market town of Devizes.

Some ten years earlier significant developments took place in south east Wiltshire when Salisbury joined the rail network with the opening, in early 1847, of the Bishopstoke (Eastleigh) to Salisbury (Milford) branch from the London & South Western Railway (LSWR) main line to Southampton. Ten years later, in 1857, the Andover to Salisbury section of the LSWR new route to the West Country opened, terminating initially at the 1847 Milford station. Two years later, on 2nd May 1859, the LSWR opened its new station at Fisherton immediately south of the earlier 1856 GWR terminus. The opening of the new station coincided with the commencement of services on the line from Salisbury to Yeovil; from that date the original 1847 Salisbury Milford station closed and all LSWR services were concentrated on the new Fisherton station. (For a detailed account of the development of rail services/stations in the Salisbury area, see the introduction to Salisbury and the accompanying plan later in this book.)

In the early 1860s the Berks & Hants Extension Railway (B&HER) developed a further route east-west across the centre of Wiltshire. The original Berks & Hants Railway opened from Reading to Hungerford on 21st December 1847. The Kennet Valley line of the Berks & Hants Extension Railway from Hungerford to Devizes opened fifteen years later on 11th November 1862, this changing Devizes from its original terminus status to a through station. The title of the B&HER was rather inappropriate in that it never entered Hampshire and ran only for two miles in Berkshire! Wiltshire was the main county served and the new line particularly assisted the development of the Vale of Pewsey (see Devizes text).

Towards the end of the nineteenth century the GWR decided to develop a new direct line to the West Country to supplement that via its original Swindon and Bristol line. This was to be achieved both by the use of sections of existing lines and construction of two sections of 'cut off' line. The first of these opened in 1900 with the commencement of services on what was then known as the Stert Valley line, running from west of Pewsey on the Hungerford to Devizes line to Westbury. This new line opened for goods traffic on 29th July and to passengers on 1st October 1900. The second cut off line, which completed the new southern GWR route opened in 1906 from Castle Cary to Cogload Junction, near Taunton.

The final major through route in Wiltshire, this time from north to south, developed in the 1880s from Cheltenham and Cirencester in Gloucestershire to Andover in Hampshire via Swindon and Marlborough. This new line opened in stages and under the auspices of different companies. The Swindon Town to Marlborough section of the Swindon, Marlborough & Andover Railway (SMAR) opened on 27th July 1881; this was closely followed by the Rushey Platt to Swindon Town (6th February 1882) and the Grafton – Ludgershall – Andover (1st May 1882) sections of SMAR. Through services between Marlborough and Grafton were delayed until February 1883 because of problems with the use by SMAR services of the GWR Marlborough branch and a section of the Berks & Hants line east of Savernake.

Later that year the Rushey Platt to Cricklade and Cirencester section of the Swindon & Cheltenham Extension Railway (S&CER) opened to goods and passenger services. Services on to Cheltenham commenced in 1891. The SMAR and S&CER merged to become the Midland & South Western Junction Railway (M&SWJR) in 1884. Fourteen years later the Marlborough & Grafton Railway (M&GR) opened on 26th June 1898; the north-south M&SWJR trains no longer were required to run on the GWR lines between Marlborough and Grafton, an operation that had been often fraught with difficulties. The M&GR was formally vested in the M&SWJR in 1899. (For further detailed text and a plan of these complicated railway developments in the Marlborough and Savernake area see the introductory text to Marlborough later in this book.)

The Marlborough branch was one of a number of such branches developed over the years to serve towns not served by the main rail network. Another important feature was the construction of lines to serve the needs of the armed forces following the development of large areas of Salisbury Plain for military purposes from 1899 on. The GWR Marlborough branch, noted above, opened on 14th April 1864; this was six months after the commencement of services on the Chippenham to Calne branch in 1863. Also developed from the main GWR London – Swindon – Bristol line were the Malmesbury branch from Dauntsey (opening December 1877) and the Highworth branch (opening May 1883).

In the south east of Wiltshire the Salisbury & Dorset Junction Railway opened in December 1866, linking the LSWR Eastleigh/Romsey to Salisbury line at Alderbury Junction to the LSWR Southampton to Dorchester line at West Moors. Two other lines in this part of the county were constructed specifically in response to increased military activity: the Amesbury & Military Camp Light Railway opened to Amesbury in 1902 and on to Bulford in 1906. This line branched north from the LSWR line from Andover to Salisbury near Newton Tony. A branch to Tidworth serving the new garrison opened to the public from Ludgershall on the M&SWJR in 1902. It had opened for military traffic a year earlier.

The last major addition to the Wiltshire rail network came in the north west of the county with the opening in 1903 of the Bristol and South Wales Direct Railway (the Badminton line) leaving the original GWR London to Bath and Bristol line at Wootton Bassett. Running through the Cotswolds, it linked to the Bristol and South Wales line at Patchway, north of Bristol. It provided a new direct route to the Severn Tunnel and South Wales and this greatly relieved congestion on the Chippenham – Bath – Bristol line. Passenger and goods traffic between London and South Wales transferred to the Badminton line. Thirty years after the opening of this cut off the Malmesbury branch was shortened and linked to the Badminton line at Little Somerford in 1933. The section of the original branch from Dauntsey to Little Somerford closed.

The final small piece in Wiltshire's rail network was a short section of the Camerton (Somerset) to Limpley Stoke line which linked to the Bath – Trowbridge – Westbury line. This opened in May 1910. However its life was short as, after temporary closures during the First World War, it closed to passengers in September 1925. This was the first of a whole series of closures of lines in Wiltshire. The principal closures (dates refer to closures to passenger traffic) were: Marlborough branch – 6th March 1933; Malmesbury branch – 10th September 1951; Amesbury and Bulford branch – 30th June 1952; Highworth branch – 2nd March 1953; Tidworth branch – 19th September 1955; Cirencester (Gloucestershire)-Swindon-Marlborough-Ludgershall-Andover (Hants) – 11th September 1961; Alderbury Junction to West Moors – 4th May 1964; Calne branch – 20th September 1965 and finally the line from Holt Junction to Patney & Chirton via Devizes – 18th April 1966.

In 1984, following the formation of the Swindon & Cricklade Railway, Blunsdon station reopened on the former Swindon Town to Cirencester section of the M&SWJR. The line has now been reopened north as far as a new station at Hayes Knoll.

THE STATIONS AND HALTS

AMESBURY

OPENED: Goods - 26th April 1902, passengers - 2nd June 1902 (as the initial terminus of the Amesbury & Military Camp Light Railway).
CLOSED: Passengers - 30th June 1952.
Goods - 4th March 1963.

With the decision of the War Office to develop military sites on Salisbury Plain, the London & South Western Railway (LSWR) applied for a Light Railway Order to build what was called the Amesbury & Military Camp Light Railway from Grateley (Hants), on the Andover to Salisbury section of the LSWR, to Amesbury. Reducing legal costs was the principal reason for authority being sought under a Light Railway Order as economies in signalling and track specification were allowed (though in this case not used). Powers were granted on 28th September 1898, the land was purchased and the contract was let to Messrs J.T. Firbank.

Unlike many light railways, the line included major engineering works with embankments varying from 10 ft to 35 ft high and cuttings as deep as 38 ft. From Grateley, some two miles east of the Wiltshire/ Hampshire border, the single track Amesbury branch ran south west for two miles parallel to the main LSWR up line before turning north west to the first station, Newton Tony. At Grateley the branch trains used a new bay platform constructed behind the main up platform. The Amesbury line opened to military traffic on 1st October 1901, to goods traffic on 26th April 1902 and to passengers on 2nd June 1902, the first train of the day apparently bringing the morning papers with news that the South African War was over!

A further Light Railway Order of 1903 authorised an extension of the line north east to recently built military camps at Bulford and Sling. This extension

Amesbury. An early view looking north towards Bulford with the main building on the down platform (left) and a shelter on the island platform. A footbridge has not yet been erected.

was constructed, unusually for the LSWR, by its own workers rather than by outside contractors, and opened for passenger services to Bulford and Bulford Camp at the beginning of June 1906. Two years earlier additional construction took place at the point where the Amesbury line left the alignment of the LSWR south west of Grateley at what was called Newton Tony Junction. A new link was made under the down main line so that through running without reverse could take place between Amesbury and Salisbury (the original single track north east to Grateley was subsequently seldom used for passenger traffic). At the same time the branch line was doubled as far as Newton Tony. To facilitate the movement of heavy army traffic, the double track was extended as far as Bulford as from May 1909.

Sited in the north east of the town immediately south of what later became the A303, Amesbury station opened as the initial terminus of the line in 1902. Expansion took place following the opening of the extension to Bulford in 1906 and it became quite an impressive station with three platforms. The principal building with two chimneys, but no canopy, stood on the down (towards Bulford) platform on the west side of the line. Opposite was an island platform; along its inner face ran the up line whilst on the outer face was a loop line. A shelter, surmounted by an elliptical roofed canopy, stood for many years on the up side island. This had been dismantled by the early 1950s. An open footbridge linking the platforms north of the principal building and shelter was subsequently erected. In 1943 an extra 'temporary' shelter, built principally of scaffold poles, was erected to the north of the main building beyond the footbridge.

Amesbury. A later view south. The military sidings are behind the main building (right). The up side goods loop (left) has been reduced to a siding.

Amesbury. Soldiers of Princess Beatrice's Own Isle of Wight Rifles on the down platform in 1910.

Avoncliff Halt. Looking south in June 1960 from the aqueduct that carries the Kennet and Avon Canal over the railway and River Avon.

Military sidings and a long loading dock were sited on the down side behind the main building. These sidings were principally used for storing troop trains, and close to the buffers was a 5 ton capacity crane. Movements to and from the sidings were controlled from the 24 lever Amesbury signal box sited south of the station on the down side, close to where the military sidings linked with the down main line. This was reduced to a ground frame as from April 1935. Movements at the north end of the station were controlled from a ground frame hut. Prior to 1906 the ground frame had only 3 levers but this increased to 18 following development of the site and the extension to Bulford. This reduced to 10 levers after 1954. The station turntable was south of the station on the outside of the up loop line.

Road access to the station was via approach roads on both the up and down sides leading from the A303 to the north. That on the down side led into the main area of the military sidings; on its eastern side stood three pairs of railway cottages occupied by Amesbury railwaymen. Throughout its life Amesbury station was principally used by military personnel and freight. The principal NAAFI stores were at Amesbury and these generated considerable rail traffic carrying military catering provisions.

With decreased military activity after the Second World War, use of the station decreased for both passengers and freight. Passenger services were withdrawn on the whole Amesbury and Bulford line at the end of June 1952 but goods services lasted a further eleven years until March 1963. Today the whole station site has been redeveloped in the London Road Industrial Estate. The original cutting north of the station has been filled in and the principal remnants from the railway era are the three pairs of former railway cottages that continue in residential use. A small red building at the head of the former down side approach opposite the cottages also appears to be a former railway structure.

AVONCLIFF HALT

OPENED: 9th July 1906 (on the Bathampton Junction - Bradford-on-Avon line originally opened through this site in February 1857).

CLOSED: Remains open as a request stop for services on the Bristol - Westbury - Southampton/Weymouth lines).

Sited on the north side of the River Avon valley and east of the Avoncliff aqueduct on the Kennet and Avon Canal, the halt opened in July 1906 nearly fifty years after passenger services commenced on the

Bath to Westbury line. A letter sent by the GWR to the Board of Trade in June 1906 requested provisional sanction for a stopping place at Avoncliff for 'rail-motor cars'. This sanction was granted and the halt quickly erected. It was subsequently inspected by Colonel Yorke on behalf of the Board of Trade who reported, 'I have inspected the new Halte at Avoncliff on the Bradford branch of the GWR. The Halte comprises two platforms each 100 ft long, 7 ft wide and 14 inches above rail level. There are no shelters but the platforms are provided with lamps and name boards. The Halte is suitable only for, and should be used only, by special rail-motor cars fitted with folding steps'.

Subsequently shelters were provided behind each platform, with a forward roof extension which protected small sections of the platforms which were raised to the standard height. West of the halt on the up (towards Westbury) side, a siding served a small stone depot to which stone was delivered from a number of local quarries. This operated until about 1936. Traffic movements in and out of this siding were controlled by a small signal box on the down side opposite the siding entrance.

Today Avoncliff (the suffix was dropped from 5th May 1969) continues to serve local residents and visitors to the canal; it is a request stop for stopping services on the Bristol/Bath to Southampton/ Weymouth lines. In the 2003/2004 timetable fifteen services were scheduled to stop if requested on weekdays in the Westbury direction. Towards Bath fourteen services were so scheduled.

Only one shelter remains, that on the platform serving Bath bound passengers. The other shelter was demolished in the 1990 gales and has not been replaced. Access to the halt is via steps from the footpath over the adjacent Avoncliff aqueduct.

BEANACRE HALT

OPENED: 29th October 1905 (on the Thingley Junction - Westbury line originally opened through this site in September 1848).

CLOSED: 7th February 1955.

Sited to the north of Beanacre village and adjacent to a minor road from the A350 to Whitley, the halt was one of four halts built and opened by the GWR at, or shortly after, a steam rail-motor service commenced between Chippenham and Trowbridge via Melksham. Such services, designed to increase patronage on local trains, had been introduced some two years earlier by the GWR in the Stroud valley of Gloucestershire between Chalford and Stonehouse.

The halt opened in October 1905 some four weeks after the start of the rail-motor service. Low level two foot high platforms were installed and the height was never raised. A standard reference book on GWR Halts (K.Robertson) states, 'this was one of the few main line halts to retain its low platforms'. Broughton Gifford halt, south of Melksham, was another example. The use of the low level platform was eased by retractable steps on the rail-motors. Small wooden shelters with roofs sloping towards the tracks stood on both platforms; an oil lamp provided illumination at the south end of the up platform (towards Chippenham). Access to the halt, as was common on this line, was via sloping paths from an adjacent road bridge to the south. Three sidings were later provided on the up side (towards Chippenham) by the War Department immediately

Beanacre Halt. A view north in 1952. Note the low level platforms which remained throughout the life of the halt. The war-time pill box just visible at the far end of the up platform (left) still survives, but not the platforms.

south of the halt and road bridge. They were in place from January 1939 to March 1948.

Beanacre Halt closed in February 1955, some eleven years before local services were withdrawn on the line. Broughton Gifford Halt, south of Melksham, also closed at that time. Lacock and Staverton Halts, the other two halts on the line, remained open until the withdrawal of local passenger services in April 1966.

Today little trace of the halt can be seen. A pill box at the north end of the up platform remains but there is no trace of the platforms. Concrete posts can be seen alongside what was the alignment of the path to the up platform.

BEDWYN

OPENED: 11th November 1862 (with the opening of the Berks & Hants Extension Railway from Hungerford to Devizes).

CLOSED: Passengers - remains open as the terminus of local services on the line west from Newbury.
Goods - 7th September 1964.

Sited in the village of Great Bedwyn alongside the north west bank of the Kennet and Avon Canal, the station opened in November 1862 with the commencement of services on the Hungerford to Devizes broad gauge Berks & Hants Extension Railway. The company was absorbed by the GWR in 1882. Originally single track through the site, a loop was added in the mid 1860s. The line west from Bedwyn was doubled in 1899, the tracks having been converted earlier from broad to standard gauge.

The principal station building, with two chimneys and a small canopy, stood on the up platform, the side closest to Great Bedwyn village. Immediately to the west of this stone structure was a smaller brick building incorporating a goods store. Further west again an open cast iron gent's urinal stood for many years. Passengers on the down platform were at first served by a small wooden shelter with a roof sloping back from the platform. This was replaced in 1919 by a larger wooden shelter with an apex roof. No footbridge was provided and inter platform connection was via a road bridge at the west end of the station accessed by flights of steps from each platform.

A small goods yard with a 3 ton crane was sited on the up side east of the station; a trailing siding ran behind the up platform to a loading dock. Traffic movements at Bedwyn were controlled from a signal box just beyond the east end of the down platform. This 17 lever box was in use from 1897 to September 1978.

In the early days of the twentieth century the majority of trains calling at Bedwyn were running on the former Berks & Hants Extension line to Devizes rather than on the new direct route to the West Country via the Stert Valley cut off line which opened in 1900. In 1903 11,711 passenger tickets were issued, a number which had fallen to 8,745 by 1933. In 1928 ten staff were based at Bedwyn, the maximum number recorded. No doubt some of them lived in the eight railway cottages that were built in the 1870s north of the station.

After the Second World War Bedwyn continued for some years to be served by limited through trains; in July 1959 eight down trains stopped on Mondays to Fridays. However, from the early 1960s Bedwyn developed as a terminus station for stopping trains starting their journey at Paddington, Reading or Newbury. By 1966 ten of the fourteen trains per day serving Bedwyn terminated at the station. At that time the terminating trains used the former loading dock siding behind the east end of the up platform. Over the period 2nd November 1964 to 5th May 1969 the suffix 'halt' was added but then dropped.

In 1976 the situation changed when a new siding was laid west of the road bridge on the up side for the short-term storage of down trains terminating at Bedwyn. The return up trains from this time pulled out of this siding and picked up passengers at the main up platform. This working method continues today, the old bay platform having now been filled in and incorporated into an expanded car park. All trains now serving Bedwyn terminate and no service is provided for west bound passengers; indeed a notice at the station indicates that west-bound passengers from Bedwyn need to change trains at Newbury; that is an eastward movement before the journey west.

Today an excellent service is provided for east-bound passengers. In the 2003/2004 timetable there were on weekdays fifteen through trains to Paddington, the first leaving Bedwyn at 0558! A further five journeys to Paddington can be made with a change either at Newbury or Reading. With all this traffic, much of it by regular commuters to Reading and London, it is unfortunate that passengers on the up side are only served by a basic 'bus shelter', the original stone building having been demolished long ago. The 1919 wooden shelter still stands on the down platform but is clearly little used

Bedwyn. Looking east in the 1960s. All the original buildings on the up platform (left) remain. The 1919 wooden shelter stands on the down platform as it does today. A terminating DMU is in the former dock siding.

as passengers only arrive on this platform and quickly leave the station.

This excellent current service is, without doubt, better than it ever has been – in the easterly direction only of course! Freight traffic was never a major feature at Bedwyn though for a time a GWR lorry delivery service was based at the station. General goods services were withdrawn from Bedwyn some forty years ago in September 1964.

BLACK DOG HALT

OPENED: Private facility - 1874, formal public use - 15th September 1952 (on the GWR Calne Branch originally opened to goods on 29th October 1863 and to passengers on 3rd November 1863).
CLOSED: Passengers - 20th September 1965
Goods - 10th June 1963.

Without doubt one of the most unusual stations in Wiltshire was Black Dog Halt, one of the two intermediate stopping points on the Chippenham to Calne branch which opened in late 1863. When the Calne Railway Company was established in 1860 (see Calne text) the Marquis of Lansdowne, a major local landowner, purchased a quarter acre of land adjacent to the point where the proposed railway crossed the then turnpike road between Calne and Chippenham (later the A4). The objective was to develop rail facilities that could bring and despatch goods to and from his adjacent Bowood estate. In both 1864 and 1869 the Marquis requested that a siding should be constructed but it was not until April 1875 that a siding, built by the GWR, finally came into use on his site. It first appeared in the Railway's working timetable as from June 1875. In the period 1886 to 1900 a second short siding was also laid and was operative until September 1932.

A temporary platform was apparently provided on the branch line itself in April 1870 for use associated with the Bowood Fête; this was provided by the Calne Railway at a cost of £4 10 shillings. A permanent platform was constructed by the GWR during 1874; some 80 ft in length, it was sited on the west side of the branch line south of the rail bridge over the turnpike. The siding area with a loading platform was on the opposite side of the line. In the winter of 1876/77 the Marquis of Lansdowne erected a small building on the platform at a cost of £59 13 2d. Some twenty years later in 1895 an extension incorporating a booking office was added

Black Dog Halt. A view on 27th July 1961 some nine years after it became a public facility. The 1895 extension to the building is at the far end.

at the northern end of the original wooden building. Photographs clearly show this addition. The original section housed a waiting room and parcels office but no toilet was provided. At the same time records indicate that a corrugated iron lamp hut was erected beyond the southern end of the platform and an existing lamp hut was converted into a lock up in the siding area. An early signal cabin and signal were also removed. The principal access to the siding and station was via an approach road leading up from the turnpike (A4) east of the bridge; passengers arriving by road were then required to cross the line by foot-boards to the platform and shelter. However a separate pedestrian access left the road west of the bridge, this led straight to the rear of the platform. The availability of both these routes to the halt and siding were for some years indicated on a large notice close to the bridge. A quarter of a mile long cinder path linking the station and estate was kept in excellent condition by Bowood staff.

The halt opened as a private facility for use by the Lansdowne family and the Bowood estate; however, the Marquis had no objection if members of the public used it. Black Dog Halt did not appear in the public timetables however for nearly eighty years and no tickets were available to the halt. Tickets to Black Dog only became available after the private status ended in 1952. On 15th September Black Dog Halt formally became a public facility and a name-board was erected just before Christmas. Hitherto no such board had been in place and indeed way back in April 1898 the GWR had been refused permission by the Marquis to provide one!

At the outset the sidings at the halt were primarily used for goods traffic to and from the Bowood estate: seven or eight trucks of coal arrived per year, pit props were despatched and horses from the estate travelled to and from various events. Stables were in place for some years adjacent to the siding. Other landowners and farmers in the area also used the siding and records suggest that this gradually increased through the years. Occasionally the short siding was used for the loading or unloading of heavy road vehicles. There were times when the Black Dog sidings were full and the wagons had to be stored in the extensive sidings at Calne. During the First World War some of the outbuildings opposite the station were occupied by the military and a War Cabinet Meeting was apparently held in a carriage in the siding.

From its early days the activities at Black Dog were supervised by a station master. An impressive house bearing the family crest, was provided by the Marquis of Lansdowne; the station master occupied the house rent free. In addition the Marquis paid part of his wages and supplied four tons of coal per year. In return the GWR agreed not to appoint any station master without first obtaining agreement from the Marquis, who reserved the right to interview all staff serving at the halt. In 1898 the staff comprised the station master and a foreman but by March 1921 this had reduced to a station master

Black Dog Halt. The site on 25th January 2004 with a section of the old platform and a re-erected nameboard. The former station master's house (background), the former stables now in residential use (left) and a section of the loading platform (centre back) remain from the earlier era.

and porter. The post of station master was abolished in 1930 (with the agreement of the Marquis!), responsibility now resting with a porter. Douglas Lovelock took up the position; he discovered that a number of the station master's privileges were no longer available. He now rented the house for £10 per annum but the rates and repairs of the house were paid by the Bowood estate. No coal was provided however. He was also advised not to express political views when dealing with the nobility and that he must endeavour to avoid the local magistrates court when the Marquis of Lansdowne was the Chairman!

In 1950 the station house, with the family crest, was put up for sale together with several outbuildings and part of the station yard. Mr Lovelock purchased them, subsequently selling off some outbuildings which were then converted into a bungalow. As from 1st February 1960 Black Dog became an unstaffed halt; the one remaining siding continued to be available providing advance notice was given to the Calne station master. Closure to goods traffic came in June 1963, the last customer being a coal merchant; the siding being lifted at the beginning of November. Passenger services continued for a further two years until they were withdrawn from the whole branch as from September 1965. The station buildings remained until the branch line was lifted in 1967. When the contractors were instructed to demolish the buildings at Black Dog, Mr Lovelock was able to gain permission personally to take them down and remove stone work on the platform. Timber from the buildings and some of the stonework was preserved at his then home in Calne. The former rail over-bridge was removed in April 1968 and the A4 road widened and straightened.

Today the former impressive station house and converted stables continue in residential use, access being via the old station access road. The former track bed through the site is now part of the National Cycle Network and north of the station site the Network crosses the busy A4 on a spectacular new bridge, approximately on the alignment of the former rail bridge. A short section of the north end of Black Dog Halt platform has been cleared on which stands a notice 'Black Dog Halt'; the remainder of the platform is hidden beneath undergrowth. Opposite the platform and towards the house, the stone wall and edging of the former loading platform can clearly be seen.

BLUNSDON

OPENED: 1st September 1895 (on the Cirencester - Swindon Town section of the Midland & South Western Junction Railway originally opened through this site in 1883).

CLOSED: Passengers - 28th September 1924.
Goods - 1st August 1937.

REOPENED: - 8th April 1984 (as the headquarters of the Swindon & Cricklade Railway).

Sited some 2½ miles west of Blunsdon St Andrew on the north side of a minor road where it crosses the River Ray, the station opened in September 1895, some twelve years after services commenced on the Rushey Platt to Cirencester section of the Swindon & Cheltenham Extension Railway (S&CER). The 176 ft long platform with a small building stood on the west side of a single track section of the line. Lighting was by gas. One writer described the facility as 'no more than a ramshackle hut'.

A sharply curved siding with a capacity of nine wagons led west from the single line immediately south of the station platform. Access to this siding was controlled by a ground frame in a small wooden hut close to the road bridge. The curvature was so severe that locomotives were not allowed to use it, only short wheel base wagons being permitted. The primary goods traffic at Blundson was milk, though

Blunsdon. Looking north in 1935. Note the two level platform, the end nearest the camera higher to assist the loading of milk churns stored under the wooden frame over which tarpaulins were hung.

Blunsdon. Looking north in April 2004. A diesel is ready to push a train to Hayes Knoll on the Swindon & Cricklade Railway. The building has been renovated after previous use at Malmesbury.

substantial amounts of cattle cake, hay and straw were also handled. The predominance of milk was reflected in the erection in 1916 of a specific milk stage behind the south end of the platform. A basic wooden frame stood on this milk platform; in hot conditions tarpaulins could be hung over the frame to protect the churns from direct sunlight: over sixty 17 gallon churns of milk were often handled per day. A small staff hut also stood on the platform between the building and the milk stage. The siding was removed and the ground frame ceased to be used in 1937, some eighteen years after the ground frame hut had been renewed.

Passenger traffic at Blunsdon was always low: in 1913 passenger receipts were only £5! As from 1922 weekday passenger services ceased to call, after which Blunsdon was unusually served by only one passenger train per week, a southbound Sunday afternoon service, principally stopping for milk traffic. This too ceased as from September 1924. In contrast the receipts from goods traffic were somewhat greater: in 1913 £922 related to parcels and £175 from other goods. These services, including milk traffic, continued at Blunsdon for a further nine years, until August 1937. From 1929 to 1934 the annual wages for the solitary employee fell from £172 to £104 and overall revenue dropped from £3,762 to £443.

Forty years on from this closure in 1937 the site saw new life with the formation of the Swindon & Cricklade Railway in 1978, based at Blunsdon. Access to the old trackbed was granted in 1979 and planning permission granted for the establishment of a new station, a short distance north of the old station. New track was laid and the station reopened formally on 8th April 1984, short train rides being offered from 1983. A great deal of development has since been undertaken, including the erection of a new platform and waiting shelter. The shelter was formerly a parcels office at Malmesbury. Following its removal from the station it was used by a Malmesbury resident for music teaching. Instead of parcels it housed a piano! It was about to be dismantled when the Swindon & Cricklade Railway heard of its history and arranged for the building to have a new lease of life at Blunsdon. A new fireplace and chimney has been installed by the S&CR at its southern end. Use has also been made in the site of equipment previously at the former rail transport depot of W.D.& H.O.Wills at Colbourne Street, Swindon, which was demolished in 1980. Building materials from the former stations at Rushey Platt and Swindon Town have also been used. A signal box, formerly at Claydon on the Bletchley - Oxford line, built by the LMS in 1944, has been re-erected. The former lamp hut from the old station is in use as an oil store. Two former passenger coaches from Norwegian State Railways are in use as a café and for staff accommodation. As can be seen, the scale of the facility at the new Blunsdon station is far in excess of that at the original. Track has been re-laid north for one mile to Hayes Knoll and trains run on certain days to this current northern terminus of the Swindon & Cricklade Railway. Work is well advanced to extend the line south from Blundson to a terminus at Moulden Hill on the northern edge of Swindon.

Box. A general view from the west showing the large stone yard on the up side. To the left is the east end of the 1845 engine shed that closed in 1919.

BOX

OPENED: 30th June 1841 (with the opening of the Chippenham - Bath section of the GWR).
CLOSED: Passengers - 4th January 1965.
Goods - 10th June 1963.

This impressive station, which opened in June 1841 with the commencement of services on the broad gauge Chippenham to Bath section of the GWR London to Bristol route, was sited west of the village adjacent to the original Chippenham to Bath turnpike (later A4). It was almost a quarter mile west of the short Box Middle Hill tunnel and one mile west of the famous Box tunnel.

The attractive large Brunel style principal building, built of local Bath stone, was sited on the down side. It was an example of a Brunel style station; the engineer had a number of standard designs of what were termed 'wayside' stations but Adrian Vaughan, in his authoritative *Great Western Architecture*, states that Box station was in fact an 'awkward customer' which did not fit into the classification of such wayside structures. He states that, 'this station was so elaborate that, although it may have been considered as a wayside station, Brunel regarded it as being of greater importance and built accordingly'.

The large chalet type building on the main station approach road featured a low pitched roof with three tall decorative chimneys. An impressive horizontal fretted canopy surrounded the building, at its widest over the platform. This canopy was supported by horizontal beams across the main building. In line with early Brunel stations, no staff accommodation was incorporated in the building, which did however include all the usual waiting and booking facilities. Some recent research suggests that the impressive building may have been erected not in the early 1840s but in about 1855, some fourteen years after the station opened, replacing original timber buildings. A separate parcels office was built later on the down platform east of the main building.

From about 1875 a small waiting shelter served passengers on the up platform beside which stood Box signal box, in use from June 1898. This replaced earlier West and East boxes. In the same year both platforms were slightly extended at the west end; inter platform connection was primarily via an impressive GWR style covered lattice girder footbridge incorporating the GWR monograph. Foot-boards were also provided across the lines at each end of the platforms. Passenger figures for Box peaked in the early years of the twentieth century. In 1903 39,266 tickets were issued; comparative figures for 1913, 1923 and 1933 were 31,116, 33,255 and 8,343. This last dramatic fall was a trend seen at many Wiltshire stations. In 1960 the number of passengers booked at Box was 12,917.

A loop line passed behind the up platform and photographs indicate that on occasions this was used by local trains travelling towards Chippenham; a section of the platform at its east end appears to have been used by passengers. For some years before the

Box. Looking east in 1963, the impressive Brunel style building on the down side with its large horizontal canopy. Through the fine GWR footbridge is the western portal of Box Middle Hill tunnel.

Second World War sidings, parallel to the loop line, serviced a large stone yard with cranes. A long loading platform ran parallel to the platform. To the west of the station a water tower, topped by an iron tank, supplied engines on the up line before they tackled the gradients to and through Box tunnel. On an adjacent site an engine shed housed a banking engine from 1845 until its closure in 1919.

To the east of the station on the down side was the goods yard with a small goods shed and a one ton crane. This provided facilities for use by local traders and also for RAF Colerne; a coal depot was sited close to the yard entrance behind the down platform. In 1843 nine staff were based at Box. By 1921 the station master was supported by one clerk, one goods clerk, three signalmen, one signalman/ porter and three porters. In 1960 there was a station master together with eight other staff. The station closed for passengers as from early January 1965 with the withdrawal of local services between Bristol and Swindon. The goods yard had closed some eighteen months earlier in June 1963. The signal box closed in August 1964.

Today there are no track side remains of Box station; the former down side approach road now forms the access to an old building that stood just beyond and behind the main building with the engraving above the door 'WRS 1902 office'. Today this is occupied by engineering and corporate events businesses, for whom the old station site itself is now a parking area. Two old gateposts stand at the entrance to the former down side goods yard. The entrance to the former stone yard on the up side is clearly to be seen; the old yard is in a rather derelict and untidy condition. Former station railings can be seen on both the up and down sides of the line.

BOX MILL LANE

OPENED: 31st March 1930 (on the Chippenham - Bath line originally opened through this site in June 1841).

CLOSED: 4th January 1965.

On the Chippenham to Bath section of the GWR main line from London to Bristol and sited between Box tunnel to the east and Box Middle Hill tunnel to the west, Box Mill Lane opened at the end of March 1930. The A4 road passes over the line between Box Mill Lane and Box tunnel. The station (the term 'halt' is sometimes used but was never displayed), built at a cost of £800, was well placed to serve the residents of Box, certainly in a better position than Box station itself, a mile to the west. The village thus had to wait eighty nine years after the line opened for a convenient station! Small corrugated iron shelters served passengers on the up and down platforms, which initially were of timber but were later replaced by concrete components. As the platforms held only four coaches, on longer trains passengers for Box Mill Lane were required to travel in the four rear coaches. The shelters remained unchanged throughout the station's life. Booking facilities were available in a timber office alongside the road at the foot of the embankment; paths led up to the two platforms from either side of a minor road bridge in Box village. Electric lighting was provided from the outset.

Box Mill Lane. Looking east on 19th August 1961. A local train to Bristol hauled by 0-6-0 No. 2232. In the far distance beyond the A4 road bridge is the western portal of Box tunnel.

A member of staff was in place from 8.15 a.m. to 6.00 p.m. to deal with passengers, parcels and other miscellaneous traffic. Outside normal working hours guards of trains were required to collect tickets from passengers who alighted, note the numbers joining and, before the installation of a time switch, light and extinguish station illumination. The Box station master visited every afternoon to collect the takings which were kept in a safe overnight. Two censuses illustrated the relatively high levels of traffic before and after the Second World War: in 1938 between January and October 13,824 passengers were booked in, total receipts being £993. Equivalent figures for the same period in 1946 were 13,989 and £1,409.

Box Mill Lane closed to passengers in January 1965 with the withdrawal of local passenger services between Bristol and Swindon. Two sidings were sited on the up side east of the station close to the road bridge; they were used for loading stone from 1896 to 1959. No trace remains today of the Box Mill Lane station or the sidings.

BRADFORD-ON-AVON

OPENED: 2nd February 1857 (with the opening of the Bathampton Junction - Bradford South Junction line).

CLOSED: Passengers - remains open for services on the Bristol - Westbury - Southampton/Weymouth lines.

Bradford-on-Avon was unique in Wiltshire, and undoubtedly rare in the whole country, in that the station buildings were ready for use some years before the rails arrived and services commenced. Normally the story is that the station was 'practically', 'not quite' or 'just' finished when the first train arrived. The Wilts, Somerset & Weymouth Railway opened from Thingley Junction, west of Chippenham on the GWR, to Westbury in September 1848. Throughout the planning of this railway branches from the main line were proposed including one west from Staverton, south of Melksham, to Bradford-on-Avon and the building was thus constructed in anticipation. However, at the last moment and before the rails were laid, work ceased, much to the concern of the local wool based businesses. It was not for another nearly nine years that the station saw rails laid, with the construction and opening in February 1857 of the single line from Bathampton on the GWR London-Bath-Bristol line to Bradford Junction north of Trowbridge on the Thingley Junction to Westbury line. Bradford thus opened as a through facility rather than as the branch line terminus originally planned. By this time the Wilts, Somerset & Weymouth Railway had been absorbed by the GWR and thus Bradford-on-Avon station was owned and operated from the start by the GWR.

Bath stone was extensively used in the construction of an attractive small station to serve this historic town in the valley of the River Avon. The buildings survive almost intact today as the best kept and best preserved of the original stations in Wiltshire. The main building stands on the up side of the line serving passengers towards Trowbridge; passengers on the down side travelling to Bath are also provided

Bradford-on-Avon. A view south through the footbridge which still has its roof on 6th June 1960. The main building stands on the up platform (left).

with a substantial stone building. These buildings, of a squat gothic style, were appropriately designed for this historic town by staff in Brunel's London offices. Features include slit windows, fine gables, a bay window at the east end of the down platform building, and diamond shaped chimneys originally built of Bath stone but later replaced by what were termed engineers' bricks. The overall design is rather similar to that at the former Melksham Station, though Bradford is a little smaller. Wide canopies originally covered passengers on both platforms; in the case of that on the up, the canopy stretched around the whole building and protected passengers entering the building from the forecourt. The forecourt side canopy of the main building has now gone but the platform canopies remain. A covered footbridge originally linked the two platforms at the west end of the two buildings. The footbridge roof has now gone; and the bridge itself was renovated in the mid 1980s. Passenger numbers at Bradford were good for a relatively small town: in 1933 72,529 tickets were issued.

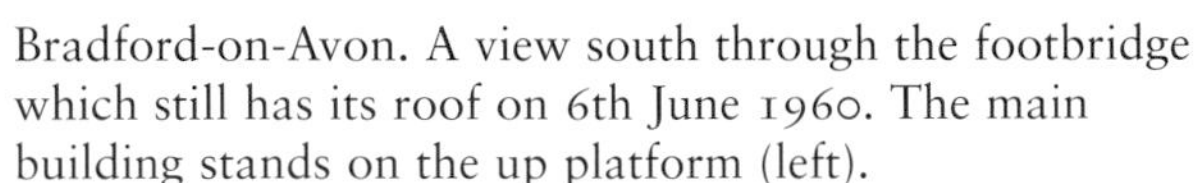

An extensive goods yard was located on the up side west of the station; the massive scale of the stone two road goods shed compared with the station itself reflected the importance for many years of goods traffic at Bradford-on-Avon, a town with old established woollen, rubber and brewing industries. The yard crane had a 6 ton capacity. Considerable traffic was also generated by the local stone quarries; the tonnage of minerals despatched varied over the early years of the twentieth century: 1903 - 3,604 tons; 1923 - 1,269 tons. Bradford-on-Avon signal box controlling movements on the main lines and in the goods yard, stood west of the station on the down side; this closed in June 1966.

The goods yard closed to general traffic in

Bradford-on-Avon. The best preserved Brunel style building in Wiltshire, dating back to the early 1850s. The 16.36 to Bristol Temple Meads arrives from Weymouth on 13th April 2004.

November 1964 though prior to this there had been major reductions in the length and number of sidings. The yard remained partially in use for a further 12 months as a coal depot. The whole yard was later converted into an extensive station car park.

The station's preservation and well kept appearance, enhanced by recent renovations, is assisted no doubt by it being staffed for long periods of the day, unusual for such a small station. GWR seats remain on the two platforms. The station is served today by trains on services between Bristol and Bath and the south coast (Southampton, Portsmouth and Weymouth). It is particularly well used by commuters and shoppers travelling to and from Bath.

BRINKWORTH

OPENED: Goods - 1st January 1903, passengers - 1st July 1903 (with the opening of the Wootton Bassett - Patchway GWR cut off line).

CLOSED: Passengers and goods - 3rd April 1961.

Brinkworth opened for passenger traffic in July 1903 on the GWR cut off line from Wootton Bassett to Patchway (the Badminton line). Goods services had commenced on the line seven months earlier (see Wootton Bassett text). Sited in the south west of the village, two tracks through the station served the 401 ft long up and down platforms. The main building, constructed at a cost of about £491, stood on the up platform. With two chimneys and a fretted canopy to the front and west of the building, it incorporated a porters' room, the station master's office, a general waiting room/booking office, the ladies' waiting room and toilets. On the down platform was a matching waiting shelter with a chimney and a canopy to the front and west; built at a cost of about £172, it incorporated a general waiting room and toilets. In design terms these station buildings were of the type used widely by the GWR for small country stations between 1902 and 1917. Of brick construction with slate roofs and with window sills and heads and chimney caps in Forest of Dean bluestone, they were built all along the cut off line in 1902/03. The Brinkworth platforms were linked adjacent to, and west of, the building and shelter by a covered metal and timber footbridge comprised of standard parts supplied by the GWR. Rail level board crossings were available for staff use at both ends of the platforms. The platforms were only partially paved, the remainder being layers of stone chippings.

At the east end of the station site a brick bridge carried a minor road from Brinkworth to Dauntsey over the lines; a tree lined approach road from the north end of the bridge led west to behind the up side main building. Two metal gateposts at the approach road head bore the inscription 'T. James, Vulcan Foundry, Cardiff 1902'. Similar entrance gate posts were in place at other stations on the cut off line. A metalled footpath at the southern end of the bridge gave pedestrians access to the rear of the down platform.

The up side approach road continued west beyond the main building providing access to a small goods yard which comprised a loop siding with head shunts at west and east ends. A small goods shed with a loading platform and 1½ ton capacity crane stood on the north side of the loop. The eastern 'head shunt' siding which terminated behind the west end of the up platform served cattle pens and a loading dock. A 12 ton weighbridge hut stood behind the up platform at the goods yard entrance.

Trains at Brinkworth were controlled from the

Brinkworth. Looking west on 28th May 1961. The main building on the up side (right) beyond which the goods shed is seen through the footbridge.

typical GWR brick signal box sited just beyond the west end of the down platform. Originally the box was staffed continuously but as early as 1910 arrangements were to close the box for limited periods during the night and at weekends. The box ceased to operate in March 1959.

From the outset a station master was appointed at Brinkworth supervising two porters and three signalmen. A detached house was built for the station master at the head of the up side approach road on the north side adjacent to the Dauntsey road. It was similar to other such houses on the cut off line, being built by Pearsons, a local contractor. They were all of a design not found elsewhere on the GWR. This Brinkworth house was unusual in that the east wall incorporated two long lengths of rail running vertically as supports; it is not known whether these featured in the original construction. During the mid 1930s the post of Brinkworth station master was abolished and supervision of the two remaining signalmen and two porters passed to the station master at Little Somerford. The Brinkworth porters undertook a number of roles including the issuing of tickets. A small terrace of three cottages was provided for the signalmen by the GWR at the end of the up side approach road north of the goods shed.

Throughout the life of Brinkworth station both passenger and freight traffic was light. An average of four passenger trains stopped on a weekday in either direction; this reduced to two on a Sunday. This small number of services was reflected in the low passenger numbers: in 1913 only 4,272 passenger tickets were issued. For the period January to November 1938 2,021 passengers were handled at Brinkworth; for the same period in 1946 the figure was 1,569. Freight trains called on an average once a day in each direction, often on a 'as required' basis. Coal was received for the local merchant but this traffic ceased in 1946. Milk was normally sent out from Brinkworth on passenger trains. It was not surprising that both passenger and goods services ceased at Brinkworth in April 1961.

Today all traces of the buildings and platforms have gone; the station master's house continues in residential use and at the entrance to the former approach road close to the house stands one of the original 1902 gate posts. The former signalmen's cottages continue as residences at the far end of the approach road, which is now in a poor rutted condition.

BROMHAM & ROWDE HALT

OPENED: 22nd February 1909 (on the Holt Junction - Devizes branch of the GWR originally opened through this site in 1857).

CLOSED: Passengers - 18th April 1966.
Goods - 10th June 1963.

Bromham & Rowde Halt was located at Sells Green very close to the northern bank of the Kennet and Avon Canal. The villages of Bromham and Rowde were some two miles north east and one and a half miles east of the site. The GWR assumed that the freight business to be generated at the proposed halt was likely to come mainly from the prosperous horticultural area around these settlements and thus the name was given. The halt opened in February 1909 having been authorised in May of the previous year. The GWR also hoped that it would generate extra passengers attracted by the rail-motor service recently introduced along the line. However, only a limited service was provided: in 1933 three trains each way called at the halt; this reduced to two trains shortly before closure.

The halt comprised one 150 ft platform on the down (south) side of the single line. Initially it was provided with a GWR style metal pagoda hut, a lamp man's hut and a milk stage. This stage was later covered by a wooden canopy; a wooden booking office was also added at the eastern end of the platform. Oil lamps to light the station approach and goods yard were installed from the outset; a scheme to introduce electric lighting at the halt itself and in the approach road was proposed in 1938 but was not implemented because of the War.

A goods loop of fifteen wagons capacity was installed in 1909 beyond the east end of the platform on the down side. A level crossing between the halt itself and the siding served the Seend brickyard and Hill View Farm. The overall cost of the facilities was in excess of £1,100, of which some £205 was spent on the halt itself.

From the outset Bromham & Rowde received significant business from the market gardens in the Bromham area, produce arriving by lorry before despatch by rail usually to the London area. Sugar beet was sent in open wagons to sugar factories in the Midlands and East Anglia. It is recorded that this traffic was so heavy in the 1940s and 1950s that in view of the limited siding space, beet growers were allocated specific weeks for loading. Earlier in the 1920s and 1930s milk traffic was particularly important and indeed more was handled at

Bromham & Rowde Halt. Looking east in the 1960s. The covered milk stage dominates the GWR style pagoda hut. The separate ticket office is beyond the stage.

Bromham & Rowde than at the nearby Seend station. The milk was delivered by road and left in a pound behind the milk stage; it was then loaded on to special trains which again generally departed for London. In 1926 62,670 filled churns were despatched, earning some £4,600 for the railway.

No cattle pens were provided at the halt, there being relatively little livestock in the area; however a further generator of traffic was the saw mills, to the east of the station beyond the station approach road. A private siding was in use from 1923 until 1963, latterly serving the Seend electric saw mills. This siding closed as from June 1963 along with the other goods siding used for the vegetable trade.

Though designated a halt, Bromham & Rowde for some years had limited staffing, normally a goods checker based at Seend. However, this ceased as from November 1951. Passenger services ended when the Holt Junction to Devizes line closed to all traffic in April 1966.

The platform remained until the mid 1990s within an agricultural yard but it has now gone, the site incorporated within the grounds of Bluemay Multicap, an agricultural machinery firm. When visiting the site, the production manager showed the author pictures of the old halt on the wall of the factory office. Only small sections of former railway posts give a clue to the original use of the site.

BROUGHTON GIFFORD HALT

OPENED: 29th October 1905 (on the Thingley Junction - Westbury line originally opened through this site in 1848).

CLOSED: 7th February 1955.

Sited about a mile south east of the village and close to the A303 Melksham to Bradford-on-Avon road, the halt was one of four halts built and opened by the GWR at, or shortly after, a steam rail-motor service commenced between Chippenham and Trowbridge via Melksham. Such services, designed to increase patronage on local trains, had been introduced some two years earlier by the GWR in the Stroud valley of Gloucestershire between Chalford and Stonehouse.

Broughton Gifford Halt opened in October 1905

Broughton Gifford Halt. A train approaches from the Melksham and Chippenham direction. Note that a small shelter is only provided on the down platform (right).

some four weeks after the start of the rail-motor service. Two low level (2 ft) 100 ft long platforms were installed and there is no evidence that they were ever raised to the normal height. Access to the rail-motors was facilitated by retractable steps. Although both platforms were provided with lamps, only the down platform had a small hut. Sloping paths led down to the platforms from the adjacent road bridge to the south.

Broughton Gifford Halt closed in February 1955 some eleven years before the local passenger service was withdrawn on this line. Beanacre Halt also closed on this date but the two remaining halts at Lacock and Staverton remained open until the service was withdrawn in 1966.

Today no line side trace can be seen although the site is clear; the alignment of the sloping path to the up side platform is visible and one old gate post remains. On the down side two vertical old rails stand in the hedge where the approach path left the road.

BULFORD

OPENED: 1st June 1906 (with the opening of the Amesbury - Bulford Camp section of the Amesbury & Military Camp Light Railway).
CLOSED: Passengers - 30th June 1952.
Goods - 4th March 1963.

The station, sited on the southern edge of Bulford, opened at the beginning of June 1906 with the commencement of services on the Amesbury to Bulford and Bulford Camp extension of the Amesbury & Military Camp Light Railway (see Amesbury text). The single platform stood on the

Bulford. Staff posing for the photographer in an early view looking north. Note the two small awnings on the platform side of the building.

down (north west) side of the line; originally with wooden edging, this was later replaced by concrete components. A loop line ran through the station from its opening but a platform was never erected on the up side. The line to Bulford was doubled as from May 1909.

The station building, with three chimneys, originally had two small awnings over entrances into the building from the platform; subsequently a large wooden canopy was added sloping up towards the line and covering the full width of the platform in front of the building. It was of such a scale as to dominate the station. At the southern end of the platform was the small Bulford signal box; this was downgraded to a ground frame as from April 1935. A small metal shelter, probably used for parcels and other storage, was a later addition between the building and the signal box.

Two sidings trailed back from the line north of the station serving Bulford goods yard sited behind the north end of the platform. The yard included a small goods shed and a cattle pen. A small water tank opposite the south end of the platform was filled by a wind pump drawing from a well in the underlying chalk.

With decreased military activity in the area, business fell markedly at Bulford after the Second World War. The train services to Salisbury were particularly affected with custom drawn away by the shorter, more direct, and cheaper bus service to the cathedral city. By the early 1950s there was only one train per weekday and the service ceased altogether

Bulford. A local train to Salisbury stands beside the large wooden canopy on 7th August 1950.

at the end of June 1952. However, goods services continued for another eleven years until March 1963. A number of excursion trains with rail enthusiasts ran as far as Bulford and Bulford Camp up to 1963.

Access to the station site was via a sloping approach up from the main road (later A3028) across which the line ran over an impressive bridge. It is on this approach road that today are found the only clear remnants of the railway era, including a house and two old cottages. On the roof of the house is a weather vane in the form of a railway locomotive. Leading off this approach road is a small new housing development, 'The Sidings'. The clearest reminder is, however, an old semaphore signal erected on the former approach road at the foot of the former railway embankment. The station site itself has been redeveloped for industrial/commercial uses and a large car park.

BULFORD CAMP

OPENED: 1st June 1906 (as the terminus of the Amesbury - Bulford Camp section of the Amesbury & Military Camp Light Railway).
CLOSED: Passengers - 30th June 1952.
Goods - 4th March 1963.

This rather desolate station opened in June 1906 when services commenced on the Amesbury to Bulford and Bulford Camp extension of the Amesbury & Military Camp Light Railway (see Amesbury text). The only facility was a long spacious platform, without any shelter, on the south east side of the line. The track alongside the platform terminated at an end loading dock. A parallel track continued until 1933 for a further three quarters of a mile to Sling Camp. Bulford Camp was never served by a regular passenger service, its principal customers being Camp personnel. It closed for passenger use at the end of June 1952; goods facilities were available for a further eleven years until March 1963. A number of excursion trains ran as far as Bulford Camp up to 1963. Today the former station site is within the large army complex which continues at Bulford.

Bulford Camp. Looking north east on 14th May 1955, a rail enthusiasts' train stands at the desolate but spacious platform which had closed to public services some three years earlier.

Calne. A view in about 1908 with station staff posing in front of the main building. Note that the canopy does not yet extend in front of the parcels office extension. Churns stand on the extended milk platform.

CALNE

OPENED: Goods - 29th October 1863, passengers - 3rd November 1863 (with the opening of the GWR Calne Branch).

CLOSED: Passengers - 20th September 1965. Goods - 2nd November 1964.

For centuries Calne has been a small but busy market and industrial town. Like many settlements in Wiltshire, it was originally important for cloth weaving but by the mid nineteenth century this began to wane with the growing competition from the steam powered mills of the north of England. Nevertheless mills continued to operate in the Calne area. The activity that stands out in the town is the bacon curing and later bacon products industry developed by the Harris family from the early 1800s, an activity for which a good transport system was critical. Early in the nineteenth century mail coaches ran along the turnpike road (later A4) from London to Bath and Bristol via Marlborough and Chippenham and through the centre of Calne, providing good facilities for conveying both passengers and light goods. The Calne branch of the Wilts & Berks Canal provided facilities for the movement of heavier goods.

The opening of the GWR on a route from Swindon to Chippenham that passed some four miles to the north of Calne left the town in a transport backwater – the through turnpike coaches ceased to serve Calne and the canal business suffered a marked decline. Local traders and residents campaigned strongly for the railway to come to Calne. An early 1845 scheme, the London, Bristol & South Wales Direct Railway, envisaged a line through Marlborough and Calne but the scheme failed. A public meeting in 1859 resolved 'that it is highly desirable and will prove very advantageous to Calne and the neighbourhood to have a line of railway from the town to join the GWR near Chippenham station'. The only opposition to this motion came from a local canal operator!

The Calne Railway Company was established and the appropriate Act received royal assent on 15th May 1860. Early discussions involved the Marquis of Lansdowne, a local major landowner including the nearby Bowood estate. Not surprisingly the Railway's Board of Directors included three representatives from the Harris family. Indeed with another family member the Harris's contributed up to one half of the capital required for the new line. The cost of construction amounted to £49,283 including £1,867 for the station buildings at Calne built on 4½ acres of land purchased from the Marquis of Lansdowne.

The five and a half mile broad gauge branch opened for goods traffic on 29th October 1863, the first train arriving at 8.30 a.m., significantly carrying a hundred pigs for the Harris factory. From the start the line was operated by the GWR, an amalgamation between the Calne Railway and the GWR taking place nearly thirty years later in July 1892. Passenger services commenced on Tuesday 3rd November 1863, a cause of much celebration in Calne, the day being declared a public holiday with all shops closed. The band of the 4th Wilts Volunteer Corps paraded through the streets and was joined by some sixty employees from Messrs G.&C. Harris. Together they proceeded to the station, where a large throng awaited the inaugural train, an excursion to Bath via Chippenham. Some 800-1000 passengers were carried but many were left behind, no space being available. The fares of Harris employees were paid by the firm which also treated its employees to a 'sumptuous banquet' (pies and sausages?). A dinner for sixty guests was hosted by the Railway directors at the White Hart Hotel.

Throughout the life of the station major business was generated by the Harris bacon factory, not only with the import of pigs for slaughter and other raw materials such as salt, ice and coal, but in the export of products such as the famous pork pies and sausages. Also exported were by-products such as fertilisers and feeding stuffs. The Calne branch was famous after the First World War for the special vans carrying the Harris products, known as Syphon C parcels vans. Leaving the station daily, yellow side plates indicated the route to be travelled – 'To work between Calne and Manchester', 'Calne and Newcastle' etc. Roof boards displayed the words 'Harris (Calne) Wiltshire Sausages'. When trains arrived at Calne conveying pigs, a special whistle was given by the station shunter engine to alert drovers to come to the station so that no time was lost in unloading the pigs and driving them down Station Road to the factory slaughter house. The wagons were then cleaned for a return to collect more animals; often these were collected from Bristol Docks where they had arrived from Ireland.

In the twentieth century considerable business was also generated, as at many Wiltshire stations, by the military. Leading up to the Second World War the

Calne. The terminus station on 27th July 1961. Note the extensive goods facilities including a glimpse of the goods shed (right), sidings of C. & T. Harris (right) and the extended milk platform (centre).

Calne. C. & T. Harris parcels being loaded at the passenger platform in about 1927. Note the van roof board 'Harris (Calne) Wiltshire Sausages'.

RAF establishments at Yatesbury, Compton Bassett and Lyneham generated much traffic, both passenger and freight. Calne station handled large quantities of materials for the construction of a range of buildings at RAF Yatesbury. At one time over 20,000 RAF personnel were stationed locally. The pattern of passenger and freight services over the years reflected the major variation in demand. At its opening in November 1863 only five passenger trains ran each way on the branch per day; this gradually increased over the years. For instance, in April 1910 twelve trains ran each way. The Calne branch was one of the lines selected by the GWR for the introduction of its steam rail-motors as from February 1905. Subsequent years saw the use of short auto trains and then, from 1958, diesel multiple units.

The station buildings at Calne evolved from the 1863 small wooden building on a single platform on the north side of the line. With the growing demands from both passengers and freight new buildings were erected in 1895, including a then standard GWR brick building with a horizontal platform canopy and chimneys. A canopy was also provided on the road approach side to give added protection. The station buildings were aligned parallel to the track, despite its terminal status, so as not to impede any possible future extension of the branch. In the early days a small locomotive shed with a slate roof and stone walls was provided west of the main building. This shed later became disused, probably following amalgamation with the GWR in 1892, and was demolished by 1906. Further to the west on the north side was the 16 lever Calne signal box, which came into operation in 1892. In the early 1900s a small eastward extension was added to the station building incorporating a parcels office; the platform canopy was extended in front of the parcels office by 1910. During the First World War a short loading platform with canopy was added at the east end of the platform. A further addition was a water tower on the west end of the platform, though this was not used for many years, locomotives generally taking on sufficient water at Chippenham.

For some years the station facilities remained broadly the same until the greater demands of the Second World War brought further expansion. In 1942 the passenger platform was extended as far west as the signal box to allow the accommodation of eight passenger coaches, many carrying troops based at the local RAF establishments. If larger trains arrived and departed alighting and boarding took place in the large goods yard. A new wooden building incorporating a booking office and waiting room was erected on the platform extension; this released space in the main station building that was taken over as a station master's office. A small shed was also built at this stage, immediately to the east of the main building, for the storage of both cycles and other goods. To the east of the station buildings and facing the main approach road a corrugated iron building was constructed for the storage of parcels and porters' trolleys.

Opposite the main station platform to the south was Calne milk platform with a direct access to Station Road that eased loading. Originally only of a short length, it was extended by 1908 west along the length of the original pre 1942 platform. It is recorded that during the First World War eight milk trains left Calne each weekday. Beyond and south of the milk platform was the main Calne goods yard including a stone goods shed with a slate roof. A siding ran through the shed but there were no doors. The number of sidings at Calne gradually increased over the years: four in 1880, five by 1900, seven in 1906 and eight by the late 1930s. A long loading platform equipped with wooden pens for the accommodation of cattle and other animals ran for much of the length of the goods yard; at the west of the platform was a hand operated light crane of 30 cwt capacity. There was also a large yard crane of a capacity of 5 tons 18 cwt. A wide variety of goods were dealt with in the yard in addition to the Harris trade; these goods were both imports and exports to and from local traders – cattle feed, farm implements, coal etc. The private siding of C.&T. Harris (Calne) built in 1927/28 began at the rear of the goods shed and ran out of the station goods yard alongside Harris's own loading platform. At one time up to twenty loaded trucks were despatched per day from the Harris platform.

With all this traffic, both passenger and freight, Calne was, without doubt, one of the busiest stations in Wiltshire. A highlight came in 1907 when King Edward VII and Queen Alexandra passed through on the way to visit Bowood House. Flowers adorned the station and it is recorded that the booking office was carpeted for the occasion! Calne developed as the focus for rail transport for a large surrounding area, in particular east towards Marlborough. There were proposals to construct a rail link from Calne station to the GWR Marlborough branch which opened in 1864. To assess the possible popularity of such a service, in 1904 the GWR inaugurated one of its very early bus services between the two towns. The service ran until 1913 but was then abandoned until 1924; it was taken over by the Bristol Omnibus Company as from 1928. No rail link was ever constructed, support for the bus service not justifying such an expensive project.

Aside from the Second World War passenger traffic levels were at their peak in the period 1900 to 1935. In 1923 35,270 passenger tickets were issued; this figure fell to 28,044 in 1933. The number of 'parcels' forwarded, many generated by the Harris factory, increased greatly during this period from 98,567 in 1903 to 357,184 in 1933. Traffic was particularly heavy during the Second World War; many passengers travelling through the station were issued with tickets at the RAF establishments and daily takings at Calne were known to exceed £1,000. This included traffic from RAF Lyneham. Although Dauntsey station on the Swindon to Chippenham line was close to Lyneham, it lacked the facilities for moving heavy goods (eg aero engines). Calne station handled hundreds of special troop trains and numbers were also great on the branch line trains, often known as the 'Calne Bunk'. During the War up to 300,000 passengers passed through Calne in a year.

These major changes in traffic levels were reflected in the staff numbers: in 1898 a station master and 7 staff; in 1903 12 staff, 1913 15 staff, in 1921 a station master and 27 staff and during the Second World War a station master and 40 staff! After the War traffic levels continued to be high during the late 1940s and early 1950s: in the twelve months ending 30th September 1952 revenue of some £150,000 was generated at Calne. From this point however, decline set in – a critical factor was the closure of the RAF

Calne. The forecourt side of the station building in its latter days; the canopy is in need of repair. The metal shed is in use as a store.

establishments at Yatesbury and Compton Bassett. The rail strike of 1955 marked the beginning of the end of Harris traffic, movements transferred to lorries and never returned to rail. By late 1963 only one freight train served Calne each way per day, in 1964 the Harris private siding closed and as from November 1964 freight services were withdrawn, the last train having run on 31st October. The sidings were lifted in 1965.

Following the introduction of diesel multiple units in 1958 a good level of passenger services was operated in the early 1960s – in 1961 there were seventeen trains each way on a weekday with an extra train on Wednesdays. The last RAF troop train ran in May 1963, coach travel having now taken much of this traffic. A survey at the end of October 1964 indicated that an average of only thirteen passengers were alighting at Calne per day. Services continued to decline and the Calne signal box closed in November 1964. British Rail at that point decided that essential work was needed on the branch line but the costs involved could not be justified. The last passenger train ran on 18th September 1965. The 'Last Post' was apparently sounded as the final train left Calne at 11.20 p.m. with 140 passengers on board.

Track lifting began on the branch at Easter 1967 and the line had gone by July. For some years the station buildings at Calne remained, though increasingly vandalised. Today the site is now incorporated in the Station Road trading estate, an agricultural merchants building standing approximately across the old buffer stops. The remainder of the site was virtually derelict when visited in late January 2004.

Chippenham. An early engraving of the first station buildings dating from the early 1840s.

CHIPPENHAM

OPENED: 31st May 1841 (with the opening of the Hay Lane - Chippenham section of the GWR).

CLOSED: Passengers - remains open on the London (Paddington) - Bristol line.
Goods - 31st December 1980.

A section of the broad gauge GWR from London (Paddington) opened from Faringdon Road (Oxon) to Hay Lane, some 2½ miles east of Wootton Bassett on 17th December 1840. The continuation from Hay Lane to Chippenham opened on 31st May 1841 and then on through Box tunnel to Bath on 30th June 1841. The Chippenham station of May 1841, designed by Brunel, was a single storey building in Bath stone with a low pitched roof that extended out to form a canopy on all four sides. A stone goods shed stood opposite the station on the north side. Records suggest that the buildings were not quite complete at the opening day.

This 1841 station was considered adequate to serve trains running on the London, Bath and Bristol route. Changes in demand began to arise during the late 1840s and 1850s with the initial development and subsequent extension of the Wilts, Somerset & Weymouth Railway (WS&WR) which formed a junction with the GWR main line some two miles south west of Chippenham station. The first section of the WS&WR from what was known as Thingley Junction to Westbury opened in September 1848; subsequent extensions were completed to Warminster (1851) and on to Salisbury (1856) and also to Frome (1850), Yeovil (1856) and Weymouth (1857). The completion of the last line to the Dorset coast saw the commencement of through trains from Paddington to Weymouth via Chippenham and Westbury.

Its new junction status was the catalyst for major expansion of Chippenham station. New buildings were erected alongside the down line which was slightly realigned southwards. Developed mainly by Rowland Brotherhood, a Chippenham based engineer, facilities were incorporated into two main buildings on the down side, separated by an impressive iron gate and topped by a low pitched roof and tall chimneys. The west building included a store room, the station master's office, a waiting room, a porters' room and a gent's urinal. To the east of the gate the building included a cloakroom, a goods lock up, the booking office and hall, the ladies' waiting room (with a large bay window), the first class waiting room, a porters' room and a store. In the early years a foot warmer room heated six to ten warmers; because of the low capacity this was abandoned in 1906, the warmers being provided to passengers at Swindon and Bristol.

At this stage, and for many years, the refreshment facilities on the down side were sited in a small separate building south west of the main buildings in what is believed to be a surviving office used by Brunel during construction of the GWR. Refreshment rooms were later provided on the platform itself as it was awkward for passengers changing trains to come out of the station to a separate building beyond the ticket barrier.

In 1857/58 a new island platform was constructed, along the northern face of which ran the main up line to Swindon and London. On the south side of the island a bay was constructed at the west end for use by trains on the Westbury, Salisbury and Weymouth lines which started from Chippenham; this was known as the Weymouth bay. A wooden building in the centre of this island platform close to the Weymouth bay buffer stop was built incorporating a refreshment room, a waiting room, a ladies' room and a gent's urinal. The down and island platforms were covered by a large train shed, apparently to mark the station's increased status. An unusual

Chippenham. A view from the west in about 1898 as a down train enters the overall train shed that was dismantled in about 1905.

Chippenham. On 19th August 1961 4-6-0 No. 6930 Aldersey Hall runs into the down platform hauling a train from Wolverhampton to Weymouth. Note the station nameboard 'Chippenham - Junction for Calne - Home of Harris' (the bacon company).

feature of this shed was that by 1898 its ends were different: the east end was enclosed above roof level whilst a glass draught screen sheltered part of the down platform. The west end of the shed was however completely open.

A further development came in 1863 with the construction of a bay platform on the south side of the island platform at its eastern end to serve trains running to Calne on the new branch line. This bay line did not however line up with the earlier Weymouth bay being slightly to the north, the island platform being narrower here than at the western end. In 1900 the Weymouth bay line was converted into a through line; through working on this line was however short lived and two sets of buffer stops were introduced recreating the Weymouth terminus bay and an eastward facing siding which for some reason became known as the New-Found-Out (NFO) siding. This through running seems to have been stopped as the two ends of the station were controlled from different signal boxes – the West on the down side, west of the station, and the East on the up side, towards the point where the Calne track veered south. At the buffer end of the New-Found-Out siding a gas cylinder truck was often stored for long periods. Following the completion of all these changes Platform 1 served the down main line, Platform 2 was the Weymouth bay, Platform 3 served the up main line and Platform 4 was the Calne branch bay. The overall train shed was removed in about 1905, protection subsequently being provided by long canopies with fretted edges.

Inter platform passenger movements were via an impressive covered footbridge based approximately in the centre of both the down and island platforms. At the west end of the station another footbridge carried local residents over the station site, linking two sections of a road severed with the construction of the GWR. There was no access to the platforms from this footbridge. Originally constructed of lattice girders, it was rebuilt in steel plates in its southern section in the 1950s; later the northern section was changed to an open girder construction. The layout and operation of the station buildings remained broadly the same from the early 1900s to the 1960s.

Passenger traffic was high in the early years of the twentieth century, generated particularly by its junction position. In 1903 106,639 passenger tickets were issued: this figure increased to 137,138 in 1923, before falling to 108,325 in 1933. Over this same period the number of parcels forwarded varied greatly: the figures were 1903 71,648; 1913 286,809; 1923 188,000; 1933 165,685.

These last figures in some way reflect the varying fortunes of firms in the Chippenham area that used the station's goods facilities. Significant developments took place at these in parallel with the evolution of services for passengers.

Prior to the coming of the railway Chippenham was already an important industrial town and its status was much enhanced by the arrival of the GWR. A major goods yard was laid out east of the station on the down side including a large (194 ft long) stone goods shed opened in 1858. The shed included a loading platform and three two ton cranes. At its western end was a workshop for railway staff: carpenters, plumber and painters. This lean-to extension was demolished in 1947 when the shed was modified so that Royal Navy trailers could be backed at right angles to the loading platform. A major complex of sidings also evolved to the north of the station beyond the up main line. A water tower was built at the western end of this yard which supplied water to pumps on the station and also to non-drinking water taps.

North east of the station on the up side just beyond where the Calne branch left the main line was Chippenham engine shed (opened in about 1858); this was surprisingly large being only a sub-shed to the main shed at Swindon. Some 95 ft x 50 ft in size, the shed often housed half a dozen GWR pannier tank engines. Also on the up side, but closer to the station, was Chippenham turntable.

A number of industrial premises operated around the station site, particularly on its northern side. These latter included a foundry, brewery, cheese factory and bacon curing factory. The last was served by a designated siding until September 1964. Also served by a siding from 1906 to 1932 was Chippenham gas works close to the engine shed. To the north west of the station was a GWR warehouse, Williams coalyard and a large weigh-bridge (which can still be seen at the north end of the western footbridge). The largest industry on the northern side was related primarily to railway brakes and signalling. Railway related activity had dated back to 1800 with the firm of Rowland Brotherhood but at the beginning of the twentieth century the firm of Saxby & Farmer signalling engineers was established. Following various mergers the well known Westinghouse Brake and Signal Company operated from 1935 in a striking factory that can still be seen to the north of the station. Much rail business was generated by Westinghouse which employed over 2,700 in 1938 and four to five thousand in the 1950s; a GWR lorry shuttled between the factory and the station whilst heavy goods and equipment was handled on a private siding which operated until 1976.

South of the station entrance a group of railway related buildings stood in the large station yard. Stables, originally used by GWR horses, were later in part converted to maintenance shops servicing the lorries based at the station. GWR lorries first ran from Chippenham station in 1918; by 1924 a number of solid tyre vehicles served the town and surrounding rural areas. Horses were also used for local deliveries during the Second World War. Also in this group of buildings were six cottages built for and used by local railwaymen, one being occupied by

Chippenham. A view east from the west end of the down platform on 4th September 1965 showing the long footbridge carrying a public right of way across the station site. The large factory of Westinghouse Brake & Signal Company can be seen in the background (middle left).

Chippenham. The east end of the station at Easter 1937. An auto-coach and gas cylinder wagon stand at the New-Found-Out siding; an 0-4-2T and van are in the fish dock and a coach and van in the parcels dock.

a railway policeman. Immediately adjacent was the detached station master's house. Many staff were based at Chippenham: in November 1920 it is recorded that the station master was supported by 52 staff. Indeed, just after the Second World War the Chippenham staff ran its own football team, 'the Railway Ramblers', who played at a field close to the East signal box, urged on by the signalman!

In the north east of the station yard, and close to the station building, was a V-shaped loading dock which can still be seen today, the northern side known as the fish dock and the southern as the parcels dock. South of the dock was a long milk platform, with a canopy used primarily for traffic associated with the Chippenham Nestle's milk factory. The platform received raw materials by rail such as sugar, tin plate for tins and wood for box construction; also exported were large quantities of condensed milk in tins packed into the wooden boxes. At one time up to ten trucks were despatched by rail per night from this platform. For some years a station horse and cart or lorry was kept busy linking the station and the milk factory. Further traffic was generated by a nearby Brooke Bond tea depot. Chippenham market operated on Fridays and cattle were often driven up to the station pens sited near the goods shed.

Like many stations in Wiltshire, Chippenham was particularly busy during, and immediately after, the Second World War. Traffic was generated not only by troop and equipment movements but also by the supply of provisions to the local ammunition stores, the RAF Camps and the Royal Navy establishment at nearby Copenacre. During the War an engine driver, then living at Station House, apparently stored bicycles for 6d a day and a shilling for the weekend, the proceeds being given to charity. Soon after the War a rank of cycle sheds was erected at the west end of the down platform.

The mid 1960s saw the beginning of a series of major changes at Chippenham station. The engine shed closed in March 1964 and the NFO siding was lifted in April. Services ceased on the Calne branch in 1965 and track in the old Weymouth bay platform was lifted on 21st August 1966. On the same day the East and West signal boxes closed, operations in the Chippenham area now being controlled from the Panel at Swindon. For the following ten years the main line trains used the old down platform and the north side of the island platform.

As from 1st February 1976, in preparation for the introduction of High Speed Trains, the down main line trains started to use the south side of the island platform, the tracks having been slewed a little to the north. This platform was longer than the down following the filling in of the former Calne up bay on the south side of the island. The track was lifted from beside the old down platform. As part of the refurbishment of facilities on the island the central wooden building was demolished in 1975, being replaced by two modern glass shelters erected on the platform. Booking facilities continued to be provided in the old down side buildings, passengers having to use the covered footbridge to reach the island platform.

Chiseldon. An early view looking east. The original tall signal box dominates the scene on the up platform. Note the milk churns.

The goods shed was demolished in about 1976 and general goods facilities were withdrawn as from 1st January 1981. A large section of the former southern goods yard was then laid out as the station car park, the remainder at the east end being sold off. The group of buildings in the station yard including the station master's house was also demolished. The old former Brunel office remains; when viewed in March 2004 it was being refurbished following a number of uses subsequent to its early role as a refreshment room. Its historical significance is indicated by a Chippenham Civic Society blue plaque on the northern wall.

To the north of the station all sidings have been lifted and redeveloped as a 200 space car park giving a total of over 650 at the station. To gain access to this car park a northern extension to the covered footbridge was constructed in a matching design to the old structure. In recent years Chippenham station has been renovated and repainted, most recently in the year 2000. The now Grade II listed buildings are in a relatively good condition, though, when visited early in 2004, the extensive canopies were beginning to show signs of decay once again. In 2000 the Beatentrack internet café was opened in the down side building. Today Chippenham station is served by a weekday half hourly high speed service to both Bristol and London. It is also a stopping point on the local service between Swindon and Southampton via Westbury.

CHISELDON

OPENED: 27th July 1881 (with the opening of the Swindon Town - Marlborough section of the Swindon, Marlborough & Andover Railway).

CLOSED: Passengers and goods - 11th September 1961.

Chiseldon station opened in July 1881 with the commencement of services on the northern section of the Swindon, Marlborough & Andover Railway (SMAR) from Swindon Town to Marlborough. Sited on a curve at the heart of Chiseldon village, the station was on a loop in the general single track line. The up platform (towards Swindon) was 344 ft long and the down 287 ft. Both platform faces and edges were initially of wooden construction but were replaced by brick sometime before 1914, probably in association with other changes at the station.

The facilities provided were similar to those at Ogbourne, the next station on the line towards Marlborough. The main brick built station building (37 ft x 15 ft) with a horizontal fretted canopy and a tall chimney stood on the up platform. Also on the up platform, in the early years, was a separate small gent's urinal. Passengers on the down platform were served by a wooden framed corrugated iron shelter.

Chiseldon. Looking west on 15th March 1958 as class 2-6-0 No. 6334 is shunting beside the down platform. The 1920 small goods shed is beyond the signal box rebuilt in 1942.

Asphalting of the platforms in front of the main building and shelter was undertaken in 1910; similar work was undertaken at other stations on the line at about this time. The remainder of the platforms had gravel surfaces.

The First World War brought increased traffic on SMAR; a long siding was laid south of the station parallel to the up line to Draycott military camp. This came into operation in September 1915 and closed in 1921. The increased traffic required extra facilities at Chiseldon station itself. A brick parcels and goods office was completed by January 1915 on the site of the original gent's urinal; this latter was moved to the east end of the up platform close to the bridge carrying a road over the line east of the station. A further wooden shed used as a store was built in 1920 at the far west end of the up platform beyond the signal box; this store was indicated as a goods shed on the official plan of 1923.

At about this time warning notices were erected encouraging passengers to cross the line by the road bridge, this bridge being accessed by steep paths from each platform. In 1911 a brick lamp hut was provided, a facility provided at a number of stations at that time following fires in the main station buildings attributed to lamp oil. Close to the lamp hut was a pump house. This was constructed in 1918 to pump water from a well to a 6,000 gallon water tank sited south of the station and road bridge on the up side. The tank supplied water to both the station itself and the station master's house. The latter stood on the down side east of the road bridge, and – unusually – had a thatch roof.

Freight traffic was, from the outset, of some importance at Chiseldon but no major facilities were provided at the two yards west of the station on the up and down sides of the line. A trailing siding served the original down yard west of the down platform. Two sidings on the up side dated from before 1905; these ran behind the signal box with the inner siding adjacent to the rear of the west end of the up platform. It is recorded that as early as 1885 considerable local freight traffic was being generated and extra siding accommodation was authorised. Local agricultural produce was an important source of traffic, in particular milk, as at peak times up to sixty churns per day were loaded onto passing milk trains. Also of importance was the arrival and despatch of racehorses based at a number of local

Chiseldon Camp Halt. The exposed platform on the west side of the single track on 8th September 1961, three days before the halt closed following the withdrawal of passenger services.

stables. An adverse effect of this was the delay often caused to through trains whilst horse vans were attached.

In 1923 1,085 tons of freight were handled at Chiseldon; this had dropped to 469 in 1933. Over the same period the number of passenger tickets issued fell from 37,000 to 22,000 though over 300 season tickets were issued in 1933. Chiseldon at that time seems to have had greater importance for passenger traffic, with many travellers going to and from Swindon for work and leisure. A commuter type service can be seen in the timetables.

During the 1920s the up loop line was partly used as a long siding for stabling passenger trains from Swindon Town; it was also used as a refuge for goods trains. During the Second World War both lines were taken back into full use for through traffic. The loop line was also extended using the track bed of the former Draycott siding. These were two adaptations made to the line because of the demands of major north-south military movements. A particular example of the change was to Chiseldon signal box. Traffic movements were originally controlled from a typical SMAR 20 lever box on the up platform supplied by the Gloucester Carriage & Wagon Company. Because of the extra demands of Second World War traffic, it was completely rebuilt in 1942. The brickwork of the early locking room was all that remained of the 1881 box. A brick extension was built doubling the length of the box and new windows inserted to match the original. The upper timber part was of a then standard GWR form.

Closure to passenger and goods traffic came in September 1961 and today no trace can be seen of the former railway apart from a small section of the adjacent bridge abutment on the up side. The remainder of the site is an open grass amenity area overlooked by a small terrace of houses one of which is called 'Sleepers Cottage'. The site of the former station master's house on Station Road is now taken by the modern Station House doctors' surgery.

CHISELDON CAMP HALT

OPENED: 1st December 1930 (on the Swindon Town - Marlborough - Andover line originally opened through this site in 1881).

CLOSED: 11th September 1961.

The 100 ft long single wooden platform, sited on the west side of the single line about two miles south of Chiseldon station, was opened at the beginning of December 1930. It was one of a number of halts opened by the GWR at that time to combat the growing threat of road transport. A small GWR style wooden hut provided shelter for the passengers, who mainly derived from the nearby Chiseldon Camp. (In the First World War the Camp was known as 'Draycott Camp' and was served by a long siding south from Chiseldon.) Over 1000 tickets were issued in each of the first three years. The halt, unstaffed and supervised from Chiseldon, was lit by electricity controlled by a switch in the shelter. Access was via a lane from the Camp, a half mile to the west. Closure came with the withdrawal of passenger services on the line in September 1961 and today no trace of the halt can be seen. The trackbed through the site is now part of the National Cycle Network.

Christian Malford Halt. Looking north east on 21st October 1962, closure came a little over two years later.

CHRISTIAN MALFORD HALT

OPENED: 18th October 1926 (on the Wootton Bassett - Chippenham line originally opened through this site in 1841).
CLOSED: 4th January 1965.

A half mile south of the village of Christian Malford the halt, authorised on 29th April 1926, opened in the following October on the GWR London - Swindon - Bristol line some four miles north east of Chippenham. Costing an estimated £650, it was sited immediately to the east of a bridge carrying the line over a minor road from Christian Malford to Foxham. Access to the two 150 ft long timber platforms was via paths and steps up from the road. Wooden huts served passengers on both platforms; unusually for such a small halt electric lighting was introduced in late 1937 at a cost of £127. Alighting passengers were required to travel in the two rear coaches. In 1928 9,104 passenger tickets were issued; by 1933 the total had fallen to 6,528.

For some years a porter attended the halt from 9.30 a.m. until 6.0 p.m. Mondays to Saturdays, after which the guard of any train calling was responsible for collecting tickets. Supervision of the halt was from Chippenham or Dauntsey and all staffing ceased as from 1st December 1954. A lad porter from Chippenham swept out the shelters weekly. Closure came in early January 1965 with the withdrawal of local stopping services between Bristol and Swindon.

Today no trace can be seen at track side. However the iron gate to the access path on the up side is still in place, although much covered by hedge and undergrowth. The alignment of the access on the down side is now used as a modern path to the line on the embankment.

CODFORD

OPENED: 30th June 1856 (with the opening of the GWR Warminster - Salisbury (Fisherton) line).
CLOSED: Passengers - 19th September 1955.
Goods - 10th June 1963.

Codford was one of six intermediate stations opened in the Wylye valley when services commenced on the single track broad gauge line between Warminster and Salisbury in 1856. The others were Heytesbury, Wylye, Wishford, Langford and Wilton GWR. Conversion to standard gauge came in 1874. The line from Heytesbury to the west was doubled in 1899 and that to Wylye to the east in 1900. The station was sited on the southern edge of Codford St Peter; a level crossing at this point carried the minor road south towards Boyton.

The principal building on the down platform (towards Salisbury) was, like others on the Wylye valley line, of a typical early GWR chalet style built of local stone with a chimney, but in this case there is no photographic evidence of a canopy. It was a design used on many parts of the GWR at that time and similar to that which is preserved today on the West Somerset Railway at Bishops Lydeard. To the south east of the main building a long wooden extension was added providing enhanced facilities. A smaller brick building with a chimney and canopy served passengers on the up platform which, together with a passing loop, was added in 1897 in advance of general doubling of the line on either side of the station. Also in 1897 the down platform was

ABOVE Codford. Looking west from the end of the up platform. Note the footbridge, the shelter on the down platform and the cattle wagons by the pens to the rear. The 1897 extension of this down platform is clearly seen.

BELOW A close up of the down side. The principal building, with a chimney but no canopy, is at the foot of the footbridge steps. The man in the top hat is sitting in front of the large wooden extension.

extended. Photographs indicate that for a time extra shelters, with large canopies sloping upwards, stood on both platforms; this was not a feature of other Wylye valley stations. The platforms were linked by a covered footbridge at the west end of the station, close to the level crossing.

Opened in March 1877, Codford signal box, of a typical GWR brick and timber design, was on the down side, immediately west of the station and level crossing. It worked the barriers from 1976, but closed in June 1982 when automatic half barriers were installed. A goods yard with a small goods shed catered for freight traffic on the down side east of the station. A dock siding served cattle pens behind the down platform. In 1938 a 3 ton capacity crane was scheduled as present, larger than at other stations in the valley where only 30 cwt lifting facilities were generally available.

As with other stations in the valley, passenger numbers fell overall between 1903 and 1933. In the former 10,539 tickets were issued, falling to 3,748 by 1933. Both passenger and freight movements were boosted in much of Wiltshire by military activity particularly during the two World Wars. Specific branch lines were often constructed, the 2¾ mile Codford Camp Railway being a good example, leaving the down refuge siding to the west of the station. Open from October 1914 to the end of 1922, it ran north to, and then beyond, the main valley road, now the A36. At the Camp a platform and sidings were provided. The GWR took over the operation of the line from May 1918 and ran it until closure, the branch being lifted in 1923.

The down refuge siding remained in place until 1968. This was thirteen years after passenger services ceased at Codford in September 1955; freight services were withdrawn as from June 1963. Today no trace remains apart from an isolated old railway post close to the automatic level crossing. The former station site and goods yard have been developed by Country Gentlemen Housing.

COLLINGBOURNE

OPENED: 1st May 1882 (with the opening of the Grafton - Ludgershall - Andover section of the Swindon, Marlborough & Andover Railway).
CLOSED: Passengers and goods - 11th September 1961.

Sited on the east side of Collingbourne Ducis, the station opened with the commencement of services at the beginning of May 1882 on the southern section of the Swindon, Marlborough & Andover Railway (SMAR). At its opening the station had two platforms (both 302 ft long) serving the through down line and an up side loop. The line was doubled south to Ludgershall as from September 1901 and north to Grafton from November 1902.

The principal brick station building, with two chimneys and a canopy, stood on the up platform (towards Grafton). A small corrugated store was later sited alongside the south end of this building. In 1912 – in common with other stations on the line – a new ticket window was installed in the booking office. On the down platform was a wooden shelter with a grey slate roof and a grey chequered brick floor. The station building and shelter were similar to those at Grafton and Burbage, being built by the same local contractor, John Dover.

Codford. A poor quality but rare photograph from the *GWR Magazine* of 1915 showing a vast number of workers who had been erecting army huts at the nearby Codford Camp.

Collingbourne. U class No. 31626 hauls a train into the station from the north. The principal building stands on the up platform (left).

A small goods yard was provided from the start south of the station on the up side; this was extended with the opening of the through route from Swindon to Andover in 1883 and later in about 1900 simplified to two long sidings. The yard originally included a small goods shed which was removed around the time of the First World War. Freight handled at Collingbourne was never high; the tonnage dropped from over 5,000 to 3,000 during the 1930s. The year 1933 was an exception with 10,308 tons handled due to the arrival of stone for local road improvements. At the north end of the station a short siding of 1906 trailing off the up line led to a horse loading dock used primarily for the transport of race horses. In 1930 three staff were based at Collingbourne, the station master living in a station house across the yard behind the up platform.

Movements at Collingbourne were controlled from a 16 lever signal box sited towards the south end of the down platform nearly opposite the rail entrance to the goods yard. Originally supplied by the Gloucester Carriage & Wagon Company, it was a tall box with a chimney. Major alterations were undertaken in the early 1930s when the box was reduced in height by about three feet and the brick chimney removed. In 1911, in line with Company policy, a new lamp house was built at the end of the down platform near the signal box. The policy of building separate lamp storage facilities became necessary after a series of fires in station buildings.

Passengers and goods services ceased at Collingbourne in September 1961 and the station buildings were subsequently demolished. Today the actual site of the former station appears to be in private ownership and landscaped with grass and a number of small trees. A section of the brick wall adjacent to the up platform loading dock can be seen alongside the approach road. Much of the former goods yard is used for storage. An old concrete post appears to mark the position of the former entrance to the station site. The old station master's house continues in residential use, the notice on the gate stating 'Station House', with an illustration of a locomotive and train.

COLLINGBOURNE KINGSTON HALT

OPENED: 1st April 1932 (on the Swindon - Marlborough - Andover line originally opened through this site in 1882).

CLOSED: 11th September 1961.

Opened in April 1932 some 1½ miles north of the much earlier (1882) Collingbourne station, the halt served the village of the same name. It was one of a number of initiatives taken by the GWR in the 1930s to combat the increasing threat of road transport, particularly where there was direct competition from a parallel road: in this case the Marlborough to Andover road (later the A338).

Collingbourne Kingston Halt. Looking south from the adjacent road bridge. A two coach train approaches the basic halt that was open for less than thirty years.

The two platforms were constructed of old sleepers supported by a wooden framework; GWR corrugated iron huts with elliptical roofs, typical of that era, stood behind the platforms. Wooden fencing ran along the back of each platform; inter-platform movements were via paths and an adjacent road bridge to the north carrying a minor road to Brunton. Electric lighting was installed after the halt's opening at a cost of £355; the lamps were mounted on telegraph type poles and were controlled by a time switch in the shelters. Records show that some 1,500 passenger tickets were issued per year in the 1930s to passengers travelling from the halt; no staffing was ever provided and passengers had to buy their tickets from an agent at 54, Collingbourne Road, Kingston.

Today the road bridge north of the halt remains in place. The actual site of the halt is covered with undergrowth but old railway fencing marks the alignment of the old track bed. Also to be seen are posts that bordered the path from the bridge to the halt on the down side (towards Ludgershall).

CORSHAM

OPENED: 30th June 1841 (with the opening of the Chippenham - Bath section of the GWR).
CLOSED: Passengers - 4th January 1965.
Goods - 10th June 1963 (except for private sidings since closed).

Sited in a cutting in the south of the town, Corsham station opened at the end of June 1841 with the commencement of services on the Chippenham to Bath section of the broad gauge GWR main line from London to Bristol. Although the station was sited away from the town centre this did not deter passengers in the early days. The *Bath Chronicle* of 20th July 1843 recorded: 'Notwithstanding the present inconvenience of the railway station at Corsham, the number of passengers who are taken up and put down at the above place surprises the most sanguine.' In December 1879 when the lake at Corsham Park froze, Lord Methuen allowed people to skate on it and, in addition to the scheduled service to Corsham, the GWR apparently stopped expresses specially for skaters, several hundred passengers arriving daily.

Because of its siting, the main station building with three chimneys was at the top of the cutting on the up (town) side of the line in Pound Mead. Shelters, with large fretted canopies sloping up towards the tracks, served passengers on both platforms, which were lengthened in 1875. Access to the up platform was via a path; passengers using the down platform crossed a high open footbridge before descending a sloping path. The footbridge also provided a public pedestrian link to a residential area south of the line. Behind the up platform the imposing Station Hotel, at the end of Station Road, dominated the station scene.

Extensive goods facilities were available at Corsham. The public goods yard, on the up side west of the station, included a large brick goods shed and loading dock. A further large siding complex, also west of the station but on the down side, dealt with extensive movements generated by the nearby stone mines. By 1864 100,000 tons of stone were despatched by rail from Corsham annually. Trucks loaded with limestone blocks often filled this area; a stone wharf at right angles to the main line was linked to the surrounding mines by 2 ft 6 inch gauge tramways. The tramways were closed in 1939 but some stone continued to be loaded on to rail at Corsham until about 1960.

Passenger traffic was at a good level during the early years of the twentieth century: in 1903 44,937 tickets were issued; 42,905 in 1923. The following ten years saw a substantial drop to 34,866 in 1933. Nevertheless this figure was much above that found in many country stations in Wiltshire at that time. Staff numbers over this period fluctuated: a total of 13 in 1903, 11 in 1922 and 12 in 1937. These staff were employed at the station itself, in the yards and at the impressive signal box which stood on the up side at the far west end of the goods yard close to a small coal depot. It appears that this box was somewhat luxurious, having running water; electric lighting was installed in about 1963.

Corsham. The up platform and shelter. Above the shelter is the station booking office; the site is dominated by the Station Hotel.

Following the major traffic flows during the Second World War, a common feature at Wiltshire stations because of the extensive military presence in the county, levels of both passenger and goods traffic fell away in the 1950s and early 1960s. The station closed in January 1965 with the withdrawal of local passenger services between Bristol and Swindon. The goods yard had closed some eighteen months earlier in June 1963. However the siding in the goods yard serving the loading dock was retained until 1978.

Corsham. Looking west from the up platform. Large shelters with wide canopies serve the passengers. Beyond the footbridge trucks can be seen in the yard that handled extensive stone traffic from the local mines.

Following closure all the principal station structures were demolished apart from the goods shed which remains today in use by 'Crash Car Repairs'. The site of the former Station Hotel has been redeveloped for new housing; the site of the former main office is derelict but the footbridge remains, providing a useful north-south link. Although the former platforms and shelters have gone, the wall bounding the path down to the up platform can still be traced in the undergrowth.

In recent years there has been a major campaign to reopen Corsham station on a site a little to the west of the original, the potential traffic from the growing town seeming to provide a good case. It was hoped that a reopened station would be served by trains on the Bristol to Oxford service. However the withdrawal of this service from May 2003 dealt a heavy blow to the reopening aspirations.

CRICKLADE

OPENED: Goods - 1st November 1883, passengers - 18th December 1883 (with the opening of the Cirencester - Rushey Platt section of the Swindon & Cheltenham Extension Railway).

CLOSED: Passengers - 11th September 1961. Goods - 1st July 1963.

Cricklade station, on the southern edge of the town, opened in 1883 with the commencement of services on the Cirencester to Rushey Platt (Swindon) section of the Swindon & Cheltenham Extension Railway (S&CER). Goods services commenced on 1st November and passengers on 18th December. The S&CER amalgamated with the Swindon, Marlborough & Andover Railway (SMAR) in 1884 to form the Midland & South Western Junction Railway (M&SWJR).

The double tracks, on a slight curve through the station, provided an important passing point on the generally single track line. The length of the loop allowed the storage of a forty five wagon goods train to allow other services to pass. In common with other loops on the M&SWJR it was lengthened in 1942 to permit the passage of long military trains.

The two 312 ft long platforms were able to accommodate nine six wheel passenger coaches. The principal red brick building stood on the down platform, the side of the station closest to the town centre. The gabled roof was topped by three chimneys; a large canopy with fretted edges supported by three columns sheltered Swindon bound passengers. An extra ticket window was added in 1912, a modification made at a number of the M&SWJR stations at the time. A shelter with a fretted canopy stood on the up platform. During 1919 this platform was widened and the shelter was re-positioned further back from the platform edge. As with other stations on the S&CER, no footbridge was ever provided, inter platform movements being via foot-boards at the platform ends. Also in common with a number of stations on the line, Cricklade station gardens were a feature.

From the outset a range of facilities were provided at Cricklade for the handling of a variety of freight. The coming of the railway at a relatively later date than at many Wiltshire towns was seen as a major boost for local industry and agriculture, which had hitherto been served by a largely inadequate road system. The main goods yard with two long sidings was sited on the down side behind and south east of

Cricklade. Looking south in May 1960. The main building and signal box are on the down platform.

Cricklade. A view north from the up platform in 1935. Three trucks are at the down platform on which stands the station lorry.

the main station building and platform. It was conveniently placed close to the station approach road that led into the station site from the Wootton Bassett to Cricklade road (now B4553). The inner siding passed through Cricklade goods shed (42 ft x 27 ft) at the north end of which was a small goods office. Two other short sidings, again on the down side, served first a dock and secondly cattle pens. Most of the activity in the goods yard related to local industry and agriculture products but, in addition, coal supplies were imported through the station for use generally in Cricklade.

The greatest activity at Cricklade was the transport of milk, indeed for some years the station was the starting point for a milk train that served a number of Wiltshire towns and villages. The traffic expanded considerably before and during the First World War and on some days over one hundred churns a day were despatched. The increased activity prompted firstly an extension of the original milk loading platform in 1915 and then a complete re-build in 1919. This latter resulted in a 175 ft platform north west from the goods shed. This 1919 work was part of a series of improvements at Cricklade at this time, other work that year included the provision of the dock siding at the south east end of the down platform, the refurbishment of the goods shed and the erection of new fences both on the station itself and along the station approach road. These facilities generally then sufficed at Cricklade though in 1944 a seventeen place cycle rack was erected in the former storage and porters' room. No new separate replacement accommodation was provided for the porters. It is also recorded that in 1941 a camping coach was sited at Cricklade for use by land reclamation labourers working in the area.

The movements of passenger and goods trains at Cricklade were controlled from the signal box sited towards the north west end of the down platform. The 14 lever box, supplied at an early date by the Gloucester Carriage & Wagon Company, was similar to those on the Swindon, Marlborough & Andover Railway section of the M&SWJR. Considerable renovation of the box took place in 1913 and an unusual small veranda was added at the south east end sometime after 1941 to increase accommodation. Following the withdrawal of passenger services, the box was reduced in status to a ground frame.

Relatively large volumes of passenger and freight traffic were dealt with at Cricklade between the two World Wars. For instance, in 1931 7,717 parcels and churns, together with 7,106 tons of general goods were handled and 5,208 passenger tickets were issued. After 1945, as with many Wiltshire stations and halts, the competition from road transport became too strong. Closure to passengers came in September 1961 and freight services were withdrawn just under two years later in July 1963. Following closure the trackbed at the station itself and west from the station was acquired by the County Council as highways authority. All railway buildings were demolished and the main alignment used for a link road between the B4040 (Malmesbury to Cricklade) and the B4553, originally B4041, (Wootton Bassett to Cricklade). The land on either side of the road was developed for housing and today no trace can be seen of former railway activity.

Dauntsey. An early view looking west. The main building stands on the up platform, a shelter serves passengers on the down. Through the lattice footbridge and road bridge can be seen the Malmesbury branch platform.

DAUNTSEY

OPENED: February 1868 (on the Wootton Bassett - Chippenham line originally opened through this site in 1841).

CLOSED: Passengers - 4th January 1965.
Goods - 10th June 1963.

The station was sited a mile and a half south of Dauntsey village at a location called Dauntsey Lock, a name reflecting its position on the former Wilts & Berks Canal. The road from Chippenham to Wootton Bassett crosses over the station site in a north west to south east direction.

Dauntsey opened in February 1868 as a small station on the Swindon to Chippenham section of the GWR main line from London to Bristol. The original station, to the east of the road bridge, was designed by G. Drew in the style of Brunel wayside stations. The principal building, of knapped flint with limestone quoins, two chimneys and a small horizontal canopy, was on the up (north) side of the line. A waiting shelter with an integral sloping roof and fretted canopy served passengers on the down side. A station master's house was sited on the down side on the east side of the road.

A major change came in December 1877 when Dauntsey became the junction station of the branch line north to Malmesbury. The up platform was extended west of the road bridge with a terminal bay on its northern side to accommodate branch trains. For a period a double ramp existed under the road bridge between the original and new sections of the up platform; this was later eliminated. A large canopy with a rounded roof and a fretted valence was erected on the up platform extension. Further extensions were later made to both platforms to accommodate longer trains on the main line. A footbridge linked the two platforms east of the road bridge as from 1885. A large GWR notice proclaimed 'Dauntsey – Junction for Malmesbury'. A water tank on the down platform was gravity fed from the Wilts and Berks Canal. Water cranes were sited at the east end of the up platform and the west end of the down. It is thought they were removed following the loss of the Malmesbury branch connection in 1933.

In 1923 16,750 passenger tickets were issued. By 1933, the year in which the Dauntsey link to the Malmesbury branch closed, the figure had fallen to 8,211. A total of ten staff was based at Dauntsey in 1921; this reduced to seven by 1933. In 1938 when the RAF opened an airfield at Lyneham, a booking clerk was appointed to handle the increased traffic. To avoid congestion at the station at weekends, either the booking clerk or the station master went to the airfield on Fridays to issue tickets.

The junction role lasted until July 1933 when the section of the Malmesbury branch north from

Dauntsey. A later view west on 19th August 1961. The up platform extension beyond the footbridge and the Malmesbury bay platform have both gone.

Dauntsey to Kingsmead Crossing was closed, the Malmesbury branch being now shortened and linked to the Badminton cut off line at Little Somerford. The terminal bay retained its track until April 1956; at this time the canopy was dismantled and transferred to Yatton in Somerset, where it remains today, at the west end of the up platform. Soon after 1956 the up platform extension at Dauntsey west of the road bridge was demolished.

A small goods yard was sited east of the station on the up side. A siding behind the east end of the up platform served both a loading dock close to the main building and also a milk platform. Milk traffic started in the early 1920s, quantities of milk from the Malmesbury branch plus three hundred churns from Dauntsey itself being sufficient to justify a whole train to the London milk depots. Apart from milk, other traffic despatched included timber, hay and also ponies for South Wales pits. Incoming goods included coal and cattle cake, the latter stored in a grounded coach and collected by farmer's wagons. The goods yard, provided with a goods shed in the 1930s, closed in 1963. Refuge sidings were sited west of the station on the down side and east of the station on the up. The former were lifted in 1963 and the latter in 1966. Traffic movements in and around the station were controlled from a signal box on the up side immediately to the west of the Malmesbury branch line. The box closed in 1966.

Dauntsey closed for passengers in January 1965 with the withdrawal of local stopping services between Bristol and Swindon. The buildings were demolished in 1977 and today there is no trace at track side. The only reminder of the railway era is 'Old Station House', the former station master's house.

Dauntsey. No.1428 is about to leave the up side bay platform for Malmesbury in 1930. Note the canopy (right) that covers the west end of the up platform and the bay platform. Following closure of Dauntsey it was moved to Yatton (Somerset) where it remains today on the up platform.

Dean. Class 460 No.471 stands at the down platform beside the impressive station house. In the foreground (left) the signal box with ornate valence and decorative wooden framing which was in place for some years.

DEAN

OPENED: 1st March 1847 (with the opening of the Bishopstoke (Eastleigh) - Salisbury (Milford) branch of the LSWR).

CLOSED: Passengers - remains open for services on the Salisbury - Southampton line.
Goods - 30th April 1962 (except for private sidings since closed).

Sited in the village of West Dean, the station lies just within Wiltshire, the county boundary with Hampshire running north to south immediately to the east of the station buildings. The eastern sections of the two platforms are in Hampshire – indeed on the up (towards Romsey) platform today stands a notice saying 'Welcome to the County of Hampshire'. Dean opened very early in the county's railway history with the start of services on the London & South Western Railway's Bishopstoke (Eastleigh) to Salisbury (Milford) branch, the first railway to reach the cathedral city some six miles to the west.

The principal buildings, including a fine station master's house, were constructed on the down (towards Salisbury) side of the line. A smaller building with a chimney and a separate wooden waiting shelter with a canopy served passengers on the up side. Early in its life ten oil lamps provided illumination on this platform. LSWR standard cast iron lamps were later introduced. A level crossing

Dean. Looking west (from within Hampshire!) on 2nd May 1964. The main station building/station house stand on the down platform (left). Behind the up platform a siding serves cattle pens.

Devizes. Looking west in about 1907 three years before the overall roof was dismantled and replaced by platform canopies. The footbridge is in its original form with steps in the direction of travel. The 1897 signal box is in the foreground.

with a minor road is sited immediately west of the station. The original wooden level crossing gates were controlled from a signal box on the west side of the crossing on the up side. Originally built with an ornate valence and decorative wooden framing, the former was later removed and the latter clad with weather boards. The box remained in use until September 1980 when automatic half barriers came into use.

Only limited goods facilities were provided at Dean, with a siding on the up side, east of the station and behind the up platform (in Hampshire). For some years this served cattle pens. A small five ton crane assisted the limited operations. Two pairs of railwaymen's cottages stood to the north-east of the siding.

Today the station has changed very little. The main building that incorporated the station master's house has been converted into two houses, 'Pullman House' and 'Tappers Cottage'. Photographs indicate that early changes were made to the original house, including the removal of a main entrance facing the road and the addition of an extra chimney. On the down platform an old corrugated iron shed remains in a derelict state virtually hidden by creeper. On the up side the original shelter remains but the small building with the chimney has gone, though a small section of the wall remains enclosing electric signalling boxes.

DEVIZES

OPENED: 1st July 1857 (as the terminus of the Holt Junction - Devizes Branch of the GWR).
CLOSED: Passengers - 18th April 1966.
Goods - 2nd November 1964.

In the mid nineteenth century the citizens and traders of Devizes, like in many towns in Wiltshire, strove hard to bring the railway to the town. Initially there was hope that the direct London to Bristol line would pass through the Pewsey Vale and Devizes, but hopes were dashed when the GWR decided to route the line north of the Marlborough Downs through Swindon. However hopes rose when, in 1845, the Wiltshire, Somerset & Weymouth Railway (WS&WR) received approval for the construction of a line south from Thingley Junction, on the GWR west of Chippenham, to Westbury, with branches in Wiltshire to Bradford-on-Avon, Devizes and Salisbury. Early ideas for the Devizes branch envisaged a connection with the main Westbury line at Melksham or Staverton but the final agreed route

Devizes. Looking east in 1962 with two DMUs, that on the right at the down platform is on route to Westbury.

ran from near Holt to Devizes. The Thingley Junction to Westbury line opened in 1848 but financial problems delayed work on the Devizes branch until 1854, by which time the WS&WR had been absorbed by the GWR.

The 8½ mile broad gauge branch eventually opened on 1st July 1857; on this opening day shops were closed and a public holiday declared in Devizes. Several hundred people assembled at the station to see the first train depart at 7.45 a.m. The station remained crowded throughout the day and newspapers reported that some local residents spent the day travelling to and from Holt, where a band played 'Hark the conquering hero comes'!

The terminus status of Devizes lasted only five years as, in November 1862, the Hungerford to Devizes (via Patney & Chirton) Berks & Hants Extension Railway opened, entering the station site at Devizes from the tunnel under Devizes Castle. The ambition of Devizes to be on a major through rail route was at last realised, trains running from London to the West Country via Reading, Newbury, Hungerford and Devizes to either Bath and Bristol or via Westbury to Taunton and Exeter. Once again there were great celebrations in the town, including a lunch at the Corn Exchange for three hundred people. Many gathered at the station to witness the first train emerge from the tunnel under the castle. Conversion of the line through Devizes from broad gauge to standard took place over the weekend of 28th June 1874.

This much enhanced status on major through routes was however reduced after only thirty eight years when, in 1900, the GWR Stert Valley cut off line opened from Patney & Chirton to Westbury. Through trains to Taunton and Exeter now passed through Lavington and Castle Cary (Somerset) to Westbury rather than through Devizes and Trowbridge.

The development of the station facilities at Devizes very much reflected the above evolution of the rail services. Some thirteen years before the railway arrived in the town it was decided that a station, when built, should be sited on level ground south of, and below, the Market Place. Constructed in 1856/1857, south of Station Road, a crescent shaped road which ran from Northgate Street in the west to the south side of Market Place, the building was described at the time in a local newspaper as 'a very pretty building affording every accommodation that can be desired in a place of that description'. The original 1856/1857 terminus station had an overall roof covering one platform (121 ft) on the northern side and two tracks which passed through to buffer stops beyond the east end of the station. The principal building on the north side faced onto Station Road. Built of Bath stone with a slate roof and brick chimneys, it also had a 7 ft wide veranda stretching 30 ft along its frontage. The building, costing £2,243, incorporated from east to west a first class ladies' waiting room and WC; a first class general waiting room, the booking office, the superintendent's office with a parcels office behind, the second class waiting room and ladies' WC, a lamp room with porters' room behind, the main access to the platform from the road and the gent's WC and urinals.

With the conversion of the track to standard gauge the resultant extra space was used for the construction of a new island down platform with a small shelter. Extensions were also made to the old up platform. In June 1889 an iron latticework footbridge with canopy was completed at the east end of the platforms just beyond the roof; in addition the waiting facilities on the island platform were improved. Further work took place in 1907 with extensions of both platforms and widening of the down. The final set of improvements, this time on a larger scale, came in 1910/1911 when the overall roof, by then in need of renewal, was replaced by conventional platform canopies. Amendments were made to the facilities on the up platform and from this time they incorporated from east to west a general ladies' room, the general waiting room, the booking hall and office, a parcels office and cloakroom, the station master's office, a ticket collectors' office behind which was the porters' room, the main passage to the platform and the gentlemen's WC and urinals. A bookstall was also introduced at the east end of the platform. The opportunity was also taken to replace the existing waiting shelter on the down platform with two buildings. That at the eastern end incorporated a ladies' room and WC whilst the other building incorporated a general waiting room and gent's WC and urinals. A new and larger covered footbridge was constructed on the same site as the original. New fencing, gates and lighting (gas) completed this significant upgrading; these facilities continued, with only minor amendments, throughout the life of the station.

In parallel with the development of the actual station, goods facilities gradually evolved as Devizes was equally busy for both goods and passenger traffic, serving a wide surrounding rural area that, over the years, was important both for the agricultural industry and activity associated with the military. At the outset a goods yard was laid out beyond the west end of the station on the up (north) side; it included a large goods shed constructed of grey Bath stone with black timber doors. The shed incorporated a road way and single track either side of an internal wooden platform on which stood a 30 cwt capacity crane. At the east end of this central platform was a small goods office (a second storey was added in 1914) and at the western end over which was a canopy, a small warehouse. The goods yard also included a 6 ton capacity crane. At an early stage a small engine shed was erected with a single line running through; on this line was a small turntable. This engine shed was removed in about 1875, the shed facilities being transferred to Trowbridge. Through the years the goods sidings were greatly extended both north of the original goods sidings and shed following widening of the

Devizes. A view west on 5th October 1962. The main building is on the up platform (right). On the down platform two separate structures beneath the large canopy incorporate waiting and toilet facilities. The goods shed is seen beyond the far end of the up platform.

cutting (1895/96) and also south of the station where there was a series of goods loops. In 1908 a six stall stable for GWR horses was erected in the yard. A large water tank was also built north of the goods shed; with a capacity of over 6,000 gallons, it was supplied by a pipe from the Kennet and Avon Canal. At the station end of the yard was a cattle dock with two pens adjacent to the end of the up platform.

During its early life as a terminus station, movements at Devizes were controlled from a small signal box (20 levers) on the east end of the goods shed; with the introduction of trains from the east a second box (16 levers) was erected at the west end of Devizes tunnel on the up side. Both these boxes were replaced in 1897 by a large (30ft x 12 ft) box on the east end of the up platform just beyond the footbridge steps. Built of blue brick and timber, it cost £858. A 45 lever frame was installed in 1911.

The above facilities at the station served a large range of passenger and freight traffic, with peaks during the First and Second World Wars. This was because Devizes station, like many in Wiltshire, was important for the transport of military personnel, equipment and stores to the many establishments on Salisbury Plain which evolved from about 1900.

In the early days, and also between the Wars, Devizes station was the starting point for many excursion trains, in particular to the south coast. It is recorded that the first, in July 1857, took some 1,000 passengers to Weymouth; the train carried members of the Royal Wiltshire Military Band who, apparently, played on Weymouth station. From 1862 to 1900 through trains to the West Country passed through Devizes, but these decreased after the opening of the cut off line. From 1906 steam rail-motors were introduced on local services. In 1903 63,609 passenger tickets were issued; this number fell to 24,013 in 1933.

The Second World War was a boom time for passenger traffic: in 1944 59,264 tickets were sold During the war years many memorable events took place at the station including the arrival of a large number of evacuees in the early days of the war and also the return of troops evacuated from Dunkirk in 1940. Large numbers of prisoners of war also passed through the station on route to POW camps. After the War, ticket sales resumed the downward trend, with 39,849 sold in 1947 and 24,269 in 1952. By that time the competition of road transport, both public and private, had once again begun to bite as it had done between the Wars. No longer were there major movements of military personnel to compensate. Services were gradually reduced, diesel multiple units taking over in the early 1960s, and the line through Devizes was singled. The final passenger service was a Newbury to Westbury service which left Devizes at 19.36 on 16th April 1966.

Freight services were of equal importance at Devizes throughout its life. Prior to the coming of the railway the majority of heavy goods to and from Devizes were conveyed by canal, but, within a couple of years, local traders found it preferable to use the trains on account of price and speed. In particular the local coal merchants soon switched. With the opening of the line from Hungerford in 1862 it was decided to attract more trade by the establishment of a cattle and cheese market. A range of services developed, including a delivery service to local establishments by horse drawn carts; later lorries took over the services. By 1889 there were three goods agents in the town.

Although the new cut off line through Lavington took away considerable passenger traffic, freight movements in the early 1900s were heavier than ever and then increased further with the build up to the First World War. Incoming goods included fruit, provisions, vegetables and also truck loads of pigs which were driven to the Central Wilts Bacon Factory in Bath Road for slaughter. Tobacco arrived for the cigarette factory of E. & W. Anstie. Exports through the station included bacon products sent to Smithfield Market in London. Cattle and sheep were despatched after sale at Devizes market; wool was sent to mills in Yorkshire. A number of firms were based at establishments in and around the station yard.

The ten year period from the mid 1920s also saw a gradual decline in goods handled at Devizes. Parcels and miscellaneous traffic delivered and despatched during 1925 totalled 143,264 items (income £10,452); by 1934 this had fallen to 109,166 (income £6,144). The despatch of milk increased during the 1920s and did not decline until 1932. The peak was registered in 1929 with 60,791 churns handled. The build up to the Second World War saw a revival in the Devizes station freight traffic; the sidings had barely sufficient space. Petrol rationing kept the rural road transport off the road but a bonus for Devizes was the number of local military and later POW camps which needed supplies of food and clothing. The goods yard was described as a hive of activity. The freight handled was considerable and varied; an unusual import was rubble from the blitzed cities of Bristol and Plymouth. The rubble

Devizes. The long main station building behind the up platform on 15th April 1965 almost exactly a year before the station closed.

was used for hardstandings at the developing military camps. Total freight handled in the years immediately after the War averaged just over 45,000 tons. Livestock continued to be on the move from the town's cattle fairs; barley and wheat was transported to the mills at Avonmouth. After a revival in the early 1950s a rapid decline in freight traffic commenced and the last freight train ran on 30th October 1964.

With all this traffic, both passenger and freight, a large number of staff were based at Devizes; in the period 1925-1929 the total was 42. By the mid 1930s the total had fallen to 30. By 1951 it had risen to 40, but after the loss of freight traffic in 1964 only 20 staff remained at the station.

Following the withdrawal of freight services in October 1964 and passenger services in 1966 the large number of station related buildings became disused and were demolished. Today the former station site has been redeveloped with housing at the western end, including the Guiness Trust development accessed by Moyne Close. The eastern half is Station Road long term car park. Incredibly there appears to be no remnant of the station itself; Devizes tunnel is used by a rifle shooting club, 'The Ranges'. The stone castellated portal is the sole reminder of the earlier era, together with the continuing Station Road.

DILTON MARSH HALT

OPENED: 1st June 1937 (on the Westbury - Warminster line originally opened through this site in 1851).
CLOSED: Remains open as a request stop on the Westbury - Salisbury line.

The halt, at the east end of the village of Dilton Marsh, two miles south west of Westbury, opened in June 1937, some 86 years after passenger services started on the Westbury to Warminster section of the GWR Westbury to Salisbury line. From Westbury this line climbs for approximately 2¾ miles towards Upton Scudamore, and half way up the incline were constructed the original two staggered wooden platforms. Each 300 ft long and 8 ft wide, the up

Dilton Marsh Halt. The timber built down platform in 1963. Both platforms were shortened to one carriage length in 1969 and then completely rebuilt in 1994.

platform (towards Westbury) was some 40 yds north of the down platform on a curved embankment. Passengers on the two platforms were served from the outset by small wooden shelters; electric lighting was also in place from 1937. The estimated cost of the halt's construction was £1,134.

No staff were ever based at Dilton Marsh; passenger tickets were issued from 1947 to at least 1969 by a local agent, Mrs H. Roberts. A notice at the gate to the down platform access path from the B3099, which passed under the line between the halt's two platforms, indicated that Mrs Roberts lived at 'Holmdale, the 7th house up the hill'.

Because of serious deterioration, the platforms were greatly shortened at the end of 1969 to accommodate only one coach. Following several attempts at permanent closure, all strongly opposed by the local community, Dilton Marsh (the suffix 'halt' had been dropped as from May 1969) was closed completely from 5th March to 30th April 1994 for complete rebuilding at a cost of some £180,000. The short platforms were retained but were now constructed of metal and concrete components. Small wooden shelters were reinstated including wooden benches. Little else was retained of the original structures, though at the path entrances old railings and gateposts were left in place.

On reopening a plaque was unveiled by the daughter of Sir John Betjeman, Candida Lycett Green, to commemorate both the rebuilding and the former Poet Laureate's poem, 'Dilton Marsh Halt', of which these are the first and last verses:

> Was it worth keeping the Halt open
> We thought as we looked at the sky
> Red through the spread of the cedar tree
> With the evening train gone by.
>
> When all the horrible roads are done for
> And there's no petrol left to burn
> Home to the Halt from Salisbury and Bristol
> Steam trains will return.

Tickets are now obtained from staff on the diesel multiple units that provide the local stopping services. In the 2003/2004 timetable fourteen trains in the up direction towards Westbury were scheduled to stop on weekdays at Dilton Marsh if requested; in the opposite direction eleven were similarly scheduled. There is little doubt that this service was better than at any time in the history of Dilton Marsh.

Dilton Marsh Halt. The gate at the entrance to the down side access path. The notice gives directions to the local agent for the purchase of tickets.

DINTON

OPENED: Passengers - 2nd May 1859 (with the opening of the Salisbury - Gillingham section of the Salisbury & Yeovil Railway to passenger traffic) goods - 1st September 1860.

CLOSED: Passengers - 7th March 1966.
Goods - 18th April 1966 (except for private siding since closed).

Sited about a mile south west of the village, Dinton opened for passenger traffic in May 1859 with the commencement of services on the Salisbury to Gillingham section of the Salisbury & Yeovil Railway. Goods services started just over a year later in September 1860.

The principal station building, including the slate hung station master's house, stood on the up platform on the north side of the line. Also on this platform, adjacent to the west end of the building, was a small wooden cabin, probably the first signal box. Passengers on the down platform were served by a small brick shelter with a sloping roof. A small goods yard with a metal goods shed, a chicken coop, cattle pens and crane was on the up side west of the station. This yard was the focus of much activity associated with local agriculture; milk churns were often a feature at Dinton. In 1936 127,690 gallons of milk were forwarded. A footbridge connected the platforms at the east end close to a north-south minor road bridge under which the platforms

Dinton. Looking east from the down platform on 5th September 1964. Note the small original signal box on the up platform. This box and the main building seen here both remain today, the latter in residential use.

extended. The second signal box at Dinton was erected beyond the west end of the down platform; this was replaced by a third 32 lever box which opened in 1942.

Passenger numbers were never great at Dinton: in 1928 7,067 tickets were issued and this fell to 1,979 in 1936. Passenger services ceased at Dinton in early March 1966 and goods just over a month later.

Like many small stations in Wiltshire, Dinton saw much traffic associated with military activity in the area. Soon after the outbreak of the First World War work began on constructing a 2½ mile long standard gauge branch south from Dinton to Fovant Camp; this left the main line just west of the station. Until this opened on 15th October 1915 transport between the station and the Camp was by traction engine. Traffic was intense during the War and after 1918 activity associated with demobilisation continued. The Fovant Camp line finally closed in 1924, the tracks being lifted in 1926.

East of Dinton station on the up side further sidings were laid for use by the Admiralty's Baverstock depot; in 1948 they served as a site for the dismantling of thirty eight Southern Railway locomotives. Also, to the west on the up side, sidings served the RAF Chilmark depot. When the line through Dinton was singled in 1967 the former up line was retained through the station serving as a link between these two sets of military sidings. Finally, south of the station, sidings were brought into use in 1938 to serve the Dinton depot of the RAF. These were laid on part of the Fovant military railway and included exchange sidings with a 2 ft gauge system. The military sidings were greatly expanded in connection with underground munitions stores in 1942. By the early 1990s most of the sidings had been lifted.

Today the substantial station building, incorporating the station master's house, continues in residential use, the original signal box is also still there. When seen in December 2003 extensive renovation of the building was in progress. The down platform and signal box have gone. The former up line is still in place through the station, but appears rusty and unused. The former down track continues in use on this single track section of the Salisbury to Yeovil line, the nearest passing points being Wilton to the east and near Tisbury to the west.

Downton. An excellent early view looking south through the rather fragile looking footbridge.

DOWNTON

OPENED: 20th December 1866 (with the opening of the Salisbury & Dorset Junction Railway).
CLOSED: Passengers and goods - 4th May 1964.

Downton opened in December 1866 with the commencement of services on the Salisbury & Dorset Junction Railway. The S&DJ connected the Salisbury to Romsey and Eastleigh line at Alderbury Junction with the Southampton to Dorchester line at West Moors in Dorset. On the opening day bells pealed in Salisbury, this apparently costing the directors of the Railway the sum of four guineas! Downton had been the site of the ceremonial cutting of the first sod for the line's construction by Countess Nelson in February 1864, the Railway having received its Act of Parliament in 1861.

The line was generally single track throughout, originally with passing places at the five intermediate stations. Downton was the only such station in Wiltshire, the others being Breamore and Fordingbridge in Hampshire and Verwood and Daggons Road in Dorset. It was worked from the start by the London & South Western Railway, which absorbed the S&DJ in January 1883.

Sited at the east end of the High Street, the station was reasonably placed to serve this elongated village. On the up platform (towards Salisbury) stood the principal building with chimneys and canopy; an annex at the north end contained the station master's office and the gentlemen's toilets. Also at the northern end of the up platform was a large metal shed used for storage. A waiting shelter with a canopy served passengers on the down platform; a small metal shed stood near the shelter on its southern side. An open metal footbridge, erected in 1903, connected the platforms at the northern end of the station. A tall 12 lever signal box was sited at the southern end of the down platform and beyond this was the station master's house.

Until 1st December 1922 Downton was one of the passing points on the line but from that date the down loop was adopted as a siding for wagon storage and the down platform taken out of use. The footbridge was retained however, as it also connected two sections of a public right of way across the station site. With no passing movements to control, the signal box closed and became only a ground frame.

Two sidings ran behind the up platform at its southern end whilst to the north of the station in the goods yard two sidings initially served cattle pens. In November 1936, in connection with a pig marketing scheme, a new dock and pens were provided in the yard and an existing siding was slewed to serve them.

Downton was unfortunately the location for a serious railway accident in the 1880s. On 3rd June 1884 a Salisbury to Wimborne train was derailed to the south of the station. Blamed on excessive speed and possibly poor track maintenance, the accident resulted in five deaths and injuries to a further 41 passengers.

Neither passenger nor freight traffic reached great levels at Downton and all services ceased on 4th May 1964. Today virtually no trace remains of the former railway activity. The former station master's house is the only surviving building, continuing in residential use. The remainder of the former station site and goods yard has been developed for housing accessed by the appropriately named road, 'The Sidings'.

EDINGTON & BRATTON

OPENED: Goods - 29th July 1900, passengers - 1st October 1900 (with the opening of the GWR Stert Valley cut off line Patney & Chirton - Westbury).
CLOSED: Passengers - 3rd November 1952.
Goods - 25th March 1963.

Sited a half mile north of the village of Edington west of a bridge over the line carrying the minor road from Edington to Steeple Ashton, the station opened in 1900 as one of two stations on the GWR Stert Valley cut off line from Patney & Chirton to Westbury. Services for goods commenced on this line on 29th July and for passengers on 1st October. The village of Bratton is 1½ miles south west of the station on the B3098, which also runs through Edington.

The principal brick building, of a design typical of the GWR at that time, stood on the down platform (towards Westbury). With one chimney and also a canopy over the platform, it incorporated the main booking, waiting and toilet facilities. A matching brick shelter, also with a chimney and canopy, served passengers on the up platform. A covered plate steel footbridge connected the platforms. The gardens on both platforms were a very attractive feature of Edington & Bratton.

There was only road access to the station on the down side; this access also served the goods yard and shed west of the station. The brick goods shed was served by a through goods loop siding. Two further sidings ran to the south of the goods shed. Edington & Bratton signal box, also of a typical GWR brick style, stood at the west end of the up platform; the box had 24 levers but eight were unused.

Passenger traffic was never at a great level: in 1903 6,765 passenger tickets were issued; in 1923 4,511. By 1933 there was a large decline to only 930 tickets. The low level of passenger numbers continued after the Second World War and it was thus not surprising that the station closed to passenger traffic in November 1952 – over ten years earlier than others on the line, and before stopping services were withdrawn. Goods services continued until 1963.

Today all trace of the station buildings has gone on the continuing main line from London (Paddington) to Taunton, apart from a long stretch of railings that originally ran behind the up side platform and building. The former goods yard is, however, a hive of activity as the Edington Station Yard Industrial Estate. The brick goods shed remains in good condition, including the small road side canopy; a Rural Development Commission project opened here in 1995. A small red building close to the approach road entrance appears to be railway related.

Edington & Bratton. A view west in 1921 showing the footbridge and the attractive gardens on both platforms.

GRAFTON & BURBAGE

OPENED: 1st May 1882 (with the opening of the Grafton - Ludgershall - Andover section of the Swindon, Marlborough & Andover Railway).

CLOSED: Passengers and goods - 11th September 1961.

Sited in West Grafton and serving also the villages of East Grafton, three quarters of a mile to the east, and Burbage a mile to the west, Grafton & Burbage station opened in May 1882 as the northern terminus of the southern section of the Swindon, Marlborough & Andover Railway (SMAR). It became a through station when services commenced in February 1883 on the missing link between Marlborough and Grafton (see introductory text to Marlborough). Although the name board at the station apparently only indicated Grafton, the timetable always used the full name Grafton & Burbage. Double track was laid at the station itself from the outset; the line was doubled north from the station when services commenced in 1898 on the new Marlborough & Grafton Railway, It was doubled south to Collingbourne from 1902.

The principal red brick building with two chimneys, a slate roof and a horizontal fretted canopy, stood on the down platform (275 ft); it was identical to the building at Collingbourne, being built by the same contractor, John Dover. A small lean-to corrugated iron store was subsequently added at the south end of the building. Passengers on the up platform (towards Savernake) were served by a wooden shelter. No footbridge was ever provided, rail level board crossings being provided at each end of the platforms. At one time an old railway van was used as a lamp store but when this burnt down a new brick hut was built at the north end of the down platform. Approach roads to both the up and down platforms led south from the Burbage to Wilton road (later A338) which passed under the railway just north of the station.

Grafton & Burbage. Looking south in about 1958. The main building and signal box are on the down platform; a small shelter stands on the up platform.

The station's small goods yard was on the up side south of the station. A loop line ran from the goods yard behind the up platform. During the brief 1882/1883 period when Grafton & Burbage acted as a terminus, a small engine shed was provided at the far end of the yard. No details of this shed have survived, but it is assumed to have been wooden framed with wood planks.

Movements at the station were controlled from an 18 lever signal box at the south end of the down platform, supplied, as usual on this line, by the Gloucester Carriage & Wagon Company. The original wooden structure was tall, with a brick chimney, but the box was reduced in height in 1907.

In 1902 a two mile standard gauge line was opened from near Grafton & Burbage station to Dodsdown, near Bedwyn, where a brickworks had been established. The line was built to assist with the supply of bricks for the building of the new garrison at Tidworth. Being of standard gauge, through transport from Dodsdown to Tidworth was possible. When this construction was completed the line closed in 1910.

Neither passenger nor freight traffic was ever high. Much of the traffic, as at many stations in Wiltshire, was related to milk ,with up to 70 churns being dealt with per day at the peak. Between 1923 and 1938 the total receipts at the station fell from £10,582 to £856, whilst freight tonnage fell from 8,644 to 1,975.

On 21st August 1925 the station building was struck by lightning, the general waiting room chimney was demolished and the roof badly damaged. In 1941 a camping coach was based at the station; it was occupied by workers employed in adapting the nearby Malmesbury Common for war-time food production.

Following closure to all traffic in September 1961, the station building was not demolished. It is now incorporated, complete with canopy, in a large house; the area between the platforms has been infilled as part of the garden. The former lamp hut at the north end of the down platform appears to be still in place.

Great Somerford. Looking north at the wooden building and platform in February 1933, six months before the station closed.

GREAT SOMERFORD

OPENED: Passengers - 18th December 1877 (with the opening of the Malmesbury Railway from Dauntsey), goods - 1st January 1879.

CLOSED: Passengers - 17th July 1933. Goods - 22nd May 1922.

The station was sited at the northern end of Great Somerford beyond a bridge over the River Avon. It opened in 1877 when services commenced on the Malmesbury Railway which ran north from the GWR London-Swindon-Bristol line at Dauntsey to the Wiltshire market town. The formal opening ceremony took place in December (see Malmesbury text). The special train from Swindon to Malmesbury passed through the station (which was incomplete) without stopping, though apparently a great crowd was present as the train was due to call on the return trip. The *Wilts Gazette and Herald* (22nd December 1877) described the station as being 'surrounded by several choice specimens of the Wiltshire peasantry who expressed wonderment at the engine and attendant carriages'! A long wooden platform with a wooden booking office stood on the west side of the single track line. A small goods yard with a single siding behind the northern end of the platform came into use in January 1879.

A single storey cottage was initially provided for a crossing keeper who controlled a level crossing immediately adjacent to, and south of, the station. This crossing duplicated an under-rail road bridge but was considered necessary as the headroom of the bridge was only seven feet. As the volume of milk traffic at Great Somerford increased (sometimes as many as 100 carts of milk churns were handled per day), it was deemed necessary for a station master to be appointed. Enhanced accommodation was required and an extra storey was added to the cottage, costing £127. By 1903 five staff were based at Great Somerford and during the year 3,000 tons of goods were handled.

The role and status of Great Somerford station changed markedly after 1903 with the opening of the Bristol & South Wales Direct Railway. This ran east-west from a junction with the GWR at Wootton Bassett to the Bristol - South Wales line at Patchway, north of Bristol. One of the classic GWR cut off routes, it became known as the Badminton line, named after one of the Gloucestershire stations opened in 1903. The new line crossed over the Malmesbury branch, some half mile north of Great Somerford and a new station opened at Little Somerford. The goods yard at Great Somerford saw increased activity during the construction stage of the new line, as it was used by the contractors as a rail head for materials. The overall impact of the new line on Great Somerford station was, however, almost entirely negative, reflected first in the closure of the goods yard in May 1922 with many of the local traders by then using the main line facilities at Little Somerford.

In 1933 a new link was constructed from the Badminton line at Little Somerford north west to the Malmesbury branch at Kingsmead Crossing. The line south from Kingsmead to Dauntsey closed, including Great Somerford station. The track from Kingsmead Crossing south as far as Great Somerford was retained however and used until 1959 for the storage of redundant rolling stock.

All these changes were reflected in a number of variations to the station name. From 1877 to 1903 it was called 'Somerford'; this was amended to 'Great Somerford' as from 1st January 1903 to distinguish it from the nearby new station at Little Somerford on the Badminton line. After the closure of the goods depot in 1922 and the withdrawal of staffing, the suffix 'halt' was added and this remained until closure in 1933.

Soon after the closure the platform and booking office were demolished, the timber being sold for £10! The station house was retained; however it was damaged in March 1959 when one of the wagons involved in final lifting of the remaining spur was derailed and ran into the house. Today it remains in residential use and the sites of the station and goods yard are occupied by Great Somerford sewage farm operated by Wessex Water Authority. There is no trace of the former bridge or level crossing. However a railway post at the road end of the former station access (now the access to the sewage farm) still stands as a remnant of Great Somerford station.

HANNINGTON

OPENED: 9th May 1883 (with the opening of the Swindon & Highworth Light Railway).

CLOSED: Passengers and goods - 2nd March 1953.

Sited about one mile south east of the village of Hannington and close to the Blunsdon to Highworth road (B4019), the station opened in May 1883 with the commencement of services on the Swindon & Highworth Light Railway (see Highworth text). The basic wooden station building stood on a short brick platform on the south east side of the line where it passed through a shallow cutting; the building had one short chimney but no canopy.

A goods loop ran parallel to the single line opposite the platform and beyond this was a small goods yard served by a trailing siding that left the goods loop just beyond the north east end of the platform. The single siding had a capacity of about ten wagons. The principal traffic at the yard related to the local agriculture (eg cattle feed and farm machinery). South west of the station a road bridge carried a minor road from the B4019 to Hannington; the approach to the goods yard left this road north west of the bridge. The station platform was primarily accessed by a footpath down from the road near the road bridge. For some years the triangular area between the road and the station approach was renowned for its attractive garden. A small signal box at Hannington closed in 1910, the function

Hannington. A fine view of the station site from the west. A long passenger train overlaps the platform and goods wagons are stored in the small goods yard. Note the churns on the small milk platform.

Hannington. A close up of the small wooden building in a very rural setting. Note the small flat roofed extension, typical of stations on the Highworth branch, which originally housed a ground frame.

being taken on by ground frames.

Traffic levels were never high at Hannington: in 1903 7,392 passenger tickets were issued; but only 273 in 1933. Milk was an important export: for some years up to a hundred churns per day were despatched by a special milk train on the branch (see Highworth text). A small milk platform stood beside the south end of the loop. The number of staff based at Hannington in the early years is not known, but only one man was there after 1923. At one stage the Hannington station master lived in Highworth. From 1932 to 1942 Hannington came under the control of Stratton, but from 1942 the Highworth station master was responsible. It became unstaffed in 1950.

Passenger and goods services ceased at Hannington in March 1953 but the siding and loop remained in use until June 1959 and were lifted soon after. Workmen's trains continued to use the Highworth branch until August 1962 and though the station building had gone one lamp was left for the benefit of workmen using the platform.

Today little remains on the site of the former station; the cutting and bridge arch have been filled in. In recent years the site has been used primarily as a farm manure dump. In February 2004 a number of wooden posts, probably dating from the station era, could be seen among trees to the rear of the platform site and one of the former gate posts at the entrance to the goods yard approach road was still in place.

HAY LANE

OPENED: 17th December 1840 (with the opening of the Faringdon Road - Hay Lane section of the GWR).

CLOSED: 30th July 1841.

The broad gauge GWR from London (Paddington) to Bristol opened as far as Faringdon Road, thirteen miles east of Swindon, on 20th July 1840. Sections of the GWR had opened east of here over the previous two years. Bad weather conditions during the autumn of 1840 delayed work on the next section in the Chippenham area and the GWR Directors decided to open the line as far as Hay Lane, four miles west of Swindon, on 17th December 1840. No station existed at that time in Swindon itself (see Swindon GWR text).

Hay Lane was some 2½ miles east of the old Wiltshire market town of Wootton Bassett, at that time much more important than Swindon. Indeed the alternative name often used for Hay Lane was 'Wootton Bassett Road'. The railway's arrival to serve Wootton Bassett was apparently a cause for celebration including, it is recorded, an exhibition of 'old English single stick play'.

Hay Lane was, of course, only a temporary terminus. Unfortunately there are no photographs or engravings of the station, and no evidence exists of the design or details of the station structure. Records suggest that the GWR intended to provide a reasonable level of facilities but such provision does not seem to have materialised. When the line opened to Hay Lane a temporary locomotive depot was, however, provided. Closing in 1842 soon after the extension on to Chippenham came into use, it only offered sidings and facilities for water and cleaning smokeboxes and ashpans.

Until the final sections of the main line to Chippenham and through Box tunnel to Bath opened in 1841, the GWR arranged with local coach companies to provide connecting services from Hay Lane to Chippenham and Bath. Although the initial view was expressed that Hay Lane station would be a permanent feature, it closed on 30th July 1841, coinciding with the opening of Wootton Bassett station. Today no trace remains of the short lived station.

Hayes Knoll. A diesel hauled train on 9th April 2004 ready to depart south to Blunsdon. The wall to the left is a facade in front of the locomotive shed.

HAYES KNOLL

OPENED: 5th December 1999.
CLOSED: Remains open as the current northern terminus of the Swindon & Cricklade Railway.

No station or halt was sited at Hayes Knoll on the Midland & South Western Junction Railway. However in the mid 1990s the Swindon & Cricklade Railway (see Blunsdon text) decided to locate its principal work base there, a mile north of Blunsdon. A large three road locomotive shed was erected on the west side of the line. On its eastern wall a long brick platform was constructed incorporating material from a number of sources including platform slabs from Kemble in Gloucestershire and also brick paving from Swindon town centre. Mock doors and windows were placed behind the platform along the shed wall and a wooden canopy was added. Much of the wood construction was undertaken by members of the Swindon & Cricklade Railway but metal work such as the brackets (incorporating the letters S&CR) that hold the canopy and a series of lights along the platform were constructed by apprentices at the Rover car works in Swindon. This passenger platform was officially opened in December 1999. There is no public access to the site, other than by train. A fine signal box has been erected, originally built by the GWR for Rowley Regis in Staffordshire in 1887. The 30 lever frame comes from Totnes in Devon.

HEYTESBURY

OPENED: 30th June 1856 (with the opening of the GWR Warminster - Salisbury (Fisherton) line).
CLOSED: Passengers and goods - 19th September 1955.

Heytesbury was one of five stations opened in the Wylye valley when services commenced on the single track broad gauge line between Warminster to Salisbury in 1856. The others were Codford, Wylye, Langford, Wishford and Wilton GWR. Conversion to standard gauge came in 1874. The line as far as Codford to the east was doubled in 1899 and to Warminster to the west in October 1900. Unlike most of the stations on the valley line, Heytesbury station was some distance from the settlement it primarily served, being nearly half a mile south of the village centre on a minor road to Tytherington which crossed the line by a bridge.

The principal building on the down platform (towards Salisbury) was, like others on the Wylye valley line, of a typical early GWR chalet style built of local stone with a tall chimney and small canopy. It was a design used on many parts of the GWR at that time and similar to that which is preserved today on the West Somerset Railway at Bishops Lydeard. An up platform and small waiting shelter were provided after the line was doubled. Surprisingly, in view of the track curvature at this point and the resulting poor sight lines, no

Heytesbury. A close up of the main building with a small canopy and tall chimney on the down platform serving passengers travelling towards Salisbury. A goods loop passes through the large goods shed.

footbridge was ever installed, unlike at other stations along the valley. A goods yard with large goods shed was provided to the west of the station on the down side. Beyond this was the down refuge siding. An up refuge siding was sited east of the road bridge. Heytesbury's brick and timber signal box stood on the up side, almost opposite the goods shed.

As with all stations on the valley line, passenger numbers fell dramatically in the thirty years 1903 to 1933. In 1903 10,908 passenger tickets were issued, but only 1,964 in 1933. This trend reflected the fall in the local rural population due to the decline in agricultural employment.

A common feature along the valley was the construction and operation of sidings and lines serving military establishments. Sutton Veny Military Camp and Hospital opened south west of Heytesbury in 1916. A 3½ mile long standard gauge branch was constructed in 1916/1917 leaving the valley up line close to the signal box. The tracks at the hospital were laid between the long lines of huts, allowing easy transfer from the trains to the wards and operating theatres. The Sutton Veny line was operated by the GWR from May 1918; it was closed and lifted in about 1926. A short length, used as a siding at the Heytesbury end, remained in use until about 1935.

Both passenger and general freight services were withdrawn as from September 1955 though the signal box remained in use until May 1968. The down refuge siding was lifted in 1954 but the up

Heytesbury. Looking north west from the adjacent road bridge. The main station building is on the down platform (right) and beyond stands the large goods shed. A small shelter serves passengers on the up platform at the end of which is the signal box.

refuge continued to be used until December 1961. Nearly fifty years on from its closure the derelict down side building is still there beside the line but there are no significant platform remains. All other traces of former rail use have gone.

HIGHWORTH

OPENED: 9th May 1883 (with the opening of the Swindon & Highworth Light Railway).
CLOSED: Passengers - 2nd March 1953 (Workmen's trains continued until 6th August 1962).
Goods - 3rd August 1962.

Following the failure of two earlier schemes in 1845 and 1863, the aim of the Swindon & Highworth Light Railway (S&HLR) was to develop a branch from the GWR Didcot to Swindon line to Highworth, a market town six miles north east of Swindon. Although the required Act of Parliament received royal assent in June 1875, problems soon arose and the first sod was not turned until nearly four years later. The ceremony took place at Highworth on 6th March 1879, declared a public holiday in the town. Construction of the line started

Highworth. Looking east on 1st May 1960 at the wooden building with small canopy on the single platform. The station master's house is prominent beyond the station.

two weeks later but the difficulties were not yet over as in March 1881, with work virtually complete, the Board of Trade declined to sanction the passage of passenger trains because of track inadequacies. By that time the S&HLR had serious financial problems and the extra money to undertake further work was not available. The solution came with the sale of the Railway to the GWR, which had previously agreed to operate the line.

With work completed to the satisfaction of the Board of Trade, the ceremonial opening of the branch took place on 8th May 1883, again a public holiday and a day of much celebration. A train comprising six 1st class saloons, four 1st class ordinary coaches and four brake coaches left Highworth station at 11 am and reached Swindon half-an-hour later. Return from Swindon came an hour later followed by a ceremonial lunch hosted by the Directors. The branch opened to the public on the following day, the initial service being five trains each way per day. The trains ran on a line whose gradient increased over the final half mile to Highworth to 1 in 44. The limited finance available in the early days for the line's construction resulted in fairly minimum standards, for instance the loading gauge height on the line (eg depth of line below bridges) was less than the normal GWR standard. Also the alignment meant that there were restrictions on the type of coaches and wagons able to use the branch (eg for some years only four wheel passenger coaches). In accord with the branch's minimum standards, the layout and facilities at Highworth, and at stations along the line, were fairly basic.

The track layout at Highworth itself was a curved line and loop through the station to the terminal buffers, together with two sidings alongside the station approach, one of which served the goods shed. The line ran approximately west-east through the station site which, when developed, was on the western edge of the town. The station itself, to the design of Arthur Pain a railway engineer involved in the construction of a number of branch lines around the country at that time, was sited on the south side of the line. The layout of the whole site was influenced to some degree by the possible plan to extend the line north to join the East Gloucestershire Railway at Lechlade.

The main wooden building with a chimney and canopy was at the west end of the platform, this

Highworth. The main building in 1947. A small canopy above the entrance protects passengers. The extension on the left originally housed a ground frame and at the other end is the hipped roof parcels office.

Highworth. In 1951 0-4-2T No. 1436 stands at the platform. The 1897 goods shed is beyond the platform. Note the large trunks on the station trolley.

being paved with diamond patterned blue bricks. The station forecourt entrance to the booking office was also provided with a small canopy. Attached to the east end of the building was a hip roofed parcels office. At the north east end of the platform were the cattle pens and a milk dock; the pens were used well for a number of years but, following the failure of Highworth market in the mid 1920s, their use declined. Beyond this again, facing onto the station approach road, was the station master's house, built in about 1911. Until the Second World War neither the house nor the station were connected to the main water supply, water coming from a small well on the hillside above the station. The station gardens were a feature and won a number of awards.

Highworth goods yard was at the west end of the station site. One siding, which ran through a timber goods shed, terminated at a loading ramp at the west end of the platform. The goods shed, probably built in about 1897 by a local builder and the largest structure on the branch, incorporated a small office and a crane of two ton capacity. A loading gauge stood in the goods yard, an unusual feature being the horizontal top section instead of a curve, reflecting the limited headroom clearance on the branch.

The layout and facilities remained relatively unchanged throughout the station's life. In 1903 32,390 passenger tickets were issued, and in 1933 4,402. Goods exported from the station included oriental mats and carpets from the Vorda works and agricultural equipment from W. Bartrop & Son; the latter factory sent out 36 tons of horseshoes in one week during the First World War! Highworth station was also a major exporter of milk, churns being brought to the station initially by horse and cart and then later by lorry. In the 1920s a special milk train served stations on the whole branch but by the early 1930s, with traffic taken away by road transport, the milk trains ceased to run. Inward goods included coconut fibre and steel as well as the normal requirements of local traders and residents (eg coal and fertilisers).

An average of five staff were employed at Highworth in the 1930s. Between 1932 and 1942 Highworth lost the post of station master, the station coming under the control of the station master at Stratton. During the Second World War the Highworth post was reinstated, the new appointee taking control of both Highworth and Hannington stations. From 1950 he was given the responsibility of all stations on the branch until its closure.

Public passenger services ceased on the Highworth branch in March 1953 but it remained open north of Stratton for goods traffic until August 1962. However during these nine years workmen's trains, particularly taking workers to and from Swindon, ran on the branch but they were not advertised for general public use.

Following complete closure in 1962 the station buildings deteriorated; by 1969 the station house had been demolished but the station building itself remained until 1970, used as a site office for the major new development, Home Farm Estate. Today Station Road follows the alignment of the former station approach road. On Station Road, senior citizen housing has been developed called 'Fairview' (apparently the name 'Beeching Folly' was considered but rejected!). The general alignment of the branch into the station from the west is followed by the eastern section of a residential road, 'Windrush'.

HOLT JUNCTION

OPENED: 1st April 1874 (On the Thingley Junction - Westbury line originally opened through this site in 1848).
CLOSED: Passengers - 18th April 1966.
Goods - 7th October 1963.

The Wilts, Somerset & Weymouth Railway opened from Thingley Junction, west of Chippenham on the GWR, to Trowbridge and Westbury in September 1848. It passed about a mile east of Holt village but no local passenger station or halt was provided at that stage. The catalyst for action came with the construction and opening of a branch line to Devizes which veered east from the main line from a point to the east of Holt in July 1857. Most sources suggest that it was only four years later, in 1861, that any facility was provided at the junction and then only a small exchange platform for passengers wishing to transfer between main line and branch trains. However recent research suggests that a facility of some kind did exist at Holt from 1857. What is certain, from local newspaper accounts, is that the opening of the branch was celebrated by Holt residents, who apparently formed a procession 'with flags, banners and music from a band' to meet the first train. It also seems that many of the villagers took a trip on the first day and thus some means of access to the trains must have been provided!

The station opened formally to local residents as from 1st April 1874 and by the turn of the century the facilities had been improved from a narrow platform with a hut, a signal box and a number of sheds to a more substantial station. The platform was widened and the original small wooden hut was replaced in 1895 by a larger wooden building accommodating a ladies' waiting room and toilets built to GWR specifications at a cost of £175. A canopy was added in 1913 to cover some 30 ft of the platform. A small separate wooden building at the north end of the platform housed the gentlemen's toilet.

In the early days of public opening there was no access road to the station. Passengers had to cross fields via a footpath to the station yard. Assisted by a public subscription of £200, a road was built in 1877, co-incident with this came the construction of a goods shed. The new road was completed to the station by November and to the goods shed by December 1877. A much needed further improvement was the construction in 1895 of a footbridge from the access road over the goods yard line to the island platform; prior to this passengers were required to use a rail level board crossing.
Over the years a number of additions and alterations were made to the station facilities including the provision of parcels offices and lamp huts. Throughout its life Holt was lit by oil or tilley lamps; no electric lighting was ever provided.

Local reports indicate that in 1890 12,226 passenger tickets were issued (receipts £637); in the

OPPOSITE PAGE TOP Holt Junction. A fine record of the Beavan's Tannery outing waiting for the train to Portsmouth on 4th July 1905.

OPPOSITE PAGE BOTTOM Holt Junction. A view north from the footbridge in about 1949. The station building is surrounded by a large canopy added in 1913.

BELOW Holt Junction. Looking north in about 1905. The 1895 open footbridge gives safe access to the island platform over the line to the goods shed.

BOVRIL
PHOENIX FIRE
Holt Station
Portsmouth
July 4th 1905

same year 4,508 tons of goods were despatched (receipts £2,189). The number of tickets issued rose to 15,518 in 1923 but then fell dramatically to 4,024 in 1933. Both through and local passenger trains stopped at Holt, the latter often being steam rail-motors running between Chippenham and Trowbridge. The passenger totals rose greatly during the Second World War with the movements of military personnel based in Wiltshire. Indeed during the War there were at times 43 trains stopping each day. For some years special excursion trains also ran from Holt, for instance the local Beavan's tannery ran special excursions to Portsmouth in 1905 and Weymouth in 1908.

Goods from a number of local factories and a large amount of agricultural produce were despatched from Holt. The tonnage forwarded rose from 2,765 in 1903 to 10,912 in 1933. Milk traffic was a particular feature at Holt. In 1897 the Anglo-Swiss Condensed Milk Company (later Nestles) purchased the former Staverton Cloth Mill. An outlet was required for rail transport of the milk products and in 1909 a large covered loading bay was constructed west of Holt station. This remained in use until 1934 when a direct rail connection was made into the factory over a mile south of Holt. Traffic was particularly heavy during the Second World War with milk production required for the troops. These private sidings remained in use until 1966; the tracks were removed a year later.

All this traffic, both passenger and freight meant that a fair level of staffing was maintained at Holt throughout the years. In 1938 it is recorded that 12 staff were based there including a station master for whom a house had been built in 1925 at the head of the Station Approach by A. & W. Mortimer Bros. at a cost of £675. Three of the station staff were housed in Foxhill Cottages in Station Road.

Throughout its life Holt enjoyed a relatively greater importance for freight rather than passenger traffic; no major housing development took place nearby to generate local passenger use. The goods yard closed in October 1963 and most of the sidings were lifted soon after. Passenger services ceased on 18th April 1966 when local services were withdrawn on the Chippenham to Trowbridge line. The signal box sited on the up side close to the Devizes branch closed in February 1967. The station buildings and platforms were soon demolished and little trace can be seen today. The goods shed had been demolished earlier in 1953 but its office remained for some years. The old milk platform was used by the local coal and builders' merchants but this has now gone, though the yard itself continues to be used for those purposes. Much of the former station site is now in use for the storage of caravans. The sole significant reminder from the railway era is the former station master's house at the end of Station Road, now used as an office by the coal merchant.

HULLAVINGTON

OPENED: Goods - 1st January 1903, passengers - 1st July 1903 (with the opening of the Wootton Bassett - Patchway GWR cut off line).

CLOSED: Passengers - 3rd April 1961.
Goods - 4th October 1965 (coal depot only from 10th June 1963).

Hullavington opened for passenger traffic in July 1903 on the GWR cut off line from Wootton Bassett to Patchway (the Badminton line). Goods services had commenced on the line seven months earlier (see Wootton Bassett text). The station was sited about a half mile north of the village on an embankment between the minor road from Hullavington to Norton to the west and the main road from Chippenham to Malmesbury to the east.

Access to the station was via a tree-lined drive sloping up from the Norton road; this led to the rear of the up platform (399 ft 6 inches long) on which stood the station's principal building. This incorporated the gentleman's toilet, the ladies' waiting room, a general waiting room/booking office and the station master's office. This building was a good example of the GWR standard design for country stations of the early 1900s, as built all along the Badminton cut off line. Of brick construction with a slate roof and a wide fretted canopy, it cost approximately £490. On the down platform stood a matching brick shelter with one chimney and a fretted canopy. The platforms were linked by a footbridge sited immediately to the east of the station building and shelter. Unlike Little Somerford to the east, the platforms were served by the through lines and not loops which also allowed goods trains to be stored whilst faster trains overtook. At Hullavington these 'refuge' facilities, accessed by trailing connections, were to the west of the station for the up line and to the east for the down line. These sidings were able to store some seventy wagons each.

The approach road continued past the up side building to the goods yard which was served by a single goods loop, with a head shunt at either end,

Hullavington. A view towards Wootton Bassett on 27th July 1961. The main building is on the up platform (left), the goods shed can be seen in the distance through the covered footbridge beyond the up platform.

and a mileage siding on the northern side. The yard had a capacity of 56 wagons. Facilities in the yard included a loading platform and small brick goods shed or 'lock up' and a 1½ ton capacity crane. The west end head shunt terminated behind the up platform and served cattle pens and a coal bunker. At the entrance to the goods yard was the weighbridge, weighbridge office and coal depot office.

Traffic movements at both the station and goods yard were controlled from a timber signal box just beyond the east end of the down platform. This traffic was of a similar level to other stations on the Badminton line – some four to six passenger trains per weekday each way and two each way on a Sunday together with a small number of goods trains calling when required. The low level of passenger movements is illustrated by the number of tickets issued: 3,902 in 1913, 1,692 in 1933, and approximately 3,500 in 1946.

The station was initially staffed by a station master, two porters and two signalmen. A substantial company house was built for the station master at the head of the station approach road; a little further towards the station a pair of cottages was provided for the signalmen. In the mid 1930s a third signalman was appointed, replacing a porter, and an additional house was built at a cost of £550. It appears that only station masters and signalmen had sufficient status in the GWR for housing to be provided at or near the stations! All the railway houses along the Badminton line were built by a local contractor, Pearsons; they were of a design not found elsewhere on the GWR. During the 1930s a country lorry service was based at Hullavington serving the local rural area. The driver became an extra member of the Hullavington staff.

Some amendments to the signalling and track layout took place in 1938; three years later both the refuge sidings were provided with facing connections thus giving greater operational flexibility. The down loop was also extended behind the down platform and signal box giving a total length of about a half mile. Much of this work was aimed at achieving greater capacity for essential war time movements of long trains.

Passenger services were withdrawn at Hullavington in April 1961; general goods services continued until June 1963 and a coal depot was served until October 1965. Today there are no traces of the platforms and the site of the main station building is occupied by a number of cabins housing electrical equipment. The former small brick goods shed still stands with a section of the loading platform, the sole building in an otherwise derelict site. On the approach road the former station master's house and pair of signalmen's cottages remain in residential use.

Idmiston Halt. Looking south west, the concrete shelter on the down platform provides protection for passengers, particularly from the adjacent military camp, travelling in the Salisbury direction.

IDMISTON HALT

OPENED: 3rd January 1943 (on the Andover - Salisbury line originally opened through this site in 1857).
CLOSED: 9th September 1968.

The halt opened in January 1943 to serve the nearby Porton Down Military Camp, which was adjacent to, and south east of, the main LSWR line. Access to the halt, sited partly in a cutting, was from a lane that connected Idmiston village to the Camp. The lane passed under the line north east of the halt. The platforms were constructed of concrete components; a concrete shelter stood on the down platform serving passengers travelling towards Salisbury, the principal destination of travellers from the halt. No shelter was provided on the up platform. Prior to the opening of Idmiston Halt, Camp personnel travelled on the Porton Down Military Railway, a narrow gauge railway that connected the Camp to Porton station some three quarters of a mile south west of the halt. Idmiston Halt closed in September 1968 and today no trace remains at lineside.

LACOCK HALT

OPENED: 16th October 1905 (on the Thingley Junction - Westbury line originally opened through this site in 1848).
CLOSED: 18th April 1966.

Sited about one mile west of the village centre, Lacock was one of four halts built and opened by the GWR at, or shortly after, the commencement of a steam rail-motor service between Chippenham and Trowbridge via Melksham. Such services, designed to increase patronage on local trains, had been introduced by the GWR some two years earlier in the Stroud valley in Gloucestershire between Chalford and Stonehouse.

Lacock Halt opened in October 1905, a fortnight

Lacock Halt. The arrival of the first train on 16th October 1905. Unusually an additional van and engine are attached to the steam rail-motor. The GWR pagoda huts have not yet been erected.

Lacock Halt. No. 1403 propelling a Chippenham to Trowbridge auto train into the halt in August 1949. The two GWR pagoda huts were erected just prior to the First World War.

after the start of the rail-motor service. Initially the 99 ft long platforms were only 2 ft high, this being overcome by the use of retractable steps on the rail-motors. Just after the First World War the platform height was raised so that all trains could use the halt. At about this time the original small metal huts were replaced by standard GWR pagoda huts. Access to the platforms was via two sloping paths down from a road bridge to the south of the halt.

To the north west of the halt six sidings were provided for the use of the Air Ministry early in 1943, as part of the operations then being planned for the invasion of Europe. A signal box was also installed at this time. This closed with the siding complex in October 1964.

The halt closed with the withdrawal of local passenger services on the line in April 1966. Today remains of the up (towards Chippenham) platform can still be seen and the gate and asphalt path (with brambles!) are still there on the down side.

LANGFORD

OPENED: 30th June 1856 (with the opening of the GWR Warminster - Salisbury (Fisherton) line).
CLOSED: October 1857.

Langford was one of six stations opened in the Wylye Valley when services commenced in June 1856 on the broad gauge single track line between Warminster and Salisbury. Sited between Wylye and Wishford, it had a very short life, closing some fifteen months later in October 1857. Unfortunately no photographs or details of Langford station are known.

LAVINGTON

OPENED: Goods - 29th July 1900, passengers - 1st October 1900 (with the opening of the GWR Stert Valley cut off line Patney & Chirton - Westbury).
CLOSED: Passengers - 18th April 1966.
Goods - 3rd April 1967.

Serving the villages of Market Lavington, one and a half miles to the east, and West Lavington, one and a half miles to the south, Lavington station was actually sited just north of Littleton Pannell on the Devizes to Amesbury road (A360). Built largely on

Lavington. An early view looking east with three staff posing on the down platform as a mixed goods train stands at the up platform beneath the covered footbridge.

an embankment immediately west of the railway bridge over the A360, the station opened in 1900 as one of two stations on the GWR Stert Valley cut off line from Patney & Chirton to Westbury.

Because of its embankment location, lightweight materials were necessary and in the early days the platforms were largely constructed of wood, though later the surface was replaced by paving and gravel. The principal brick building, of a design typical of the GWR at that time, stood on the down platform (towards Westbury); with one chimney and a canopy over the platform, it incorporated the main booking, waiting and toilet facilities. A matching brick waiting shelter, also with a chimney and canopy, served passengers on the up platform. A plate steel footbridge, with cover both over the bridge itself and approach steps, connected the two platforms beyond the west ends of the building and shelter. On the down side platform a metal store was added later. Approach roads led up from the A360 to both up and down platforms; in the case of the latter the road also served Lavington goods yard and shed which were sited to the west of the station on the down side.

A loop siding ran through the brick goods shed; the goods yard also included further sidings both beyond and to the south of the shed. A short siding also led back to a loading dock at the west end of the down platform. On the up side a long siding was added in 1914 for military use; in 1944 this was lengthened and converted into a long loop thus giving greater capacity on the line for the intensive use by war-time traffic. The loop closed in 1964.

The rail traffic at Lavington was principally controlled by the 22 lever typical GWR style brick West signal box at the west end of the up platform. In its latter years it was used only at peak times and ceased to operate after 22nd January 1979, some twelve years after the station closed. From about 1903 to 1914 there was also a small East box at the east end of the down platform. This was demolished when both platforms were lengthened in 1914.

In 1903 fourteen staff were based at Lavington; the number had dropped to six by 1913. A total of nine or ten was normal between the wars but after the Second World War the number decreased and, as from November 1965, Lavington station was unstaffed. Passenger trains ceased to call after 18th April 1966 and the goods yard closed just under a year later.

Today there is no line side trace of the station as high speed trains continue to pass through on the London (Paddington) to Taunton route. A scrapyard occupies the site of the former downside buildings and goods yard. The former Railway Hotel standing south of the junction of the down side approach road

Lavington. Another view this time looking west - the goods shed and the West signal box are seen through the footbridge.

with the A360 was empty and to let when seen in early March 2004. Behind the hotel building was the Littleton Pannell Mobile Home Park. At the former entrance to the up side approach road, adjacent to the A360 and north of the rail over bridge, an old gate post supported by a small section of track and a short section of fencing appears to be the only remnant of the former Lavington station.

LIMPLEY STOKE

OPENED: 2nd February 1857 (with the opening of the Bathampton Junction - Bradford South Junction line).
CLOSED: Passengers - 3rd October 1966.
Goods - 4th January 1960.

Limpley Stoke station was sited below the village in the valley bottom of the River Avon between Bathampton and Bradford-on-Avon. The line, originally a broad gauge single track connecting Bathampton on the GWR London to Bath and Bristol line and Bradford South Junction on the Thingley Junction to Westbury line, opened in February 1857. It was, and continues to be, in a classic narrow transport corridor along with the A36 road and the Kennet and Avon Canal. In the course of building, the track bed was laid sufficiently wide to accommodate a double track; this did not come into use however until 1885, and by that time the line had been converted to standard gauge (July 1874). The station, as originally built, consisted of a short platform sited on the west side of the single track with a timber station building. A timber platform with a waiting shelter was provided to serve the doubled line from 1885.

A significant event for Limpley Stoke was the opening in 1910 of the Cam Valley line from

Limpley Stoke. The main building on the down platform following major redevelopment when the line to Camerton opened in 1910. Note the tall water tower and the original small signal box (left).

Limpley Stoke. The 1910 North signal box at the north end of the down platform dominates this photograph, the main station building and the original signal box are beyond. The small goods shed can be seen through the footbridge beyond the end of the up platform (left).

Camerton and Hallatrow. This served both residents of the valley and more important, the collieries. The passenger service commenced in May 1910 with a rail-motor service of five trains each way per day, normally starting and terminating at Limpley Stoke. The service only lasted 15 years with trains ceasing in 1925; a long temporary withdrawal of services during the First World War lasted from March 1915 until July 1923. Coal and mineral traffic continued for another 25 years with goods services ceasing in February 1951. The large Camerton Colliery had closed in April 1950.

The Cam Valley line branched west some 700 yds north of Limpley Stoke station, the track running initially parallel to the main line. The station itself was redeveloped, including the extension of both platforms by 200 ft. A 150 ft bay platform was also added at its northern end on the down side to serve the Camerton line trains. A replacement station building was also provided. Constructed of a timber frame mounted on a brick plinth, the walls were constructed of 2 ft square artificial stone slabs. It is possible that some fittings from the original structure were used. The roof was covered with artificial tiles. Standing at the southern end of the down platform (towards Bath), facilities comprised a booking office, booking hall (which doubled as a waiting room) and a ladies' waiting room with WC. Gent's toilets were provided in a brick structure between the footbridge and the North signal box. A wooden shelter with a small canopy served passengers on the up platform (towards Bradford-on-Avon).

Both platforms were originally built of wood to reduce weight on the embankment site but sections were later reconstructed with concrete components. The platform lighting was changed from oil to incandescent gas in 1905, and the platforms were linked by an open plate metal footbridge, running from north of the main building on the down platform to south of the waiting shelter on the up. The bay platform became disused after the Cam Valley passenger services ceased in 1925 but the bay line continued in occasional use until 1958. Access to the station for passengers was via a flight of steps to the down platform from the adjacent Limpley Stoke to Freshford road. In 1903 25,695 passenger tickets were issued; this fell to 13,239 in 1933.

At the extreme south end of the down platform stood the original small wooden signal box. It is not known when this was provided. It was replaced from

1910 by two signal boxes, one, the North Box, at the northern end of the same platform and another (the South Box) a little to the south of the station. The North Box was reduced in status to a ground frame in 1927 and the South Box eventually closed in August 1969. The original box remained in use for some years as a parcels office. Another feature of the station was a tall water tank immediately south of the station on the down side.

Two goods sidings were laid parallel to the main line south of the station, that on the down side being used for the loading of local stone. In 1903 2,736 tons were despatched; by 1913 this had reduced to 577 and in subsequent years it often fell below the 100 ton mark. The siding on the up side served a short platform on which was a timber goods lock up. It was sited close to the mills from which most of the traffic originated.

A further important feature of Limpley Stoke was the extensive area of sidings laid in 1910 south of the station towards Freshford station (Somerset). This complex was extensively used by coal trains coming down the branch line from Camerton and other Cam valley collieries. The sidings were sited there as there was insufficient room available in the valley any closer to where the branch joined the main line. It meant however, that all the coal trains passed through Limpley Stoke en route to the siding complex. These sidings, then in use for other purposes, continued beyond the closure of both the local collieries and the Cam valley line. They were eventually lifted during the large scale 1960's rationalisation programme.

During the 1950s camping coaches were often sited at Limpley Stoke Station. Staffing ceased in March 1961 and the station was re-designated as a halt. It closed to passenger traffic in October 1966, goods traffic having been withdrawn more than six years earlier in January 1960.

Following closure the platforms and waiting shelter were dismantled but the main building survived. It was taken over in the early 1990s by a transport bookseller and given the name 'The Titfield Thunderbolt', after the famous 1952 film largely shot on location on the Camerton line at Monkton Combe. Today however, the building appears to be derelict with the gate to the access steps locked. South of the building sections of old railway railings and posts are still in place as is a notice, 'Beware of the trains'.

LITTLE SOMERFORD

OPENED: Goods - 1st January 1903, passengers - 1st July 1903 (with the opening of the Wootton Bassett - Patchway GWR cut off line).

CLOSED: Passengers - 3rd April 1961.
Goods - 10th June 1963.

Little Somerford opened for passenger traffic in July 1903 on the GWR cut off line from Wootton Bassett to Patchway (the Badminton line). Goods services had commenced on the line seven months earlier (see Wootton Bassett text). Sited at the southern end of the village, four tracks ran through the station, up and down main lines and two loops serving the up (399 ft) and down (401 ft) platforms. The prefix 'Little' was included from its opening; at the same time in 1903 the prefix 'Great' was added to the 1877 Somerford station on the Malmesbury branch to avoid confusion between the two stations.

The principal brick building, with two chimneys, a fretted canopy and a slate roof, stood in the centre of the up (towards London) platform. From west to east it incorporated a porters room, the station master's office, a general waiting room/booking office, the ladies' waiting room and a gent's toilet. A small brick waiting shelter, incorporating toilets, with one chimney and a fretted canopy stood towards the west end of the down platform. This offset siting was apparently due to foundation difficulties. Linking the two platforms was a metal covered footbridge. The canopy on both the main building and shelter extended to the footbridge steps. Initially the platform had timber and gravel surfaces but, following deterioration, this was later replaced by paving slabs. The buildings at Little Somerford were typical of the GWR country station design used throughout the Company's system in the early 1900s; the approximate cost of the main building was £491 and the shelter £172.

All access to Little Somerford station was on the up side via a long drive from the Swindon to Chippenham road which passed beneath the lines just west of the station. This drive led to the rear of the up side building and then past the weighbridge to the goods yard which incorporated a goods loop, mileage siding, goods platform (58 ft) with goods lock up, loading dock and cattle pens. A 6 ton capacity crane alongside the mileage siding and a one ton crane next to the goods shed completed the yard facilities.

The Little Somerford wooden signal box stood at

Little Somerford. Looking east on 28th May 1961. The covered metal footbridge crosses the four tracks from west of the up side building (left) to east of the down side shelter. Malmesbury branch trains used the up platform from 1933 to 1951.

the east end of the down platform at a point where the signalmen were able to view both ends of the station loops where they connected with the main lines. These loops were used not only by passenger trains stopping at the platforms but also by goods trains halting to allow fast passenger trains to overtake on the two through lines. In 1912 short sidings or 'head shunts' were added at the trailing ends of both loops to give more room for manoeuvring goods trains, particularly if these were longer or nearly as long as the loop itself. This was a problem that arose more in the Second World War with the movement of long military trains and in 1941 both loops were lengthened.

A significant change in the role of Little Somerford station came in 1933 following the decision to shorten the south-north Malmesbury branch. From its opening in 1877 the branch had linked with the main GWR London to Bristol line at Dauntsey, between Swindon and Chippenham. When the GWR Badminton cut off line was constructed and opened in 1903 it crossed the branch at right angles just west of Little Somerford. The GWR decided, as an economy move, to abandon the southern section of the branch from Dauntsey north to Kingsmead Crossing and to introduce a link spur from the cut off line leading west from Little Somerford station. This new arrangement commenced in July 1933. The new spur which was, in fact, a westward extension of the 1912 headshunt on the up side loop, led into the up platform at Little Somerford. No bay platform was constructed, a contrast with many other GWR main line stations when subsequent branches were constructed. In the case of Little Somerford it was not really needed as there were four tracks through the station, with non-stop trains not passing immediately along the platforms giving more capacity to accommodate the branch line trains at the up platform. The bridge over the road west of the station was widened to accommodate the branch line. This new role as a junction station lasted just under twenty years until passenger services ceased on the Malmesbury branch in 1951. During this period the name-board at Little Somerford proclaimed 'Little Somerford – Change for Malmesbury'.

Both passenger and freight traffic was relatively light throughout the life of Little Somerford. An average of six passenger trains stopped at the station each way on weekdays and two each way on Sundays. This low level of service was reflected in the number of passenger tickets issued: in 1913 these totalled 4,662; the figure fell to 2,853 in 1933. Goods handled at the station were principally linked to livestock and milk; in some years the receipts for such traffic exceeded, by a large margin, that for passenger traffic, particularly in the 1930s (eg in 1933 passengers £488; goods £2,991).

At its opening a station master was appointed who supervised two porters and three signalmen. For some years a lad porter was also at Little Somerford but this post was abolished in 1946. From 1922 the station master also supervised operations at Great Somerford on the Malmesbury branch; in the mid 1930s the supervisory role was again extended to include Brinkworth. At both Great Somerford and Brinkworth the post of station master had been abolished. Accommodation for the Little Somerford station master was originally provided in a company house about a third of a mile away, but later a detached house was built nearer the station. This and a pair of semi-detached cottages were sited in a private lane on the down side west of the station.

Records suggest water supply problems arose at Little Somerford, both for the station and the accommodation. For a period water was brought in by a rail borne tanker and then distributed in churns. There was a failed attempt at sinking a well but the final solution was the installation of a pump house to take water from the nearby River Avon.

Passenger services were withdrawn in April 1961 and goods traffic just over two years later in June 1963. The station loops were abandoned in 1966 and the signal box closed in 1967. Today at track side the down platform is clearly visible. At the head of the station access drive the two original gateposts stand. They are exactly the same as can still be seen at Badminton, Coalpit Heath and Brinkworth stations on the cut off line, and carry the inscription 'T. James Vulcan Foundry, Cardiff 1902'. The old station master's house and the pair of cottages continue in residential use on Meadow Lane, the former named 'Station House'.

Ludgershall. Looking west in about 1905. Staff pose for the camera in front of the main building (right) and on the very wide up platform. Note the very small shelter on the latter and the long covered footbridge.

LUDGERSHALL

OPENED: 1st May 1882 (with the opening of the Grafton - Ludgershall - Andover section of the Swindon, Marlborough & Andover Railway).

CLOSED: Passengers - 11th September 1961.
Goods - 24th March 1964 (except for sidings that remain open for military traffic).

Sited just within the eastern boundary of Wiltshire, the original station at Ludgershall opened with the commencement of services in May 1882 on the Grafton to Andover (Hants) section of the Swindon, Marlborough & Andover Railway (SMAR). In 1884 the SMAR amalgamated with the Swindon & Cheltenham Extension Railway to form the Midland & South Western Junction Railway (see Swindon Town text). The original 1882 SMAR station had a simple layout with two through tracks with crossing facilities serving two platforms on the otherwise then single line. In addition there was a small goods yard of two sidings and a small corrugated iron goods shed.

These facilities served Ludgershall for some fifteen years, but in the late 1890s the Government began to make use of Salisbury Plain for military purposes and by 1900 the War Office had decided to base both camps and a new barracks in the area. In particular it was decided to develop a major garrison and barracks at Tidworth and a new branch line was proposed from Ludgershall to Tidworth (see Tidworth text). This opened for military traffic in July 1901, to War Department traffic in May 1902, to public goods traffic in July 1902 and to public passenger traffic in October 1902. The new role as a

Ludgershall. The impressive covered footbridge designed to cope with large troop movements between the extensive platforms.

centre for military traffic and also as a junction for the Tidworth branch was the catalyst for the major re-modelling and extension of Ludgershall station over the period 1900-1902. This led to it becoming the largest station in area on the Midland & South Western Junction Railway (M&SWJR) system, covering some sixteen acres.

The SMAR line was doubled south east to Weyhill (Hants) in 1900 and north to Collingbourne a year later. A long down bay line was laid through the north side of the station site behind the very long (943 ft) down platform; this bay line reached almost to a bridge at the west end of the station site which carried the Ludgershall to Tidworth road. This bay line effectively transformed the down platform into an island; in addition a bay line was constructed on the south side of the station behind the west end of the up platform (735 ft) for use by Tidworth branch trains. The principal station building stood on the down (towards Andover) 'island' platform; constructed of brick with three chimneys, a series of short canopy sections provided cover for waiting passengers. Only a small wooden shelter served passengers on the up (towards Collingbourne) platform.

The outstanding feature of Ludgershall station was the extensive and wide platforms designed to accommodate the large numbers of troops and volumes of freight. It is recorded that at times up to ten troop trains arrived per day. The platforms, generally with a gravel surface, were connected in 1902 by a covered lattice footbridge that crossed both the long down side bay line and the two through main lines. It was one of only three footbridges on the M&SWJR; at its northern end the foot of the steps was immediately adjacent to a booking office erected in 1900. Prior to this, when the station was much smaller, tickets were issued in the main building. The new booking office faced east onto the station approach road which led south from the main Andover Road in the centre of Ludgershall. Access from the booking office to the platforms was primarily over the footbridge; however a level passage was possible across the down bay line via a rail level board crossing linking to dips in the platforms. On the south east corner of the Approach Road and Andover Road the large Prince of Wales Hotel was constructed in the 1900-1902 period in anticipation of major business associated with the new military activity. This never really materialised, as the focus of activity in the area developed at Tidworth, some two miles away.

In parallel with the redevelopment of the station itself, a major goods yard was laid out west of the Tidworth Road bridge in the V between the main line to Swindon and the Tidworth branch. The yard incorporated a long loading platform (655 ft) and a timber framed corrugated iron goods shed. A two road engine shed with a wooden frame covered by wooden boarding was erected in 1903 for use by Tidworth branch engines. It stood south of the loading platform adjacent to the branch line. Further sidings were also laid south of the Tidworth branch. Movements at Ludgershall, both at the station itself and in the extensive yard, were largely controlled from the signal box on the up platform between the footbridge and the Tidworth bay platform. The original 1882 box was replaced on about the same site in 1901 by a larger 40 lever brick box supplied by Pease and Company of Worcester. The sight lines into the yard from the signal box were hindered somewhat by the Tidworth Road bridge. A further

Ludgershall. Australian troops on the wide up platform in about 1906.

signal box known as the Perham Box stood a short way along the Tidworth branch.

With the increased train movements, there was great demand for water to supply the locomotives and a large water tank of 10,000 gallon capacity was erected in 1916 south of the station on the embankment. This tank supplied water to pumps at each end of the two platforms. The M&SWJR however avoided using these pumps as far as possible because of the high cost of the water supplied by the War Office!

The level of all types of traffic was high for many years at Ludgershall, in particular during the two World Wars. Even in the inter-war period passenger movements were large and in 1923 29,000 passenger tickets were issued. Passenger traffic was particularly great at the time of the annual Tidworth Tattoo. Freight handled at the station rose from 8,000 to 14,000 tons over the 1923-1938 period. Staff levels varied from 15 in 1923 to 12 in 1938; it was reported that during the times of major troop manoeuvres the staff worked 12 hours per day for six days a week. One early highlight came in November 1917 when King George V stayed for three days in the Royal Train stabled in the down bay line at Ludgershall.

The Tidworth branch engine shed closed as early as 1925 but otherwise the extensive facilities largely remained in operation until the 1950s. The Tidworth branch closed for passenger traffic in September 1955 and the Ludgershall bay line was lifted. Public goods traffic on the branch only continued for a further two months. The branch continued in use for military purposes until the end of July 1963. By that time Ludgershall station had closed for passenger traffic with the withdrawal of passenger services on the Swindon to Andover line in September 1961. Public goods services continued until March 1964. The two lines through the station were retained,

Ludgershall. King George V inspecting the troops at the station on 8th November 1917. The booking office is to the right with the footbridge beyond.

serving the yard west of the road bridge. This is still the case today though the old bridge has been replaced by a new structure immediately to the west. The old yard lines are all MoD property protected by fencing. They are used for military purposes, including the storage of rolling stock, with use being particularly heavy at times of major military activity (eg Balkans and Iraq Wars). The lines through the former station site are still in place. The sole remnants of the former extensive station are sections of the former brick edging of the up platform. The main station site north of the through lines has been redeveloped for housing. South of the lines landscaping has taken place alongside a road serving further housing development.

Malmesbury. Staff pose in this 1905 south facing view. Malmesbury Abbey dominates the skyline. The engine shed is to the left and the goods shed beyond the platform. Note the attractive bay window on the north end of the main building.

MALMESBURY

OPENED: 18th December 1877 (with the opening of the Malmesbury Railway from Dauntsey).
CLOSED: Passengers - 10th September 1951 (temporary closure 12th February 1951 - 2nd April 1951).
Goods - 12th November 1962.

Malmesbury opened as the northern terminus of the Malmesbury Railway in December 1877. An earlier scheme, the Wiltshire & Gloucestershire Railway, authorised by an Act of 1864, envisaged Malmesbury as an intermediate station on a through line connecting the Stonehouse & Nailsworth Railway (authorised in 1863) with the GWR London to Bristol line at Christian Malford, north east of Chippenham. This ambitious scheme did not materialise, although in July 1865 limited work was undertaken on a tunnel section at Malmesbury.

The Malmesbury Railway Act 1872 authorised the construction of a 6½ mile branch north from the GWR London - Swindon - Bath - Bristol line at Dauntsey; the GWR agreed to contribute half of the estimated cost of £60,000 and to work the line on completion. The day of the line's formal opening, 17th December 1877, was one of great rejoicing in Malmesbury, and was declared a public holiday. A special train from Swindon via Dauntsey was greeted by a large crowd, with a procession of local dignitaries being led to the station by the Malmesbury Town Band. Free tickets were issued to shareholders and promoters of the Railway and some three hundred passengers made a return trip to Dauntsey. Such a scale of activity was seemingly never repeated, even when the large Sunday school trips used the branch. At the evening celebration dinner, held at the Kings Arms, tributes were made to all those who had striven hard to bring the railway to Malmesbury. The Town Band played outside the hotel and balloons were released. The costs of all these festivities were borne partly by the GWR. Regular services began the following day, the initial service being six trains each way per day, except on Sundays. The journey time between Dauntsey and Malmesbury varied from 16 to 23 minutes.

The site of Malmesbury station was unusual in that, as a terminus, it was beyond the centre of the town rather than short of it, as was common on many branch lines. Such a siting was dictated partly by the presence of the hill dominated by Malmesbury Abbey; it was also influenced by the alignment of the earlier failed Wiltshire & Gloucestershire Railway on which some early work had been undertaken relating to the 105 yd tunnel under the hill, a tunnel which featured on the Malmesbury branch. Whatever the final reasoning, the station, overlooked from the south by the impressive abbey, was attractively sited in the valley between a steep slope to the east and a tributary of the River Avon to the west. There was the added bonus that it was close to a main road.

The main station building on the single platform west of the line was aligned north-south; of grey stone construction with a slate roof and tall chimney, it incorporated two waiting rooms (one for first class passengers), a ticket office and toilets. The joint contractors were Brock & Bruce and a Mr G. Drew of Chalford. Originally a wooden entrance lobby led from the forecourt into the building, but this was demolished in 1946. The large platform canopy was supported by three cast iron pillars. Three stay wires were added in later years to give extra support. The canopy, surrounded by a typical GWR fretted valance, incorporated a skylight adjacent to the first class waiting room, thus giving extra natural light. Attractive bay windows were a feature of the building, one overlooking the forecourt and one in the northern wall. Gas lamps provided illumination on the platform at the north end of which was the lamp hut together with both the original and replacement parcels offices. A loading bay was sited at the south end of the platform. A long siding on the down (west) side led south from the platform to a stone goods shed with a crane and a coal yard. Close by were the coal company offices and a weighbridge.

Opposite the station building and platform were two loop lines, on the outer of which was the stone engine shed. Close by was a water tower and coaling stage. The single storey signal box stood opposite the goods shed on the up side south of the station. It became a ground frame only from 1933 and was taken out of use in 1956; the box's function was clearly shown by the striking long cast iron name plate. The main gates into the station site were to the north west on Gloucester Road and opposite the Railway Hotel. These gates were closed on Sundays from the 1920s to enable the GWR to class the station yard as private land under the 1921 Rights of Way Act.

The early years of the twentieth century brought a significant change to the operation of the branch to Malmesbury. In 1903 the Bristol & South Wales Direct Railway opened; known as the Badminton cut off line, it ran from Wootton Bassett on the original GWR London - Swindon - Bath - Bristol line through

Malmesbury. Looking north on 5th June 1954. The engine shed, which still remains today, and the water tank are to the right. A truck stands at the loading bay at the south end of the station.

Malmesbury. A view of the station building overlooking the forecourt. Note the wooden entrance lobby with large Van Houten's cocoa advertisement. The lobby was demolished in 1946, five years before the station's closure to passengers.

the Cotswolds and north of Bristol to Patchway on the Bristol to South Wales line. The cut off line crossed the Dauntsey to Malmesbury line to the west of Little Somerford; during the building of this new line a temporary siding was laid west from the Malmesbury branch to convey construction materials. Some thirty years later, as an economy measure, it was decided that a permanent link should be laid from the cut off up line at Little Somerford to the Malmesbury branch at Kingsmead Crossing. Such a link allowed the closure of the section of the original Malmesbury Railway between Dauntsey and Kingsmead Crossing. Work on the new link was completed by early February 1933 but because of legal complications that prevented actual closure of the redundant section, it was not opened until July. The length of the Malmesbury branch was now 3¾ miles instead of the original 6½ miles. The track on the original section from Dauntsey north to Great Somerford was soon lifted but the short section from Great Somerford to Kingsmead Crossing was retained for some years used for stock storage. These revisions were the cause of some regret in Malmesbury, particularly because of the much longer rail journeys now required to Chippenham and Bath. Instead of a connection at Daunstey, passengers now had to travel east via Little Somerford and change to westbound trains at Wootton Bassett. As compensation nine trains a day now ran each way on the reduced length branch.

Contemporary accounts indicate that the coming of the railway had a substantial impact upon life in Malmesbury and the surrounding rural area. Local industries and agriculture benefited particularly and there was a new lease of life for Malmesbury market. As from February 1878 an extra train was run to the town on market days – the attendance at the market on the opening day of the new service was the largest for over thirty years. The conveyance of milk churns was a particular feature, especially in the 1920s. Passenger excursion trains both to and from the town were a feature – for instance special trains came to Malmesbury for the annual flower show. Sunday school outings, usually to Weston-super-Mare, took place for many years; thirteen coach trains were apparently not unusual. This was the maximum size that could be handled at the station.

Passenger numbers were high in the early days of the branch, there being little competition from road transport. In the period from the opening day on 18th December 1877 to 30th January 1878 23,776 passengers were carried on the branch; in addition 5,727 tons of general goods, coal and minerals were conveyed. The local paper, in reporting these figures, described it as 'a gratifying state of things'. Figures for 1879 showed that 41,005 passengers were carried on the branch. During the latter years of the nineteenth century a limited Sunday service was introduced comprising one evening train in each direction. This service ceased in 1935. A feature of operations on the branch was the running of mixed trains of both passenger coaches and goods wagons.

As with many branch lines, operations were affected by the two World Wars. Unlike many other lines in Wiltshire, the Malmesbury branch, in the absence of many nearby camps, did not see major movements of military personnel and equipment. However, during the First World War Red Cross hospital trains brought the wounded to the military hospital at Charlton Park. Malmesbury received a large number of evacuees during the Second World War: on 1st September 1939 a train arrived at the station with a large group of children from a London school, identification labels around their necks. In June 1940 another influx occurred when thirteen passenger coaches, the maximum the station could handle, arrived. A marquee was set up in the station forecourt where food was provided; the children were then taken to Malmesbury Grammar School for medical checks before dispersal to their war-time homes.

The number of passenger tickets issued fell dramatically from 20,624 in 1903 to 5,891 in 1933. In contrast the goods traffic levels held steady,

Manningford Halt. Looking west on 24th February 1965, just over a year before closure.

illustrated by the number of parcels handled: rising from 58,796 in 1903 to 70,338 in 1933.

Passenger services during the inter-war years suffered from the competition of road transport and this increased further after the Second World War. Passenger numbers handled on the branch dropped 50% between 1938 and 1950, and passenger services ceased permanently in September 1951. Twenty passengers rode on the last train but there was no great ceremony. An Alderman Jones who travelled on the first train as a school-child also travelled on this last service. Goods services continued for another eleven years on the Malmesbury branch until, despite local protests, these too were withdrawn. These services were used by a number of local industries, in particular by the local agricultural contractors A. B. Blanch. During the eleven year period occasional charter passenger trains used the branch line and station. When the last goods train ran on 11th November 1962 it passed the home of Alderman Jones, by then aged ninety five.

The branch line itself was lifted in October 1963 but then there was a legal wrangle concerning the ownership of the station site. Eventually the whole site was bought by the Borough Council and planning permission given for the use of part for light industry and warehousing. By this time the station building was in a dangerous condition and, together with the goods shed, was demolished. The former engine shed survived.

Today the station site has been redeveloped, largely as the Gloucester Road Industrial Estate. The former engine shed, now much altered with the ends filled in, is used as a tyre fitting deport. The town's fire station stands near the old station entrance and the southern part of the site is a long stay car park. It is also suggested that a grassy mound on the main estate road opposite the former engine shed has a base comprising rubble from the former station platform.

MANNINGFORD HALT

OPENED: 20th June 1932 (on the Newbury - Patney & Chirton line originally opened by the Berks & Hants Extension Railway through this site in 1862).
CLOSED: 18th April 1966.

Sited north of the village of Manningford Bruce and immediately west of a bridge carrying a minor road over the line from the village north to Wilcot, the halt opened on the original Berks & Hants Extension Railway in June 1932. By that date the line had, for some thirty years, been part of the GWR route from London (Paddington) to the West Country via Newbury and Westbury. The halt was intended to boost passenger traffic on local stopping services running on the lines to Westbury and also to Devizes, the latter veering north from the main line west of Patney & Chirton.

The up and down platforms were originally of timber construction but were later rebuilt of concrete slabs; a corrugated iron shelter stood on each platform. The estimated total cost of the original halt was £625. Access to the up platform (towards Pewsey) was via steps down from the Wilcot road north of the bridge; access to the down platform was via a level footpath linking with the road a little way south of the road bridge.

In 1932 903 tickets were issued in the half year of its operation; whole year figures for the following six years 1933 to 1938 ranged from 1,619 in the former to 1,238 in the latter. The maximum receipts of £236 were received in 1933. Passenger services ceased on 18th April 1966 with the withdrawal of local stopping services on the line.

Today there is no line side trace of the halt nor of the up side access. However, the alignment of the former access path to the down side platform is clear; at its junction with the road there appears to be the surviving original gate.

MARLBOROUGH

The following sets out a résumé of the complicated history of the rail network in the Marlborough and Savernake areas. The aim is to provide a context for the accounts on the two stations at both Marlborough and Savernake. This résumé should be read in conjunction with the diagram.

In the mid nineteenth century Marlborough was, as it is today, an important centre for a wide rural area on the Wiltshire Downs. Early in the century mail coaches ran along the turnpike road from London to Bath and Bristol via Marlborough and Chippenham. The coming of the railways to Wiltshire brought no favours to the town: in particular the main GWR London to Bristol line opened east-west some eight miles to the north in the 1840s. Later, in the 1880s, the Berks and Hants Extension Railway again by-passed the town some five miles to the south through Savernake. The Marlborough area was avoided in both cases because of the surrounding hilly terrain. Local businesses suffered, in particular with the withdrawal of many mail coaches, their role being taken over the trains. A local campaign was launched and the situation was much improved with the opening in April 1864 of the Marlborough Railway, a branch from the GWR at Savernake (later Low Level) to Marlborough (later High Level). Initially of broad gauge, the branch was converted to standard gauge in late June 1874.

Some ten years later plans for a north-south rail link through Wiltshire began to be fulfilled with the authorisation of the Swindon, Marlborough & Andover Railway (SMAR). Following a number of delays because of problems in the Swindon area (see Swindon Town text), the line opened from Swindon Town to Marlborough in July 1881, another Marlborough station (later Low Level) being provided a short distance from the 1864 terminus of the Marlborough Railway. Nine months later the southern section of SMAR opened from Grafton to Andover. For the following nearly twenty years the intervening section between Marlborough and Grafton was to prove a major problem, a problem faced initially by SMAR and then by the Midland & South Western Junction Railway (M&SWJR) which was formed following the amalgamation of SMAR with the Swindon & Cheltenham Extension Railway (SCER) in 1884. The SCER had opened from Swindon to Cirencester in 1883 and the line was extended by the M&SWJR to Cheltenham in 1891, thus completing a link between the two major rail networks of the Midland and London & South Western Railways. This link was to prove vital, in particular during war time when the extra traffic in many cases had a significant impact upon the stations, with the lengthening of loop lines and construction of new and expanded facilities.

Reverting to the Marlborough - Grafton missing link SMAR, on account of its difficult financial situation, negotiated an agreement with the Marlborough Railway and the GWR to operate over the 1864 branch line to Savernake and then a short section of the GWR main line east to just north of Grafton, from which point SMAR provided a short curved link to Grafton station. Operations over these lines was delayed until February 1883 because of Board of Trade requirements for improvements at Savernake station, which the GWR was in no hurry to complete.

Not surprisingly the operation of two rival companies over the Marlborough branch proved to be problematical. For instance the M&SWJR was not allowed to carry passengers on its trains who wished only to travel to Savernake Low Level to transfer to through GWR services; such travellers had to use GWR trains operating over the Marlborough branch. Rigorous ticket inspections were undertaken by GWR staff at Savernake to enforce this rule! A further problem for M&SWJR was that it was charged £1,000 per annum to use the branch line.

In 1893 discussions began between the M&SWJR and local landowners, in particular the Marquis of Ailesbury. The outcome was the passing of the Marlborough and Grafton Railway Act for a new line running through Savernake Forest and over land

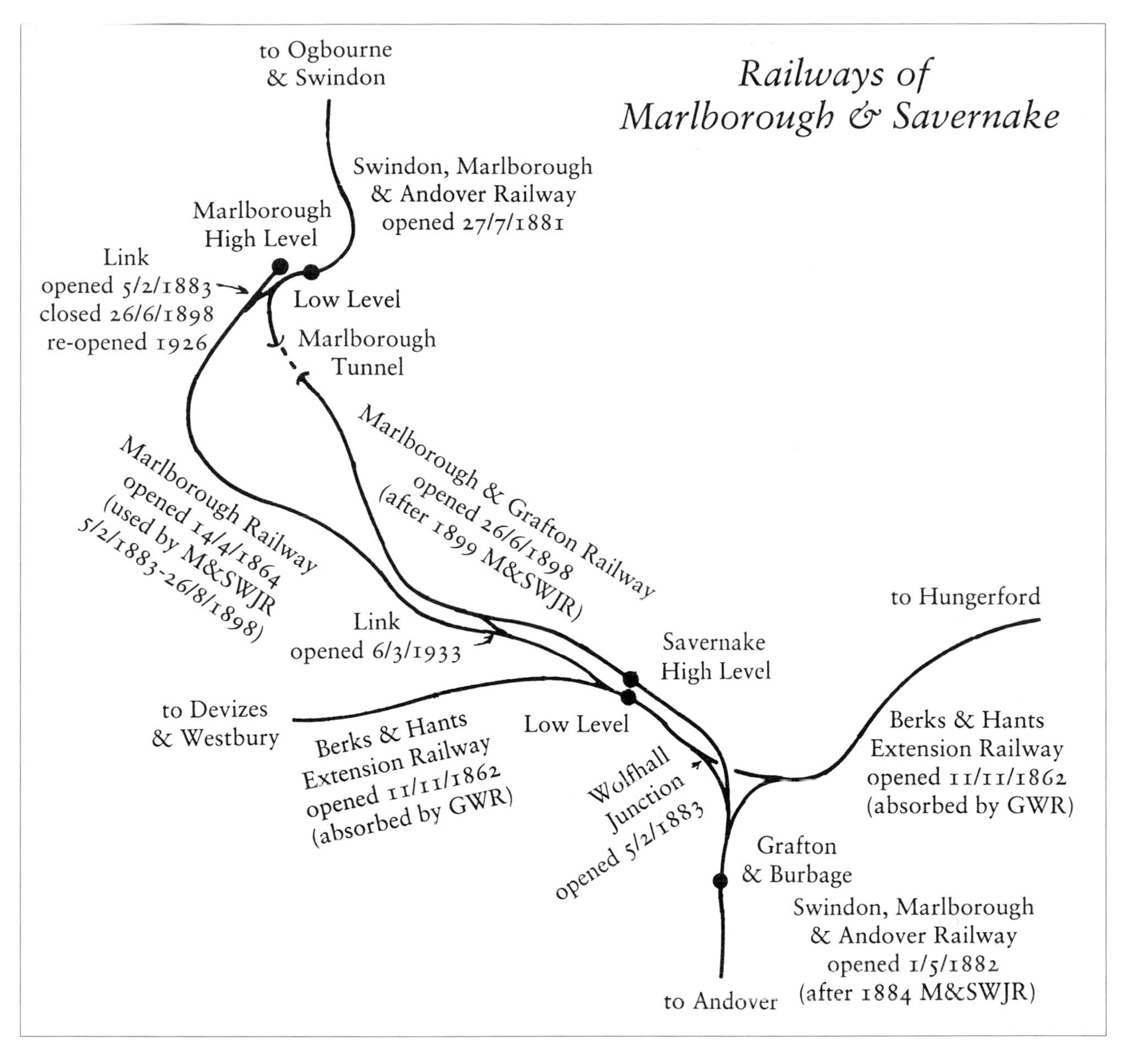

owned by the Marquis. Running south from the M&SWJR station at Marlborough, the line passed through a 640 yd tunnel bored through chalk and then south over the GWR to join the southern section of line at Grafton. A new station at Savernake (later High Level) was opened. This new line opened on 26th June 1898. The Marlborough & Grafton Railway was vested in the M&SWJR in 1899 and for the following thirty four years the new line and the original GWR branch ran broadly parallel to each other between Marlborough and Savernake. The link between the lines just south of Marlborough was lifted in 1898 but restored in 1926.

In 1933 the GWR, which had taken over ownership of the M&SWJR following the major grouping exercise of 1924, decided to rationalise operations in the Marlborough/Savernake area. The majority of the branch line north from Savernake Low Level was closed and passenger services withdrawn. The 1864 GWR Marlborough terminus closed to passengers. All services to Marlborough were concentrated on the former M&SWJR, a link to the original branch being laid just north of Savernake Low Level. This allowed local trains to take passengers from Marlborough to connect with GWR trains at Savernake Low Level. The 1898 M&SWJR lines were henceforth operated as two single lines, the original down line continuing to carry trains on the through Marlborough to Andover route and the original up carrying the local trains. A link between the two parallel lines was maintained at the north end to permit continued access to the original Marlborough GWR goods yard. Operations continued generally in this manner from 1933 until the closure of the whole M&SWJR to passengers in 1961 and to goods services in 1964. Some enhancement of services came during the Second World War. During the last two years of operation of through passenger services all trains transferred to the route via Savernake Low Level because of major chalk falls on the route through the High Level station.

Marlborough High Level. A view prior to the First World War showing the main building with its canopy supported by five cast iron pillars. Note also the large signal box beside the building. The track is receiving attention.

MARLBOROUGH HIGH LEVEL

OPENED: 14th April 1864 (with the opening of the Marlborough Railway Savernake - Marlborough).
CLOSED: Passengers - 6th March 1933.
Goods - 19th May 1964.

The station opened in April 1864 as the terminus of the broad gauge Marlborough Railway from Savernake where it connected with the Berks & Hants Extension Railway from Hungerford to Devizes. The opening marked the culmination of many years of effort to bring the railway to Marlborough. Earlier schemes which failed to materialise envisaged the town as a stopping point on north-south routes, an ambition that was finally realised in 1881 with the opening of the SMAR line (see introductory Marlborough text).

Marlborough High Level. A 1950s view of the L shaped station building some 20 years after closure to passengers. Note the attractive bay windows, the narrow slit windows and the tall chimneys.

The coming of the Marlborough Railway was due in no small measure to the support of local businessmen and Marlborough College. The Marlborough Railway was later absorbed by the GWR and converted to standard gauge in late June 1874 at the same time as the main line. The suffix 'High Level' was officially added as from July 1924 following the major grouping of railway companies. Known for some years as the GWR station, it was sited in the south east of Marlborough at a slightly higher level than the nearby Marlborough station of the Swindon, Marlborough & Andover Railway (SMAR) which opened in 1881 (later Midland & South Western Junction Railway - M&SWJR). The inaugural service to Savernake was five trains each way with a journey time of fifteen minutes, at an average speed of 22 mph, a speed which led to the train being called 'the Marlborough Donkey'.

The main building was on the north west side of the tracks. Erected by the contractors Dalrymple and Findley, the original cost of the station was recorded as £788. With an L shaped plan and a total floor area of some 1,000 sq ft, it was constructed of red brick, in what was termed a 'contemporary gothic style', with freestone quoins under a slate roof and two chimneys. The usual facilities were provided: a booking office which probably also served as the station master's office, a general waiting room, a first

Marlborough High Level. After its 1933 closure to passenger traffic. In the distance from left to right: the water tower, the engine shed and the 'black house'. The last included the station master's house and other staff accommodation for the Marlborough Low Level station which is seen in the distance below the GWR loading gauge.

class waiting room and a ladies' waiting room. The booking office and the general waiting room were, in effect, one room – separating the two was an L shaped curved counter. Entry to the building from the station approach was through a substantial wooden panelled door; a similar door led to the platform from the waiting room. Within the building entry to the first class waiting room was via a door from the general waiting room; a further door from the first class room led to the ladies' waiting room and toilet. Entry to the gent's toilet and urinals was from the outside of the south west end of the building. Passengers on the platform were protected by a canopy which stretched the length of the building and also slightly over the track. The canopy was supported by five cast iron columns.

At the north east end of the platform were cattle pens with direct access from the station yard. A 15 lever signal box stood on the platform immediately south west of the building; it was erected in 1892 at a cost of £529. A goods yard with a goods shed was sited on the west side of the tracks south west of the station. The shed was of a conventional design with a single through siding and a loading platform. At the station end was a lean-to office and on the loading platform was a hand-operated 30 cwt capacity crane. The goods handled related mainly to local agriculture with a peak at the time of the annual sheep fair in late summer. Unlike Marlborough Low Level, the High Level station did not make a great contribution to the First World War effort. An engine shed was sited north east of the station near the buffer stops; built in the broad gauge era, it was subsequently provided with off centre doors. Alongside the engine shed was an ornate water tower.

The Swindon to Marlborough section of the SMAR opened in 1881 and from this date the two stations catered for the passenger and freight traffic generated by the town and the surrounding rural areas. There was fierce competition between the two stations until the grouping in 1924, at which point the GWR took control of both Marlborough High Level and Marlborough Low Level stations. The passenger services served the needs of the local residents, local industry, visitors to Savernake Forest and, importantly, the pupils at Marlborough College – for which many school specials ran over the years. The number of passenger tickets issued at Marlborough High Level varied from 38,296 in 1913 to just over 5,000 in 1932, the year before closure. In 1903 8 staff were based at the station; this rose to 13 in 1923, but had fallen to 7 by 1933. No specific living accommodation was thought to have been provided for the station master, though it might have been rented. Despite the relatively high

Marlborough High Level. An excellent picture in about 1909 of an early GWR bus on the Marlborough - Calne service standing in the station forecourt. Note the solid tyres, open top and exposed staircase.

passenger numbers, the station closed in March 1933 with all passenger movements being transferred to the former M&SWJR Low Level station. This action derived from rationalisation following the grouping of 1924.

During its early life Marlborough High Level developed as a focal point for road services serving the local area. Originally operated from 1864 by horse buses, the GWR Marlborough to Calne motor bus service commenced in 1904 (see Calne text). Other services also followed, operated by the GWR. The signal box closed as from February 1933 and the engine shed was formally closed four months later, although it is believed that limited use was made of the shed for some years with freight facilities continuing to be provided in the former GWR goods yard until May 1964. When the former GWR branch was lifted for much of its length access to the goods yard was maintained via a link to the former M&SWJR line. The station buildings remained in place for some years after 1933, mainly used in conjunction with the freight services but were demolished following complete withdrawal of the station facilities.

Today no trace can be seen of railway activity on the former station site; the north east section has been redeveloped for housing accessed off Cherry Orchard; the south west half, including the former goods yard, is today occupied by buildings operated by the Kennet and North Wiltshire Primary Care Trust, including Postern House. At the junction of Salisbury Road and Cherry Orchard (which aligns at this point with the former station approach road) there is a section of old railway fencing, ending with an original post.

MARLBOROUGH LOW LEVEL

OPENED: 27th July 1881 (with the opening of the Swindon Town - Marlborough section of the Swindon, Marlborough & Andover Railway).
CLOSED: Passengers - 11th September 1961 (college traffic continued until 1st May 1964).
Goods - 7th September 1964 (coal depot only from 19th May 1964).

Opened in July 1881 as the southern terminus of the Swindon to Marlborough section of the Swindon, Marlborough & Andover Railway (SMAR), it became a through station in February 1883 with the commencement of SMAR services via the GWR lines to Grafton (see introductory text). The suffix 'Low Level' was officially added on 1st July 1924, following the major grouping of the railway companies.

The principal brick station building with four tall chimneys (shortened in 1910) stood on the up platform (towards Swindon) east of a road under bridge through which passed the Marlborough to Andover road. West of this SMAR station, beyond the road, was the earlier 1864 GWR station. A large horizontal canopy supported by decorative pillars covered the full width of the platform in front of the building; a canopy was also attached to the building over the forecourt passenger entrance. Passengers on the down platform were served by a wood frame

Marlborough Low Level. Staff and passengers pose for the camera in about 1912 under the canopy on the up platform. In the distance over the canopy is the staff housing in the 'black house', including accommodation for the station master.

Marlborough Low Level. Looking east at the main building and refreshment room (left) on the up platform. The goods shed can be seen beyond the right hand end of the building.

corrugated iron hut; the slate roof extended forward over the platform providing shelter. A water tank was initially provided on the down side close to the road bridge; this was particularly required for the short time (1881-1883) when Marlborough was a terminus station. Once the Marlborough & Grafton Railway was opened in 1898 via Savernake High Level, the tank was used even less and in 1912 was dismantled and subsequently used at Foss Cross station in Gloucestershire.

The goods yard was sited behind the up platform on the north west side of the site; a large goods shed surpassed in size on the M&SWJR only by those at Cirencester and Swindon, it stood close to, and east of, the main building. Of a basic corrugated iron construction on a wooden framework, there was a small canopy on the road side and inside was a wooden loading platform and a 1 ton 10 cwt capacity crane. The size was apparently justified in the early days as in 1885 it was reported that goods traffic was 'considerable'. Much traffic was generated by the three Marlborough sheep and cattle fairs. The local stables also brought much traffic including the movement of race-horses. This was of a scale that justified the early provision of a special siding and loading platform immediately west of the road bridge on the down side, horse vans being often attached to passenger trains. However, the volume of motor traffic increased on the road beneath the rail bridge; the sudden noises began to frighten the horses and the loading platform was moved to the eastern end of the up platform, far away from the road.

The original signal box stood on the down platform at the Swindon end. This was in use until the 1933 rationalisation when a new box on the down side, west of the road bridge, came into operation. This new box controlled movements in the Marlborough area on the two operational single lines north from Savernake.

At the station itself business was such that in 1884 a brick refreshment room was built on the up platform west of the main building. Originally 'Refreshments and Teas' were advertised but 'Teas' was later dropped; at one stage the facility was advertised on the roof of the building in white tiles! In 1924 the refreshment room, which had been leased to the station master, was taken over by the Great Western Hotels organisation; it continued to serve both passengers and local residents until closure of the line to passengers in 1961.

Marlborough Low Level handled a good volume of passenger traffic for some years, in particular in the 1920s and 1930s: local residents, boys travelling to and from Marlborough College (with their luggage), College visitors and visitors to the Marlborough Fairs and to Savernake Forest etc. Some 28,000 passenger tickets were sold in 1923; this total fell to 19,000 by 1930, over the same period the tonnage of goods handled rose from 8,000 to 14,000. At this time an average of seven men were based at the station. Accommodation was provided for the station master and another local railway employee in a pair of semi-detached houses west of the road bridge on the up side. Just before the

Marlborough Low Level. An excellent close up of the main building with its fine canopy supported by four pillars. The large refreshment room is to the left.

First World War the house's exterior was covered in tar like material, hence the local name of the 'black house'. The pedestrian link between the houses and the station was via a path alongside the up line over the bridge.

Public passenger services at Marlborough Low Level ceased in September 1961; general goods services continued until September 1964. The last 'passenger' train at Marlborough Low Level ran on 1st May 1964 nearly three years after official closure to passengers. It was a special train for pupils at Marlborough College. This was not without incident as, in running round the train, the diesel locomotive ran out of track, the driver not being aware that the tracks north of the station towards Ogbourne had already been lifted!

Since 1997 the site has been developed primarily as a Wiltshire C.C. highways depot, the approach road being approximately on the line of the old station approach up from Salisbury Road. Within the site today an old loading platform and some concrete bunkers near to the depot entrance appear to be survivors from the station facilities. All other railway structures have gone.

MELKSHAM

OPENED: 5th September 1848 (with the opening of the Thingley Junction - Westbury section of the Wilts, Somerset & Weymouth Railway).
CLOSED: Passengers - 18th April 1966.
Goods - 2nd November 1964 (except private sidings since closed).
REOPENED: 13th May 1985.

Sited in the west of the town, Melksham was the only intermediate station on the Thingley Junction to Trowbridge section of the Wilts, Somerset & Weymouth Railway when it opened between Thingley and Westbury in September 1848. Traffic was generated not only by the local residents but also by a range of industries that evolved and changed before and after the coming of the railway.

The station itself was built in what has been described as the Brunel 'road side' or 'chalet' style to the designs of Geddeth and Nollath, two of Brunel's assistants. The original principal stone building on the down side (towards Trowbridge) was similar to that which can still be seen today at Bradford-on-Avon, though later an extension was built on the southern end in a matching style. A stone waiting shelter stood on the up platform; canopies on both the principal building and the shelter protected passengers. A standard metal plate covered footbridge connected the two platforms at the northern end of the station.

North of the station on the up side was the goods

yard with a large Brunel era stone goods shed and cattle pens. Also north, but on the down side, was the foundry and engineering works of Spencer Engineering. Much of the output of girders and conveyers was transported by rail, the factory being served by a number of sidings.

South of the station, beyond a road bridge, a number of industrial premises were rail connected. Massive grain silos built by the Ministry of Works during the Second World War were served by two sidings. Taken over first by Wiltshire Farms Ltd and later West of England Farms they closed in the late 1980s. On the up side was the 1932 siding of the Co-operative Wholesale Society; this closed in 1965.

General goods services at Melksham were withdrawn with the closure of the yard in November 1964; passenger services ceased in April 1966. The signal box, sited north of the station on the down side closed in February 1967 following the singling of the line through Melksham. An oil depot was established and by 1981 often required two trains per week; a local fertiliser depot was served by one train but both of these movements had ceased by 1985.

Melksham. Staff pose in this view looking north. A good example of a Brunel style building stands on the down platform, similar to that still standing at Bradford-on-Avon.

The year 1985 saw a significant up-turn in fortunes as, after considerable local pressure and with a single line still open through the station site, a limited passenger service was re-introduced. All the station buildings and the up platform had been demolished after closure in 1966. Only the former down platform remained and on this was erected a 'bus shelter'. Later additions have included an open cycle shed and now small lockable cycle sheds. A number of small industries are established along Station Approach and the southern end of the former station site on the down side is occupied by Melksham Tyre Services. The 2003/4 winter timetable provided a much improved service over that which was originally re-introduced in 1985. Five trains per weekday ran in each direction on the Swindon-Westbury-Southampton route. On Saturdays this reduced to four and on Sundays to three.

Melksham. A splendid view on 6th June 1960 as class 4-6-0 No. 6879 Overton Grange passes through on its way north towards Chippenham.

MIDFORD HALT

OPENED: 27th February 1911 (on the Camerton - Limpley Stoke line originally opened through this site in 1910).
CLOSED: 22nd March 1915.

Just within the western boundary of Wiltshire, and north east of the Bath to Frome road (now B3110), the halt opened at the end of February 1911. Approval for construction had been given in November 1910 under the name of Midford Bridge Halt. It is uncertain whether the halt was provided following local pressure or whether it was a speculative initiative by the GWR, seeking to attract business away from the nearby Midford station (in Somerset) on the north-south Bath extension of the Somerset & Dorset Railway.

Midford Halt was sited on the west-east Camerton to Limpley Stoke line which had opened for passenger traffic in May 1910; these passenger services were the shortest lived of any provided in the West Country, being withdrawn permanently after only fifteen years in September 1925. The services had also been subject to a temporary war-time suspension from March 1915 until July 1923 and thus in total they ran for only about seven years. In the case of Midford the service provided was even less as, unlike other halts on the Camerton line, it did not reopen in 1923 and thus only served Midford residents from May 1910 until March 1915, less than five years.

Perched on an embankment on the north side of the single line, and costing £483, the halt's three foot high platform (150 ft x 10 ft) was constructed of timber baulks covered with timber decking. A standard GWR pagoda style shelter stood behind the platform. Access was via a steeply inclined (1 in 6) footpath up the embankment from the Bath to Frome road. Lighting was by oil lamps. The short life of the halt was not surprising; the Somerset & Dorset line gave a more direct rail route to Bath (and to Radstock). Early bus services also passed through the village. Unfortunately no photograph is known of Midford Halt and today no trace can be seen on the ground.

MINETY & ASHTON KEYNES

OPENED: 31st May 1841 (with the opening of the Swindon Junction - Kemble section of the Cheltenham & Great Western Union Railway).
CLOSED: Passengers - 2nd November 1964.
Goods - 1st July 1963.

Sited at the north east end of Minety village and some two and a half miles south west of Ashton Keynes, the station opened in 1841 with the commencement of services on the first section of the broad gauge Cheltenham & Great Western Union Railway from Swindon to Kemble. The line was converted to standard gauge in May 1872. Originally named 'Minety', the suffix '& Ashton Keynes' was added as from August 1905.

Minety & Ashton Keynes was an excellent example of the early Brunel 'road side' or 'chalet'

Minety & Ashton Keynes. A view on 30th April 1960 as Castle Class 4-6-0 No. 7000 Viscount Portal passes through this fine example of a Brunel style station.

style station. Distinctive features of the main building on the up platform (towards Swindon) included a steeply pitched roof topped by a tall chimney together with a canopy around the whole building supported by ornate brackets. The building was constructed in brick with stone dressings. Subsequent to its opening the up platform was extended beyond the road bridge south east of the station. On the down platform stood a small brick and stone shelter with a canopy on the line side. This platform extended north west some way beyond the end of the up; at its north west end stood the small signal box. An open iron plate sided footbridge connected the two platforms at the Swindon end close to a road bridge. The goods yard with a small wooden goods shed was sited on the up side north west of the main building. A loop siding ran through the goods shed. Plans indicate an early small wagon turntable close to the Kemble end of the up platform where a loading dock was served by a short siding.

Few alterations were made to the station building over its 123 year history. Today such an attractive early Brunel station would surely have been preserved, but unfortunately it was demolished soon after closure to goods traffic in July 1963 and to passengers in November 1964, the latter with the withdrawal of local stopping services on the Swindon to Gloucester line. When visited in late December 2003 the only trace of former railway use at lineside was a small remnant of the down platform. The former approach roads to the station on both up and down sides provide access to residential properties. 'Station House' stands at the head of the down side approach, adjacent to the former station site. A former public house in the up side forecourt is now in residential use; close by one of the original gate posts is still in place.

MOREDON PLATFORM

OPENED: 25th March 1913 (on the Cirencester - Swindon Town section of the Midland & South Western Junction Railway originally opened through this site in 1883).
CLOSED: 1st October 1932.

This small 40 ft long sleeper faced platform with a gravel surface was sited on the west side of the Swindon Town to Cirencester section of the Midland & South Western Junction Railway immediately south of a bridge carrying the west to east Lydeard Millicent to Pinehurst road north west of Swindon. A sleeper built small structure (8 ft x 9 ft), known as a checker's hut, was erected in 1914, some eight months after the platform itself came into operation. Moredon Platform was primarily built for milk traffic and no public passenger service was ever advertised. Contemporary reports suggest however that it was used both by milk traffic and by workmen from its opening. In its last years records suggest that milk trains only called at Moredon. However even this is not entirely certain as some passenger receipts were recorded up to 1935, despite the fact that the official closing date for the Platform was 1932!

Almost opposite the platform on the east side of the line a goods loop (1923) and a siding (1928) served Moredon Power Station. In 1950 as many as a hundred coal wagons arrived daily, but this traffic ceased in 1969 and all generation ended in March 1973. The siding was removed in the mid 1970s, and the power station was demolished in 1979.

NEWTON TONY

OPENED: Goods - 26th April 1902, passengers - 2nd June 1902 (with the opening of the Newton Tony Junction - Amesbury section of the Amesbury & Military Camp Light Railway).
CLOSED: Passengers - 30th June 1952.
Goods - 4th March 1963.

The station, sited on a hill to the west of the village, opened as the only intermediate station on the Amesbury & Military Camp Light Railway when it opened from Grateley (Hants) to Amesbury in 1902 (see Amesbury text). The line was doubled as far as

Moreden Platform. Looking south west from under the road bridge, the checker's hut can just be glimpsed behind the parapet. The wooden frame could be covered to provide shelter for milk churns.

Newton Tony. An early view south of the up platform showing the main building (centre) with the lean-to gent's annex nearest to the camera. The small signal box is beyond the building; the corrugated iron hut in the foreground is a store.

Newton Tony in 1904 and from that date there were two sleeper faced gravel platforms. The principal corrugated iron building, incorporating the main facilities, stood on the up platform (towards Grateley). A small lean-to annex at its northern end initially housed the gent's toilets. A corrugated iron building to the north of the building served as a store. A small shelter protected passengers on the down platform. The main building was later rebuilt and extended with the gent's now incorporated into the southern end. This southern extension was over the site of the original small signal box, which was replaced by a larger box off the north end of the up platform close to a level crossing with the Newton Tony to Allington road. All station buildings were also rendered with a form of pebble dash at the time of rebuilding. The old wooden edges of the platform were also later replaced with standard Southern Railway concrete components.

A long goods siding trailing from the up line south of the station ran behind the main building almost as far as the Allington road. A short siding behind the south end of the down platform served a cattle pen. Adjacent to the Allington road, east of the main station building, was the station master's house with two semi-detached cottages behind.

Passenger services at Newton Tony ceased at the end of June 1952. Goods services continued however for a further eleven years until March 1963. The line from Newton Tony to Amesbury was singled from October 1953 and south from Newton Tony a year later, after which the remaining track was slewed between the platforms, connecting the single tracks to the north and south.

Today no trace remains of the station itself; when visited in February 2004 the only occupants of the site were two donkeys and some geese in a grassy paddock. The alignment of the former track bed could be clearly seen north of the Newton Tony to Allington road. The station house continues in use as a fine residence, 'Station House', the front garden edged by former railway sleepers.

OAKSEY HALT

OPENED: 18th February 1929 (on the Swindon - Kemble line originally opened through this site in 1841).

CLOSED: 2nd November 1964.

Following a number of petitions over the previous twenty years, the halt, built at an estimated cost of £640 opened in February 1929. Sited about three quarters of a mile east of the village and two miles north west of Minety & Ashton Keynes station, stone platforms were provided on the Swindon to Kemble line. Both platforms were 150 ft long; the down (towards Kemble) being 10 ft wide and the up (towards Swindon) 8 ft wide. Access was via two paths down from an adjacent road bridge to the north west carrying a minor road. Shelter on each platform was provided by basic galvanised corrugated iron huts. In addition to passengers, milk traffic was also handled. Closure came in November 1964 with the withdrawal of local stopping services on the Swindon to Gloucester line. Today both

Oaksey Halt. Looking south east from the adjacent road bridge on 21st August 1963. Corrugated iron shelters give protection on both platforms; these platforms are still visible today beside the Swindon - Kemble - Gloucester line.

platforms remain clearly visible but the now single track has been aligned away from them. When visited in late December 2003 an area behind the former up platform, accessed from the road, was in use for the storage of tracks and sleepers.

OGBOURNE

OPENED: 27th July 1881 (with the opening of the Swindon Town - Marlborough section of the Swindon, Marlborough & Andover Railway).

CLOSED: Passengers and goods - 11th September 1961.

Ogbourne station opened in July 1881 with the commencement of services on the northern section of the Swindon, Marlborough & Andover Railway (SMAR) from Swindon Town to Marlborough. Sited at the northern end of the small village of Ogbourne St George, and immediately west of the north-south Swindon to Marlborough road (now A346), the station was on a loop in the general single track line.

The principal building, with two chimneys and a horizontal fretted canopy, stood on the down platform (towards Marlborough); a corrugated iron store was later attached to the south end of the building. Behind the north end of this down platform

Ogbourne. Looking north from the south end of the down platform in the early 1930s, showing the main building (right), the up platform shelter and the original signal box which had been renovated in 1914.

were cattle pens, a lamp hut and brick built gent's urinals. The north end of the platform was slightly higher than the remainder, apparently to ease the loading of milk churns and cattle. Passengers on the up platform were provided with a wooden framed corrugated iron shelter. Wooden posts and rail fencing ran behind both platforms and illumination was given by lamps on attractive brackets. No footbridge was provided and inter platform connections were via rail level board crossings at both ends. In its latter years the up platform was seldom used, the tracks through Ogbourne being signalled for bi-directional use.

The small goods yard was on the down side to the rear of the south end of the platform; a siding ran immediately behind the rear of the platform to a loading dock. An outer siding stretching a little further north behind the platform was sited almost adjacent to the parallel road. An original short siding which ran on the down side towards the railway bridge south of the station was removed at an early date. Goods traffic volumes were never great at Ogbourne, race horse movements in horse vans being the dominant feature. Traffic movements at the station and in the goods yard were for many years controlled by a signal box sited on the up platform south of the shelter. Opened with the station in 1881, the 12 ft 6 inch square box, supplied by the Gloucester Carriage and Wagon Company, was originally all wooden, but in 1914 it was renovated up to floor level with brickwork. This box was superseded as from January 1943 by a new box north of the station on the down side; this was required because of the major northward lengthening of the loop to cope with the long trains carrying war time equipment and troops. This lengthening of the loop was apparently undertaken by American troops based in the area. The siting of the new box was considered inadequate by some, as the sidings south of the station could hardly be seen from the box, even on a clear day! The old signal box was retained as a permanent way office. All services were withdrawn from Ogbourne with the closure of the line on 11th September 1961.

Today much of the former station site is now covered by a new section of the A346 that has used the rail alignment in by-passing the village of Ogbourne St George. The former station site was close to the point where a bus shelter now stands on the west side of the road immediately north of a new bridge (on the site of the old rail bridge) north of the village. The alignment of the former track bed veers from the new road line north of the shelter and approximately follows a footpath through a small area of woodland towards an old railway cutting.

PANS LANE HALT

OPENED: 4th March 1929 (on the Devizes - Patney & Chirton line originally opened through this site in 1862).

CLOSED: 18th April 1966.

Sited in the south-eastern outskirts of Devizes, Pans Lane Halt opened in March 1929 some 67 years after services commenced on the Berks & Hants Extension Railway between Hungerford and Devizes. The halt was in a cutting which, when originally excavated for the Berks & Hants, revealed a number of Roman relics, the site having been the focus of a Roman settlement in the second century A.D. The settlement was known as 'Punctuabice' and it was even suggested that the Latin name should be adopted, an idea apparently rejected on the grounds that it was too long a name for such an insignificant halt! It has also been suggested that the name given to the halt, which relates to that part of the town, originated because of the numerous finds 'panned' in the area.

When it opened in the late 1920s there were few houses in the immediate vicinity, but there were plans to develop the area and the provision of a railway halt on the existing line was thought to be a beneficial factor. Both the Devizes Isolation Hospital (later Roundway) and the Wilts United Dairies Factory were within walking distance of the halt.

Pans Lane Halt comprised one normal height platform; 208 ft long, it was sited on the down (south) side of the single line. The gravel surface was held in place by a wall of old railway sleepers. A corrugated iron waiting shelter, supplied by a Joseph Ash, stood on the platform. The overall cost of construction was £196. Access was via a flight of steps and a path from the Pans Lane road bridge to the south east of the halt. The path was lit by two oil lamps whilst a tilley lamp, serviced daily by a porter from Devizes, illuminated the halt itself. The guard of the last train calling at Pans Lane was required to extinguish this lamp.

During the 1930s auto-trains were used extensively on the line; these comprised a carriage or set of carriages with a small steam locomotive at one end. The train was capable of operation from both ends – either from the locomotive itself or from a cab in

Pans Lane Halt. A view south east on 14th February 1965. Note the access gate and steps by the bridge seen above the waiting shelter. The road side wall of the bridge appears to be damaged next to the gate.

the end carriage. Such an arrangement meant that these auto-trains could be used for services starting or terminating at small stations or halts where no run-round facilities were available for locomotives to change ends. Thus Pans Lane Halt was, on occasions, the terminating/starting point for local services, in particular from the Trowbridge direction, through Devizes. Such an arrangement often occurred on Sunday afternoons when visitors to the nearby Roundway Hospital were carried.

Pans Lane Halt was also the stopping point for a number of through trains, including some to and from London. The platform was, however, too short to take a train longer than two coaches. In this case passengers wishing to alight were required to travel in the last two carriages, and the drivers were instructed to ensure that they were correctly positioned at the platform!

Despite the early hopes, Pans Lane Halt did not prosper – from its opening in March 1929 to December of that year only 1,476 tickets were issued with receipts of £83. The halt was principally used by local residents and visitors to the hospital. Large quantities of milk and milk products were sent daily to London from the nearby factory until its closure in 1940, but this was sent from Devizes, Pans Lane not having the appropriate access nor handling facilities.

During the Second World War the halt closed for a period after October 1941 but some request stops were apparently made. After the War a limited service was re-introduced – in 1953 only two up trains called on weekdays and three on Saturdays. After protests an improved service was provided and during the 1960s both London and local stopping trains called every day. The halt survived until the complete closure of the line in April 1966.

Today there is no trace of the halt, the track bed to the east of the remaining road bridge is laid out as open space. The former site of the halt itself is now incorporated in rear garden extensions of houses in 'The Breach'.

PATNEY & CHIRTON

OPENED: 29th July 1900 (with the opening of the GWR Stert Valley cut off Patney & Chirton - Westbury on the line originally opened by the Berks & Hants Extension Railway in 1862).

CLOSED: Passengers - 18th April 1966.
Goods - 19th May 1964.

When the Berks & Hants Extension Railway opened from Hungerford to Devizes in 1862 it passed just to the north of Patney village. During the planning of the line requests were made for a station to serve the village and its surrounding rural area. These requests were however rejected on the grounds that a station at Woodborough, some two miles to the east, was adequate to meet the needs of that part of the Vale of Pewsey.

For some thirty five years this remained the situation, but the proposed GWR Stert Valley cut off route leaving the Hungerford to Devizes line about one mile west of Patney brought a change of mind with the identified need for a junction station to serve trains on the Devizes and cut off lines. The site

Patney & Chirton. Looking west in 1927 at the substantial buildings on both platforms. The long footbridge beyond these buildings carrying a public right of way across the site survives today but without its roof. No other significant station structures remain.

Patney & Chirton. A 1910 photograph of troops on the military platform erected the previous year on the north side of the station site.

chosen was just to the west of Patney bridge north of Patney on the road to All Cannings. Building started in 1899, the name initially being Patney Bridge; this was soon changed to Patney & Chirton to avoid confusion with Putney Bridge station in London. Chirton is a village a half mile south of Patney.

Of a design used by the GWR at many stations in the early days of the twentieth century, the main building, accessed by an approach road from the north end of Patney village, stood on the 500 ft long down platform. Constructed of red brick with a slate roof and two chimneys, it incorporated the general waiting room, the booking office, the ladies' waiting room and a gent's WC. A substantial wooden canopy extended over the full width of the platform. Opposite was an island platform, the inner face serving trains on the main up line and the outer trains on the Devizes line. This island platform had similar accommodation to the down, but lacked a booking office; the facilities were incorporated in two separate buildings with a space between the general and ladies' waiting rooms. Substantial canopies covered the inner and outer platforms. Lighting on the station was by oil lamps. A long footbridge west of the buildings provided access to both platforms; there were also extensions to both the north and south of the station as the bridge also carried a public right of way across the site. For many years a glazed canopy covered that part of the bridge between the platforms but had gone by the early 1950s. A large 70 lever signal box was installed beyond the west end of the down platform, the building materials matching that of the station. The cost of building the station and the signal box, together with the track work required, was £10,692. Soon after its opening a goods yard, with a number of loops and a loading dock behind the signal box, was developed. A weighbridge and office was also provided; although the new cut off route was opened to goods traffic in 1900 the goods yard at Patney & Chirton did not come into use until October 1904.

As with many stations in Wiltshire, Patney & Chirton took on an important military role following the Government decision to develop Salisbury Plain for military training. The catalyst in this case was the staging of an exercise for the Territorial Army in August 1909, involving some 40,000 troops. Patney & Chirton was selected as a major arrival and departure point for transporting the troops, leading to the hurried construction of what was termed the military platform. Sited north of the station and with a separate access from the All Cannings road north west of Patney bridge, it was 650 ft long and built of old railway sleepers with a gravel and earth surface. This large platform was required in order that the troops, together with their horses and other equipment, could be rapidly unloaded. Records suggest that some 140 trains brought the troops to Patney & Chirton; a large number of temporary camps were erected in fields around the station. The military platform again had significant use during the First World War with troops arriving for training exercises on the Plain before leaving for active service. The platform was again used to a limited extent in the Second World War, but was dismantled in the early 1950s.

Civilian passenger numbers were never high at Patney & Chirton, a reflection of the low population in this part of the Vale of Pewsey. In 1903 10,124 passenger tickets were issued; this gradually fell to 3,650 in 1933. During late 1939 and early 1940 a number of evacuees from the London area arrived at the station, a separate school being opened in the village hall for the children. In the early 1950s the number of tickets issued averaged about 3,000 per year, a reflection of the then limited number of local stopping trains. The station closed for passenger services with the withdrawal of all services on the Devizes line as from April 1966.

Reflecting its location at the heart of a flourishing agricultural area, the majority of freight handled at Patney & Chirton related to farming, in particular, dairy farming. Milk was sent to the London area from a number of stations in the Vale of Pewsey, especially during the 1920s and early 1930s. Churns arrived by horse and cart and by lorry. The peak came in 1930 when 46,721 churns were handled at the station giving receipts of £2,542. There was a major decline by 1933 when only 893 churns were handled: road transport had taken the trade away. Livestock was also transported through the station, an average of 50 livestock wagons being handled per year between the Wars. The facilities were not as good as at some Wiltshire stations; there were reports of animals escaping during loading and unloading! Following a slight revival after the Second World War the decline continued and freight services ceased as from May 1964. In view of this rather limited freight traffic it is a little surprising that in 1947 a new red brick building was added on the down platform to act primarily as a parcels store and also as a messroom for staff.

Through the years an average of ten staff were based at Patney & Chirton, including the station master. These staff not only served the passenger and freight traffic but also kept the station in excellent condition, the gardens being an attractive feature. They were the recipient of a 'Best Kept Gardens Award' on five occasions. Staffing ceased in November 1965.

Following closure of the station, the signal box remained in use until July 1966 but demolition of the platforms and buildings soon followed. The principal survivor was the footbridge which today remains in place across the old station site and main West Country line. No lineside trace can be seen, but at the former road entrances to the station yard to the south and the military platform to the north two substantial posts appear to be remnants from the original gates. A brick on the top of the road bridge is engraved 'Joseph Hamblet 1897 West Bromwich', recording the date of its reconstruction associated with the rail developments at that time.

PEWSEY

OPENED: 11th November 1862 (with the opening of the Berks & Hants Extension Railway from Hungerford to Devizes).

CLOSED: Passengers - Remains open for services on the London (Paddington) - Westbury - Taunton line. Goods - 13th July 1964 (coal depot only from 19th May 1964).

Sited on the northern edge of Pewsey immediately to the west of the road to Marlborough (A345), the station opened in November 1862 with the commencement of services on the broad gauge Berks & Hants Extension Railway from Hungerford to Devizes. A passing loop was installed in the mid 1860s at Pewsey, the gauge was reduced to standard in 1874 and the whole line was doubled in 1899 in conjunction with the construction, to the west of Pewsey, of the Patney & Chirton to Westbury Stert Valley cut off line.

The attractive principal building, of soft pink coloured brick, was constructed on the down platform on the town side of the line served by the main approach from the Marlborough road. In a typical Berks & Hants Railway style, it had two impressive chimney stacks and a recessed sheltered waiting area, but no platform canopy. It housed all the main station facilities including waiting rooms, the booking office and toilet facilities. Passengers on

Pewsey. An eastbound goods train passes the up platform in 1962. All the original structures remain in place. Some twenty years later the up side shelter is replaced by a fine brick structure.

the up side platform, to which there was also an access from the Marlborough road, were provided with a wooden shelter; also on this platform was an open shelter with a canopy for the storage of mail and other goods awaiting loading. An open lattice footbridge connected the two platforms at the east end of the platforms.

The Vale of Pewsey is a rich agricultural area and for many years the station provided a range of freight facilities serving the farming community. The goods yard, with a large goods shed, was on the down side at the west end of the station; the siding into the yard trailed from the up line, there being no direct link from the down, thereby avoiding the provision of facing points. A 30 cwt capacity crane was sited in the goods shed, road access to which was from the down side main approach road. Controlling movements at the station, the original signal box stood at the west end of the up platform. This survived until 1923 when it was replaced by a larger box with 26 levers on a site immediately adjacent. This second box operated until May 1966.

In the early years of the twentieth century both passenger and goods traffic was brisk. In 1903 21,345 passenger tickets were issued, the figure fell significantly to 10,555 in 1933. After the Second World War levels of all traffic fell greatly. By the mid 1960s services were limited, for instance only two down trains from Paddington called at Pewsey in the early evening. The goods yard closed in July 1964.

Despite this low usage, Pewsey survived the widespread station closures of the 1960s and subsequently underwent a major revival in fortunes. In 1984 work was undertaken on the buildings. Although the chimney stacks were removed, the original main building was renovated; the principal work was however the replacement of the old up side wooden shelter by an impressive brick structure matching the architectural style of the surviving down side building. The open wooden goods shelter on this platform was retained. The lattice footbridge had been replaced in about 1969 by a plate sided structure which had originally served passengers at Cookham on the Maidenhead to Marlow branch. In 1985 Pewsey station received a First Class Award in the Best Preserved Station competition organised by the Association of Railway Preservation Societies and Ian Allan Ltd.

In the 2003/2004 timetable Pewsey was served by 8 direct trains to Paddington, the first leaving at 07.24 and the last at 21.10. When visited in early March 2004, the station was in very good condition, the waiting rooms provided with magazines such as *Country Life* as well as railway literature. The 1984 up side shelter featured a poster commemorating the 100th anniversary of Brunel's Saltash Bridge 1859-1959. Outside this shelter a small garden was

Pewsey. The replacement up side shelter, erected in 1984, photographed twenty years later in early March 2004.

Pewsey. The fine renovated down side building in early March 2004.

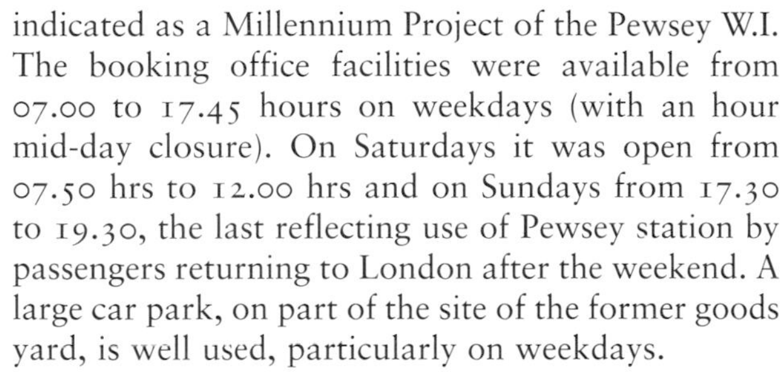

indicated as a Millennium Project of the Pewsey W.I. The booking office facilities were available from 07.00 to 17.45 hours on weekdays (with an hour mid-day closure). On Saturdays it was open from 07.50 hrs to 12.00 hrs and on Sundays from 17.30 to 19.30, the last reflecting use of Pewsey station by passengers returning to London after the weekend. A large car park, on part of the site of the former goods yard, is well used, particularly on weekdays.

In summary, the attractive Pewsey station today provides a good service for the Vale of Pewsey residents; a rare survivor from the many similar country stations that suffered closure in the 1960s.

PORTON

OPENED: 1st May 1857 (with the opening of the Andover - Salisbury (Milford) section of the London & South Western Railway).

CLOSED: Passengers - 9th September 1968.
Goods - 10th September 1962.

Sited at the south eastern end of Porton village on the hillside above the Bourne valley, the station opened at the beginning of May 1857 with commencement of services on the Andover (Hants) to Salisbury (Milford) section of the London & South Western Railway (LSWR). The typical early LSWR two storey building, incorporating accommodation for the station master, stood on the up platform (towards Andover); two large chimneys rose above the steeply pitched roof. An annex on its north eastern side provided shelter for passengers and a

Porton. Looking north east with all the main buildings on the up platform, shelter for passengers being provided in a small recess beyond the station house. Note the squat LSWR signal box (left).

further extension included the gent's toilets. To the south west of the building two further small buildings provided staff accommodation and storage; also on the platform was the Porton signal box, a squat wooden structure on a stone base. The box had 17 levers and remained in use until May 1968. Passengers on the down platform were served by a shelter with a wide canopy stretching to the platform edge. The two platforms were connected by an open skeleton bridge north east of the main building and shelter.

A trailing siding north east of the station led into Porton goods yard, sited behind the up side platform and main building. The original siding ran immediately behind the platform; two further sidings across the station forecourt were added in 1899. Yard facilities included a goods lock up and a cattle pen. Adjacent to the goods yard was the terminus of the 2 ft gauge Porton Down Camp Military Railway which crossed the main LSWR line by a bridge beyond the Andover end of the station on route to the Camp, almost a mile north east of Porton. These narrow gauge lines were in use from 1916 until 1946 and were mainly operated by petrol locomotives. A two ton capacity crane aided with the transfer of goods between the narrow gauge wagons of the Military Railway and the standard gauge trucks in the goods yard. The main access road up from the village directly served both the up side main building and the goods yard. A short distance down the hill was the Railway Hotel.

Goods services ceased at Porton in September 1962 but passenger trains continued to call for a further six years. Today the whole site of the station itself and the goods yard is occupied by the Porton Garden, Pets and Aquatic Centre. The former Railway Hotel is now the Porton Hotel; close to the hotel is an old post which appears to be one of the original gate posts at the station entrance.

PURTON

OPENED: 31st May 1841 (with the opening of the Swindon Junction - Kemble section of the Cheltenham & Great Western Union Railway).
CLOSED: Passengers - 2nd November 1964.
Goods - 1st July 1963.

Sited at the northern end of the village, immediately to the west of, and adjacent to, a bridge carrying the Wootton Bassett to Cricklade road, the station opened at the end of May 1841 with the start of services on the first section of the broad gauge Cheltenham & Great Western Union Railway from Swindon to Kemble. The line was converted to standard gauge in May 1872.

The main building was on the up (towards Swindon) side of the line. The original building was of timber construction with two chimneys; it was replaced in about 1960 by a flat roofed modern brick building. A timber waiting shelter served passengers on the down platform throughout the life of the station; an additional small shelter was a later addition on this platform. Inter platform connection was via the adjacent road bridge and steps linked to each platform. These steps were initially preceded by foot-boards at the platform ends.

Purton. Staff pose for the camera in about 1910 on the up platform on which stands the original timber building, replaced in about 1960. The wooden shelter on the down side survived throughout the station's life.

Purton. In 1960 a young boy stands in front of the very new replacement building on the up platform. It survives today, albeit not in good condition, as 'Station Garage'.

The goods yard to the west of the station on the up side was accessed by the main station approach road. The yard incorporated a brick and timber goods shed through which ran a goods loop. A short siding led east from the goods loop to a loading platform at the rear of the west end of the up platform. Further west, beyond the goods yard, a private siding led to Hill's Brickworks; this facility ceased in 1963. At about this date the up refuge (to the west of the station) and down refuge sidings (east of the station) also closed. Traffic movements at Purton were controlled from a small signal box on the down side opposite the goods shed.

The station closed to goods traffic in July 1963 and to passengers in November 1964. Today the 1960 up side building survives as 'Station Garage' standing on a section of the old up platform. Close by is the 'Ghost Train' public house. Trains continue to pass through the station site on the now single track.

Rushey Platt. Looking north in 1934, some thirty years after the station's closure. To the left the double tracks lead towards Cirencester whilst at the low level is the main building on the line to the GWR west of Swindon.

Rushey Platt. The former main station building in residential use in 1934. The three original platform side doors are all bricked up.

RUSHEY PLATT

OPENED: Goods - 1st November 1883, passengers - 18th December 1883 (with the opening of the Cirencester - Rushey Platt section of the Swindon & Cheltenham Extension Railway).

CLOSED: Passengers - 1st October 1905.
Goods - 19th May 1964 (except for private sidings since closed).

Rushey Platt station, on the western edge of Swindon, had a brief, but complicated, history. As set out in the text relating to Swindon Town, the section of the Swindon, Marlborough & Andover Railway (SMAR) west and north from Swindon Town to a junction with the GWR west of Swindon GWR opened in February 1882. In parallel with these developments progress was being made on the completion of the Swindon to Cirencester section of the Swindon & Cheltenham Extension Railway (S&CER). This opened to passengers in December 1883. The junction of the original link line to Swindon GWR and the line north to Cirencester was at Rushey Platt and a station evolved here to serve both lines. Low level platforms were constructed, slightly staggered, on the link to the Swindon GWR line and high level platforms (at a slightly higher level) to serve the S&CER.

The main station building was on the down

platform on the inside of the curve of the Swindon GWR link line, a brick construction with three chimneys and three doors on to the platform. The main station access road led to the back of this building; the station master's house was probably sited on this road. Access to the up platform (towards Swindon GWR) and the down Cirencester line platform was via rail level boards but a subway linked the up and down platforms of the S&CER. This subway was largely blocked off in 1907.

A small goods yard was sited on the Swindon GWR side of the main building on the inside of the curve; this incorporated a small goods shed. Goods outwards averaged about 1,200 tons 1929-1937; coal imports were about 1,700 tons over the same period. The low level platforms only served passengers for fifteen months until March 1885, the shuttle service between the two Swindon stations being withdrawn because of the high charges made by the GWR for use by SMAR trains on the 1½ miles of track into GWR Swindon. The high level platforms continued in use for a further twenty years, until they too closed in 1905.

The low level station building was converted into a house, and for some years an unofficial stop was made at the high level platform by the passenger trains on the Cirencester line so that its residents could board or leave.

A 30 lever signal box opened in 1917 at the south end of the high level down platform, replacing an earlier box and remaining in operation until June 1965. For a number of years the remaining platforms at Rushey Platt were used for the loading of milk products, whilst general goods traffic continued to use the yard until 1964. A private siding to timber mills continued for a short period. The station building and platforms remained in place for some years up to the 1960s but all has now gone, much industrial development having taken place in the area. The former embankment that carried the Cirencester line over the main GWR is still clearly to be seen.

SALISBURY

The railway came to Salisbury with the opening of the London & South Western Railway (LSWR) branch from Bishopstoke (Eastleigh) to Milford on the south-east edge of the city. Bishopstoke was on the LSWR main line from London to Southampton and thus residents and traders were able to benefit from their first rail link to the capital and the south coast. A special train arrived from London on 21st January 1847 conveying LSWR officials and journalists from the London newspapers. Coal traffic started on 27th January and, following a Board of Trade inspection on 23rd February, public passenger services commenced on 1st March. The occasion was marked by a banquet at the White Hart Hotel where one of the speakers expressed the aspiration of Salisbury now becoming the 'Manchester of the South'. This was clearly an unrealistic, and perhaps unwelcome, ambition but there is little doubt that the railway played a major role in the development of Salisbury's commercial life.

Further development of Salisbury's rail network came nine years later. The GWR through the Wilts, Somerset & Weymouth Railway had, for some years, planned a branch from its main line at Westbury south-east to Salisbury. The section to Warminster opened in 1851 but the further extension on to Salisbury was delayed a number of times. However, under pressure from interests in the city and along the Wylye valley, the broad gauge branch was completed to a terminus station on Fisherton Street in 1856, opening to passengers on 30th June.

Thus by the mid 1850s Salisbury was served by two branch lines of different gauges and could be reached from London via Bishopstoke (Eastleigh) (96 miles) or via Swindon and Westbury (136 miles).

A more direct line arrived when another LSWR line reached the city from London via Andover, opening on 1st May 1857. The LSWR had decided to build a new station at Fisherton just south of the 1856 GWR terminus. This was, however, not ready to receive traffic in May 1857 and thus, for two years, trains on the direct line via Andover used Milford Station, having to reverse into the station (see diagram). The new section of line across Salisbury north of the city centre through the Salisbury tunnel to the new LSWR station at Fisherton opened on 2nd May 1859. This was coincident with the opening of the first section of the Salisbury & Yeovil Railway west to Gillingham in Dorset, trains being worked by the LSWR. From this date all LSWR trains both via Andover and Bishopstoke (Eastleigh) used the new Fisherton Station, the 1847 Milford Station closing to passenger traffic. This old terminus continued in use for many years as Salisbury's principal goods depot (see below), closing in 1967. The LSWR Fisherton station was finished to serve an inaugural train

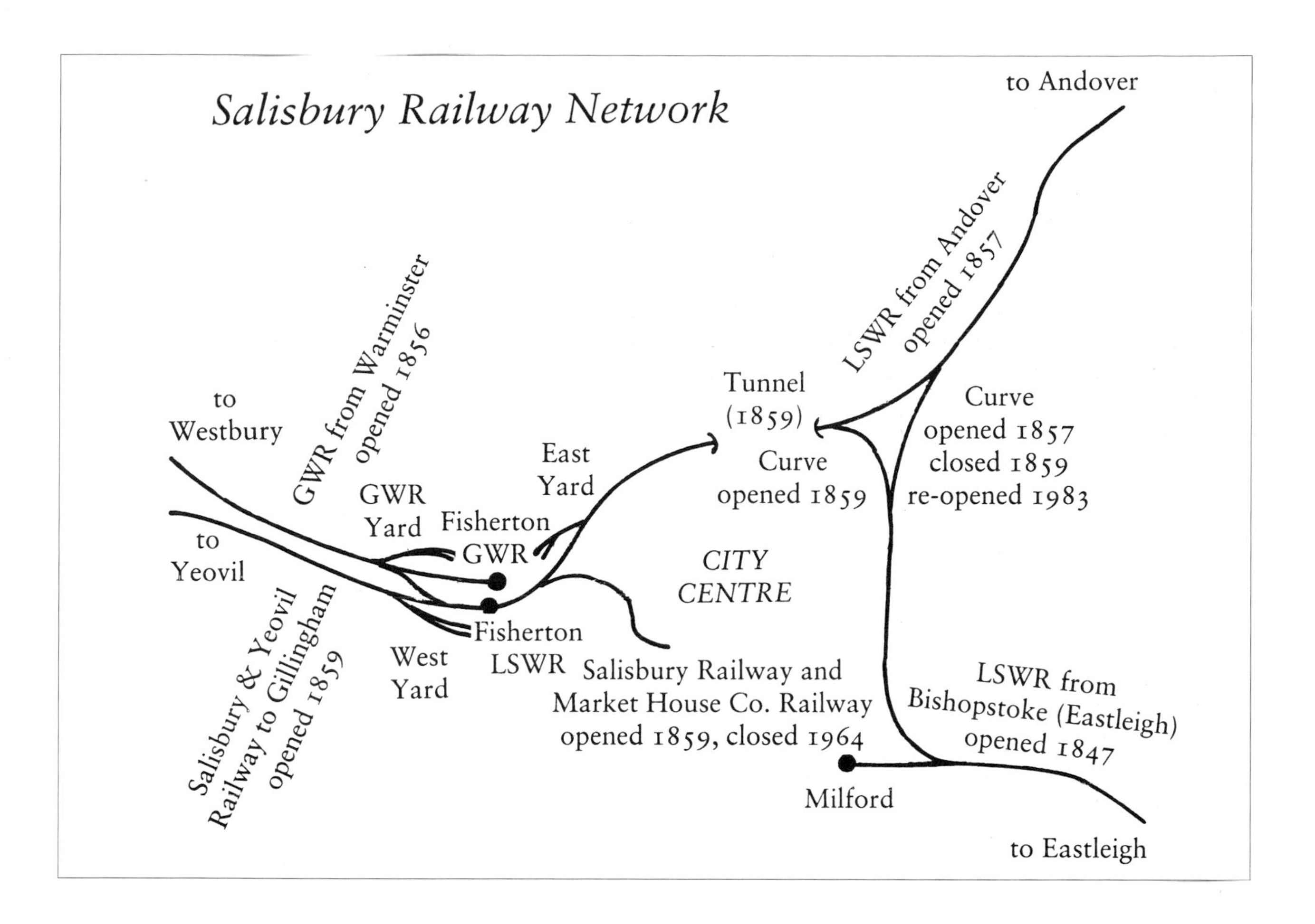

transporting LSWR officials on the completed through line from London to Exeter on 18th July 1860. The Exeter line opened to the public on the following day.

Two stations now operated just west of Fisherton Street: to the north the original 1856 broad gauge GWR terminus and to its south the 1859/1860 LSWR station with standard gauge tracks. In 1860 a goods transit shed for the exchange of traffic between the two gauges was opened, the shed incorporating one track of each gauge separated by a transfer platform. Sited on land between the GWR and LSWR systems west of the two stations, the shed was in use for fourteen years until the gauge conversion of the GWR branch in 1874. A connecting siding between the GWR and LSWR systems was brought into use in 1878, each company paying 50% of the estimated £80 cost. It was apparently not used for through working as reversal was necessary. However with the inauguration of a through Cardiff to Portsmouth service in 1896 a more direct connection came into use. This operated for some four years until the changes associated with the major expansion of the LSWR Fisherton Station in 1901/1902. This new station remained basically in the same form for the following hundred years; the GWR terminus closed to passenger traffic in 1932. Details of these two stations are set out below.

Finally, in this brief review of Salisbury's railway network, the 460 yd long Market House branch must be noted. The Salisbury Railway & Market House Company was formed in 1856 by local businessmen concerned at the remoteness from the city centre of the stations then existing at Milford and proposed at Fisherton. A new Market House opened in 1859, served by a branch line which left the main LSWR line just east of Fisherton Station, the line being maintained and worked initially by the LSWR and then by the Southern Railway and British Railways. Over the years a great variety of goods were carried over the short branch including barley to a maltings, cheese, corn and also coal to a local generating company. The track within the Market House was removed prior to the First World War and traffic ceased on the Market House branch in 1962, the official closing date being 1st July 1964.

Salisbury Fisherton (GWR). A view east of the terminal building with its impressive train shed. To the right, behind the lamp post, is the covered footbridge linking to the adjacent LSWR station.

SALISBURY FISHERTON (GWR)

OPENED: 30th June 1856 (with the opening of the GWR Warminster - Salisbury (Fisherton) line).
CLOSED: Passengers - 12th September 1932.
Goods - Early 1991.

The GWR Fisherton Station opened in 1856 with the completion of the broad gauge line to the city from Westbury and Warminster. Very similar to the GWR terminus at Basingstoke, it was built in a typical GWR Brunel terminus style. It comprised two platforms under an overall roof with a glazed end and a smoke hood over the down platform track. At right angles to the tracks and buffers were the imposing brick built offices with a canopy. Under the roof of the timber built train shed were two platform roads and two centre sidings. These latter appear to have been generally used for the storage of stock and at some stage may have been linked to the platform roads by wagon turntables and a transverse line. Fisherton GWR was described at its opening as a 'small, neat and functional station'. A covered footbridge built in 1860 at the western end of the train shed linked to the LSWR station, completed in that year. The bridge survived for nearly a hundred years, being demolished in 1956.

A two road broad gauge engine shed was opened in April 1858 close to the GWR train shed. It was replaced in 1899 by a three road shed with a 'northlight' slated and glazed roof, some way to the west, close to Ashfield Road, the cost being borne by the LSWR which had taken over the site of the original 1858 shed for its major station expansion.

The GWR Fisherton terminus station remained in use for passenger traffic until September 1932. From 1902 through services from Westbury towards

Salisbury Fisherton (GWR). An interior view of the timber-built train shed; iron trusses assist in supporting the roof.

Salisbury Fisherton (GWR). An engraving showing the scene after a cattle train pulled by two engines ploughed through the buffers and wooden platform and demolished the ladies waiting room in 1856, four months after the station opened. The leading engine came to a halt when parallel with the street, but though most of the livestock perished, only two people were killed.

Southampton and Portsmouth used the expanded LSWR station but local branch services continued to use the original terminus station for another thirty years. Following the withdrawal of passenger services the station building was used as a goods depot until early 1991.

Today the original terminus offices, now listed, are in commercial use by a car hire firm and chartered accountants. A disused large water tank, immediately to the west of the station, remains as does the platform structure on the south side. The overall shed roof was removed many years ago. The area of the original GWR track complex west of the terminus is now within the major new West of England Traincare depot where locomotives and rolling stock of South West Trains are maintained and serviced.

BELOW Salisbury Fisherton (GWR). The impressive main building, sited at right angles to the tracks behind the buffers, incorporating the main booking and waiting facilities. Now a listed building, but without the canopy, it is used as offices.

SALISBURY FISHERTON (LSWR)

OPENED: 2nd May 1859 (with the opening of the Salisbury - Gillingham section of the Salisbury & Yeovil Railway to passenger traffic).

CLOSED: Passengers - remains open for services on the London (Waterloo) - Salisbury - Exeter and Cardiff/Bristol - Salisbury - Southampton/ Portsmouth lines.
Goods - 1970s.

Opening in May 1859 and completed in 1860, the original LSWR station comprised one long platform on the south side of the line with a bay at the east (London) end. The main platform was covered by a large roof supported by a series of pillars. The principal offices were within an impressive building immediately behind the platform. The long platform could accommodate both up and down trains simultaneously, the main problem being that up trains, towards London, could not always run directly into the designated 'up' east end of the platform, but had to run through the station and then reverse back into the platform for passengers to alight from or join the train. A similar manoeuvre was also needed for down trains using the west end of the platform. In both cases trains usually stopped initially at what was known as 'ticket platforms' before manoeuvring to their final positions at the main platform.

ABOVE Salisbury Fisherton (LSWR). In 1959 the white building (centre and right) with canopy over the entrance is the 1859/1860 structure that acted as the first station building behind the original long platform that served both up and down trains. Beyond is the later 1901/1902 building. Both buildings survive today.

BELOW Salisbury Fisherton (LSWR). A rare photograph of the separate up platform, to the east of the Fisherton Street bridge, that served travellers in the London direction from 1879 to 1902. The photographer is on the east end of the original long down side platform.

A covered glazed footbridge was built in 1860 providing a pedestrian link with the 1856 GWR terminus immediately to the north. Although this terminus closed to passengers in 1932, the footbridge survived until 1956.

By the mid 1870s, with widespread congestion and delays, the LSWR sought to co-operate with the GWR in plans for the major enhancement of the 1859/1860 station. Such co-operation was not however forthcoming and the LSWR decided to take unilateral action with plans for, and construction of, a separate up platform on the inside of the curve east of the down platform. This new platform, 683 ft long with a bay at the eastern end, was separated from the down by Fisherton Street bridge. Provided with a booking office, waiting room and refreshment room, it opened on 19th August 1878. It had direct access from Fisherton Street below, and a subway from its extreme western end connected with the east end of the down bay platform which extended over the Fisherton Street bridge.

By the mid 1890s the LSWR was again concerned at problems created by ever increasing passenger and goods movements at Salisbury – a major re-modelling seemed essential. After long and difficult negotiations, the LSWR and the GWR reached an agreement dated 28th January 1898. The main problem for the LSWR for station expansion was the 1858 broad gauge GWR engine shed but, financed by the LSWR, this was demolished and a new GWR Dean pattern shed was built further west, north of the operating lines of both companies adjacent to Ashfield Road. It opened in 1899 and functioned until 1949. A major land exchange took place and the LSWR gained enough land to allow the introduction of three additional platforms, two up and one down, two of them on a central island. With the LSWR moving its original engine sheds (see

Salisbury Fisherton (LSWR). The scene in July 1906 after a boat train from Plymouth overturned on the curve outside the station, killing 24 passengers.

later), the original single platform was extended west, all four platforms now being between 650 and 700 ft long and covered by canopies. A subway was constructed to connect all platforms. The first of the new platforms came into use in April 1902.

A key part of the expanded facilities was a new station building constructed west of, and linked to, the original 1859/1860 building. Built of red brick and with a canopy on the forecourt side, it incorporated an entrance hall, booking office, buffet and waiting rooms. The 1878 separate up platform east of Fisherton Street was closed in April 1902 and the site was subsequently included in a large marshalling and transfer yard with 16 roads. The original 1859/1860 station building on the down side was used for some years primarily as a parcels office, and since 1981 it has housed the Salisbury signal panel. This panel replaced signal boxes beyond the east and west ends of the station; an earlier box on the island platform was used, following closure, firstly as a heating point for foot warmers (!) and then as an office for carriage examiners.

Some four years after its major expansion Salisbury station was the scene of a very serious accident. At 1.57 hrs on 1st July 1906 an up express boat train from Plymouth carrying passengers from the *S.S. New York* overturned on the sharp curve east of the station, an incident caused by excessive speed (67 mph as against the restriction of 30 mph). Of the 43 passengers (mostly American) on the train 24 were killed, together with the driver and fireman of the boat train and the guard and fireman of a milk train with which the train collided. The casualties were treated at Salisbury Infirmary and subsequently a 'thank you' was received from the then U.S. President Roosevelt.

Ever since the major reconstruction and expansion of the early 1900s, Salisbury has continued to act as a major railway node at the crossing of the London - Salisbury - Exeter and Cardiff/Bristol - Salisbury - Southampton/Portsmouth routes. The station has also for long periods been the starting or terminating point for local services in Wiltshire. The LSWR

Salisbury Fisherton (LSWR). A view soon after completion of the 1901/1902 building; the earlier 1859/1860 building is seen to the right. The buildings survive today very much as in the photograph.

Salisbury Fisherton (LSWR). A view west from the bay platform at the east end of the main down platform. Dominating the scene is the impressive covered footbridge that linked not only the LSWR platforms but also to the adjacent GWR station to the north.

station buildings have undergone relatively little change; in contrast the former GWR terminus to the immediate north closed to passenger traffic in 1932 but continued as a goods depot for over twenty five years.

In parallel with these developments at the station itself, a series of LSWR locomotive sheds were provided. With the opening of the original 1859/1860 station, a three road loco shed was constructed a short distance west of the station. A 45 ft turntable, coal stage, stores, a small shed surmounted by a water tank, water column and an inspection pit supplemented the facilities. Further improvements included the provision of a 50 ft turntable, a lengthening of the shed and extension of the coal stage. Further growth in traffic led to the construction of an additional shed adjacent to the original. With the expansion of the main station building westwards in 1901/1902 these two goods sheds were demolished and replaced by a major new locomotive shed with ten roads some distance west of the station, abutting onto Cherry Orchard Lane. This large shed continued in use until the end of the steam era and finally closed in July 1967. For a further two years it was used as a signing on point for crews and also, for a period, was sadly used as storage for redundant steam locomotives. It was eventually demolished.

Although goods sheds were provided west and north of the station, as well as sidings (West Yard), the principal goods facilities were concentrated east of Fisherton Street (East Yard). After the separate up platform ceased to be used in 1902 the site was incorporated in this large sixteen road marshalling yard. Goods traffic also used the Market House branch (see text above). The large goods depot in the south east of the city at Milford continued in use until August 1967 (see Salisbury Milford LSWR text).

Today Salisbury station continues to be busy, served largely by the 1901/1902 buildings, most of which are in good condition. The canopies remain; the 1860 covered footbridge linking to the early GWR terminus to the north was demolished in 1956. Currently three through platforms are in use, from north to south No. 2 and 3 (on the island platform) and No. 4 on the down side. The bay platform (No. 6) at the east end of the down platform is in use for terminating trains mainly from London (Waterloo). The other original bay platform at the west end of the down platform (No. 5) is only used for stock

Salisbury. A view, again from the east, but much later on 15th May 1965. The footbridge has gone, the inter platforms link is now only via a subway. To the right is a wall of the former GWR station and a large water tower both of which survive today.

Salisbury Milford (LSWR). A rare view of the wooden structure, part of which served as the station building from March 1847 until its closure in May 1859. It subsequently served for over 100 years as the city's main freight depot before its demolition in 1968.

storage. Finally No. 1 platform on the northern side is indicated as being unused apart from the storage of cycles. The site of former sidings to the west of the station behind the down platform is now used as a car park. The large former siding complex north of the current station and west of the former GWR terminus is completely covered by the modern West of England Traincare depot where a large number of South West Trains are maintained and repaired. The former large East Yard is no longer in rail use. The original LSWR and GWR engine sheds have thus been replaced by a modern facility at the heart of southern England's railway network.

SALISBURY MILFORD (LSWR)

OPENED: Goods - 27th January 1847, passengers - 1st March 1847 (with the opening of the Bishopstoke (Eastleigh) - Salisbury Milford branch of the London & South Western Railway).
CLOSED: Passengers - 2nd May 1859.
Goods - 21st August 1967.

Opening for goods traffic in January 1847 and passengers just over a month later, the LSWR Milford terminus comprised a single 350 ft platform, together with a collection of timber built structures. A goods shed and warehouse were also provided, passengers and goods trains running to and from Bishopstoke (Eastleigh) where connections were made with services on the London to Southampton line. A two road brick built locomotive shed was also in use from the start. Nearby was a 25 ft turntable. From 1859 the loco shed was used as a store.

For two years May 1857 to May 1859 Milford also acted as the terminus and starting point for trains on the more direct LSWR line to London via Andover. Such use required reversing movements both into and out of the station. Following completion of the line north of the city centre through Salisbury tunnel and the opening of the LSWR Fisherton Station, Milford closed to passenger traffic.

It remained in use for a further 108 years as the major goods depot for the city, closing on 21st August 1967. At its peak the yard handled about 250 wagons per day; coal, cattle and sheep were important commodities. Clearance of the site took place in 1968 and today there is no trace of former railway activity in what is now the Milford Trading Estate, the actual site of the old station now being occupied by an office block. The Railway Inn at the entrance to the estate is today the only reminder of the earlier era.

SAVERNAKE HIGH LEVEL

OPENED: 26th June 1898 (with the opening of the Marlborough & Grafton Railway).
CLOSED: Passengers - 15th September 1958 (last train ran). Official closure 22nd June 1959.
Goods - 22nd June 1959.

This second station at Savernake opened with the commencement of services on the Marlborough & Grafton Railway (MGR) in June 1898. It was some 200 yards north of the 1862 GWR station; the suffix 'High Level' was added as from July 1924, a result of

Savernake High Level. Looking east when both platforms were in use prior to 1933 and when the footbridge was still in place. Note the large wooden canopies. The private waiting room for the Marquis of Ailesbury is beyond the building on the down platform (left).

the major railway company grouping of that year. The MGR was constructed to overcome the problems of north-south Midland & South Western Junction Railway (M&SWJR) trains operating on the GWR Marlborough branch line and the GWR main line through Savernake (see introductory text to Marlborough). When the MGR route was being planned and agreement sought to cross his land, the Marquis of Ailesbury stipulated that, in return for his permission, a second station should be constructed at Savernake (despite the small local population) and that it should have facilities at least equal to those at the 1862 GWR station. He further stipulated that he should be provided with a private waiting room for use when waiting for down trains to Andover, where he would change for trains to London. Thus a special brick built waiting room, with a tall chimney, was constructed on the 465 ft long down platform beside the waiting shelter with a canopy used by other passengers.

The principal building was on the up side (towards Marlborough) platform. Topped by two chimneys the dominant feature was a large wide fretted canopy of full platform width supported by cast iron columns. Few changes were subsequently made to the station buildings; in 1912 a ticket window was inserted in the booking office wall, an action taken at the time at many M&SWJR stations, and in 1917 the waiting room floor of the main building was replaced by pitched pine. An open footbridge connected the two platforms north west of the main building and shelter. The provision of a footbridge was unusual at M&SWJR stations of this size but was in response to the Marquis of Ailesbury's stipulation that facilities at the new Savernake station should be equal to those at the earlier station (note though the Savernake Low Level bridge was covered in 1899!).

The goods yard was behind the up platform and included a loading dock and cattle pens. A horse loading dock was sited at one end of the up platform, served by a short siding. No goods shed was provided but for some years a Wiltshire Farmers milk depot operated beside the goods yard, generating much milk traffic for both Savernake stations. Incoming traffic was primarily related to the local agriculture industry, including fertilisers and feed stuffs. A signal box was sited on the down side opposite the rail entrance to the goods yard. Between the box and the south east of the down platform was a water tank and pump.

The absorption of the M&SWJR by the GWR with the major railway grouping exercise of 1924 led to some staff rationalisation. The station master at what was now officially called the High Level station was withdrawn, the control new vesting with the Savernake Low Level station master. This reduction in staff levels was no doubt a reflection of the low level of business: in 1930 only 3,619 passenger tickets were issued at Savernake High Level, less than half the average figure at that time at the Low Level station.

In 1933 much of the original GWR branch from Savernake Low Level was closed and the former double track south of Marlborough was adapted to operate as two single lines (see introductory text to Marlborough). Through Savernake High Level station the former down line was henceforth used only as a goods loop, all passenger traffic being concentrated on the former up platform. The former waiting room built for the Marquis of Ailesbury was left isolated on the disused down platform. The footbridge was removed.

General goods traffic ceased at Savernake High Level as from June 1959; permanent closure of passenger services came on the same day although trains had ceased to call as from 15th September 1958 after a major chalk fall blocked the line. All north to south trains were diverted to use Savernake Low Level.

Following closure the station buildings were not demolished and the original station building has been incorporated into a large residence. A number of the former station structures now survive in the garden, including the water tower, the shell of the signal box and the former down shelter and private waiting room. A goods truck is also in place in the garden. The residence and the garden are strictly private property. The disused platforms can however still be seen from the adjacent road bridge.

SAVERNAKE LOW LEVEL

OPENED: 11th November 1862 (with the opening of the Berks & Hants Extension Railway from Hungerford to Devizes).

CLOSED: Passengers - 18th April 1966.
Goods - 19th May 1964.

The station opened in November 1862 with the start of services on the then broad gauge Berks & Hants Extension Railway (B&HER) from Hungerford to Devizes. The station was sited in a 30 ft deep cutting at the summit of the line between Reading and Devizes. The suffix 'Low Level' was officially added following the major railway company grouping of 1924, only to be dropped in 1961 after the closure of the nearby Savernake High Level station. At its opening there was only one platform on the up (north) side of the single line; on this stood the station's principal building. A passing loop on the down side was in place from the opening but no platform served the loop. At this time this was the only loop on the B&HER line between Hungerford and Devizes. In 1864 a slightly curved bay platform was constructed on the up side at the west end of the station beyond a road bridge. The bay was to serve trains on the new Marlborough Railway branch line; this new junction status was reflected in the nameboard which read 'Savernake Junction – Change for Marlborough'.

The principal 1862 building on the up platform was a basic single storey brick structure with twin gables and tall chimneys; a distinctive feature was the ornate brickwork on the end walls created by criss-

Savernake Low Level. Looking west on 3rd August 1959. Seen through the fine covered footbridge and road bridge, a Marlborough branch train stands at the bay platform. Note the unusual criss-cross brick pattern on the main building.

Savernake Low Level. A Marlborough branch train stands in the up side bay platform at the west end of the station on 2nd June 1959.

cross lighter brick work. This was incorporated to match brickwork at nearby lodges owned by the local major landowner, the Marquis of Ailesbury. Within the building the accommodation originally comprised the usual booking and parcels offices, together with first and second class waiting rooms and a general waiting room and lobby. A separate station master's office was apparently not provided though a station master was in post from an early date. Over the years the uses of the rooms in the building varied according to different requirements. As from October 1863 a refreshment room opened alongside the main building operated by the nearby Savernake Forest Hotel, which opened at about the same time as the station.

A 300 ft down platform with a small waiting shelter was added by December 1882, a requirement of the Board of Trade before the Marlborough Railway branch and the GWR line could be used by the north to south trains of the Swindon, Marlborough & Andover Railway (see introductory text relating to Marlborough). An open footbridge was provided immediately to the east of the road bridge. The main line through the station was converted from broad to standard gauge in June 1874, as was the Marlborough branch.

The tracks west from Savernake were doubled in 1899 in readiness for the opening of the Stert Valley GWR cut off line west from Patney & Chirton to Westbury. With greater numbers of longer trains serving Savernake a number of improvements took place over the period 1898 to 1903: the platforms were lengthened, the original footbridge was roofed, and a red brick waiting room with a canopy was built on the down platform replacing the original small shelter. The canopy ran the whole length of the building and covered the full width of the platform.

From early days a separate goods facility, known as Burbage Wharf goods station, was developed three quarters of a mile west of the station. It was at a convenient point for the interchange of goods between the railway, the local roads and the canal. As a result the provision for the handling of goods at Savernake station was limited. Two short parallel goods sidings trailing from the up line ran behind the up platform at the east end of the station, one provided by 1877 leading to a loading dock. A down goods loop, also to the east of the station, served a cattle dock and pens. Through the years there were proposals to close the separate goods station at Burbage but it remained open until November 1947.

Two signal boxes controlled operations in the Savernake area after 1883. The West Box, to the west of the station on the up side in the V with the

Marlborough branch, had 32 levers and was in use until November 1978. The box was rarely switched on during its latter years. The East Box with 18 levers was at the east end of the down goods loop; this closed in February 1968. A water tank also stood for some years on the down side beyond the west end of the platform and opposite the West Box.

The station, much of which was built over the Bruce Tunnel of the Kennet and Avon Canal, handled a fair volume of passenger traffic during the early years of the twentieth century. In 1903 18,031 passenger tickets were issued, a number which had more than halved by 1933. That same year the original GWR branch to Marlborough High Level closed, but a link to Marlborough Low Level station was substituted. Express trains passing through Savernake non-stop on occasions dropped slip coaches which were then shunted on to Marlborough branch line trains. The branch was always operated by locomotive hauled coaches, the gradients being too steep for the steam rail-motors used on some other GWR branches (eg Calne). A total of fifteen staff were based at Savernake Low Level in the 1920s, supervised by the station master who lived in a house provided in about 1912 above the station on the down side, at a cost of £450. The post of station master was abolished in 1958.

For the period 15th September 1958, until the closure of the original Midland & South Western Junction Railway in September 1961, the north-south through trains were diverted to Savernake Low Level because of a major chalk fall which blocked the line through Savernake High Level.

Savernake Low Level was re-designated a halt as from November 1965. Passenger trains ceased to call in April 1966; goods services had ceased two years earlier. The station buildings were demolished and today no trace can be seen at line side; the derelict station site can still be identified east of the road bridge, as can the alignment of the former Marlborough branch line as it veers north, west of the bridge. The former station master's house remains in residential use as 'Beeching Villa'. The former Savernake Forest Hotel, south of the line, developed for use by rail borne passengers coming to Savernake Forest, was vacant awaiting new uses when viewed in early February 2004. The canal tunnel under the site remains in use on the reopened Kennet and Avon Canal.

SEEND

OPENED: 1st September 1858 (on the Holt Junction - Devizes branch of the GWR originally opened through this site in 1857).
CLOSED: Passengers - 18th April 1966.
Goods - 10th June 1963.

Fourteen months after the broad gauge line opened from Holt Junction to Devizes (see Devizes text), services commenced at Seend station. Located nearly a mile north west of the village and half a mile north of the Kennet and Avon Canal, the siting was the subject of early debate, an alternative being at Sells Green, about a mile to the east. The decisive factor was the traffic potential offered by the iron ore mine and iron works at Seend, which had recently commenced operations.

When originally opened in September 1858, the station comprised one short platform with a simple station building on the north side of the single track. A small brick signal box with only 10 levers was added on the east end of the platform in 1875. A small corrugated iron cabin between the building and the box acted as the station goods lock up and tool cupboard.

Major developments took place at Seend in 1908. A downside (towards Holt) loop line was added to allow the trains to pass; a down platform (400 ft) was constructed with a waiting shelter of red brick with a slate roof and wooden canopy. The original up side platform and building were reconstructed, the latter in red brick with a platform canopy and two chimneys. The cast iron gent's urinal was repositioned at the west end of the platform. The goods lock up was moved to the site of the original signal box, the box having been demolished and replaced by a larger (28 lever) box at the west end of the new down platform. To the west of, and to the rear of, the new down platform, sidings were laid and finally a new approach road led to the rear of the up platform main building. By 1911 a tall metal cabin had been sited at the far east end of the up platform beyond the goods lock up; it housed a tap and an elevated water tank supplying water for station use.

These extensive improvements were partly in response to the good level of business at the turn of the century. In 1903 13,912 passenger tickets were issued and 10,208 parcels were handled. A marked decline eventually set in with traffic, as in many rural stations, being affected by the competition of road transport, in this case to towns such as Devizes and

Seend. A two car DMU at the up platform on route to Devizes in 1962. A loop line passes behind the down platform. Note the 1911 tall cabin on the up housing a water tank that supplied the station.

Trowbridge. In 1933 only 3,631 tickets were issued. During the Second World War there was a revival with increased use by military personnel based in the area, in particular at RAF Melksham and the USAF base at Keevil. Contemporary accounts indicate, for instance, that local trains were used by airmen to travel to dances and other social activities in Devizes. Although passenger levels remained at a reasonable level for some years after the Second World War, decline accelerated and passenger services ceased at Seend in mid April 1966.

As noted at the outset, the decision to site the station at Seend was influenced to some degree by the operation of the Seend Iron Works. For a period in the mid 19th century a narrow gauge tramway led north from these operations, initially to a wharf on the Kennet and Avon Canal and then to Seend station. The tramway ceased to operate in about 1875. For many years there was a fluctuating level of iron ore activity with a number of different operators. Even after the foundry ceased operations and was demolished in about 1900, iron ore continued to be extracted and for the period 1911 to 1924 aerial ropeways delivered ore to sidings at Seend. When this ceased deliveries came either by horse and cart or by lorry. A final minor revival in the traffic came during the Second World War.

In addition to the iron ore movements, Seend station saw considerable business with the more usual agricultural trade typical of Wiltshire. For many years milk was despatched both to the large milk processing factory at Staverton, near Trowbridge, and to London. The 1920s and early 1930s saw the maximum movement: in 1928 30,264 churns were handled giving receipts of £1,922. However, there was a major decline to only 36 churns in 1934, road transport having taken the traffic away. Coal movements also generated significant traffic serving a number of local merchants; for a while after closure, the station yard was used by a local coal merchant though the coal came in by road! Freight ceased to be handled in June 1963, some three years before the station closed to passengers.

Compared with many small rural Wiltshire stations staffing levels were relatively high at Seend. In 1925 there were 7 staff based at the station; the station master, 3 porters, 1 goods checker and 2 signalmen. This total increased by a further two during the Second World War. However, as from 1952, Seend came under the control of Devizes; the sole remaining porter was withdrawn in 1962.

In the mid 1950s the station loop line was removed and the signal box closed in June 1956. Trains now could only pass at Devizes. Final closure came in April 1966 with the withdrawal of passenger services along the whole Holt Junction to Devizes and Patney

& Chirton line. Following closure the main buildings were demolished and the site is today occupied by a builders merchant. The up side platform survives and old railway sleepers separate supplies of sand, gravel etc. To the north of the road bridge, at the east end of the station site, two original decorative gate posts survive at the entrance to the former up side approach road as does the remains of a wooden kissing gate adjacent to the bridge that originally gave access to steps linking to the up side platform.

SEMINGTON HALT

OPENED: 1st October 1906 (on the Holt Junction - Devizes branch of the GWR originally opened through this site in 1857).
CLOSED: 18th April 1966.

The halt, sited north of Semington village on the Melksham to Westbury road, opened in 1906 with the introduction of rail-motor services on the Trowbridge - Devizes - Patney & Chirton line. Such services had proved successful on other GWR lines since their initial introduction in 1903. Semington Halt was of a basic construction with a short platform lower than the standard height of three feet. In such instances it was a duty of the train guard to lower a set of steps from the rail-motor on arrival at the stations (on some occasions the guard forgot to raise the steps following departure from these low level halts, with unfortunate results when the rail-motor entered a platform of standard height!).

The halt stood on an exposed embankment west of, and above, the main north-south road. The single line crossed the road and the disused Wilts and Berks Canal by a three arch bridge; originally of brick, it was replaced in 1939 by a box girder structure that had extra strength to bear the weight of heavier engines pulling long war-time trains. The only access to the platform, on the north side of the line, was via a footpath cut into the embankment leading up from the road. A much needed wooden shelter gave protection to passengers after July 1907. The platform itself was renewed as from 1909 with old railway sleepers and a gravel surface. Two lamps provided illumination, one on the platform and one alongside the approach path; originally oil, they were later converted to electricity.

With no vehicular access, the halt almost exclusively handled passenger traffic, though as from February 1909 limited parcels traffic was handled by a local agent and carried on passenger trains. Virtually all stopping trains ran on local services between Devizes and Westbury; tickets were obtained either from the guard or at the destination. Passenger numbers were boosted by military personnel from RAF Melksham, about a mile to the north east. Seend station was actually closer but the RAF personnel could easily reach Semington across the fields from the back of the Camp.

The halt closed with the withdrawal of all services on the line on 18th April 1966. Today the road bridge has gone, as has any trace of the halt. A house south of a remaining section of the embankment on the west side of the pre March 2004 alignment of the A350 bears the name 'The Halt'. East of the road close to the former Railway Farm, now the Outmarsh business area, stands the eastern abutment of the former long east-west bridge.

Semington Halt. Looking east in about 1955 at this basic halt with a small wooden shelter on the single track.

Semley. Looking east from the west end of the up platform. Note the large covered footbridge and the nameboard 'Semley for Shaftesbury' (right).

SEMLEY

OPENED: Passengers - 2nd May 1859 (with the opening of the Salisbury - Gillingham section of the Salisbury & Yeovil Railway to passenger traffic) goods - 1st September 1860.
CLOSED: Passengers - 7th March 1966.
Goods - 5th April 1965.

Sited about three quarters of a mile west of Semley village and some three miles north of the Dorset market town of Shaftesbury, the station opened in May 1859 with the commencement of services on the Salisbury to Gillingham section of the Salisbury & Yeovil Railway. Goods services started just over a year later in September 1860. For many years the station name-board stated 'Semley for Shaftesbury'.

The main station buildings, including the station master's house, were grouped on the up platform on the north side of the line. A canopy supported by pillars gave protection for Salisbury and London bound passengers. A waiting shelter with a large fretted canopy served passengers travelling towards Gillingham and Yeovil from the down platform. The platforms were linked by a typical LSWR design footbridge at the west end; it was originally covered and fully glazed but by the 1950s the roof had gone. Later improvements included platform lengthening and illumination of the board crossings across the tracks. In 1928 13,531 passenger tickets were issued, by 1936 the figure was 6,906. In 1910 the Bradshaw timetable indicated ten up and twelve down trains per day; there was little variation from this pattern over the years.

Semley. A view west on 2nd June 1963. The 1961 modern design signal box stands on the up platform, the footbridge has lost its roof. Both the main building and signal box remain today, both in residential use.

South Marston Platform. The brick platform in 1958, a year after it reopened for six months during the Suez fuel crisis. The former booking office/waiting room is at the far end.

Semley was equally, if not more, important for the handling of freight traffic. The large goods yard with shed, feed store, coal bunkers, cattle pens and a 5 ton capacity crane was east of the station on the up side. It extended under and beyond a road bridge. A siding was also laid east of the station on the down side. A wide variety of freight was handled, largely relating to agriculture.

An important feature throughout the life of the station was the transport of milk and milk products. The LSWR from 1874 provided facilities to serve the large milk factory sited north west of Semley station. Until 1931 churns were the primary means of milk transport by the railway (83,165 from Semley in 1928); from that time transport was by rail milk tankers (4,780,186 gallons in 1936). The tankers were marshalled in a dock siding behind the up platform at the west end of the station. A gantry carried a pipe from the milk factory over the adjacent road; this fed milk direct into the rail tankers. This milk traffic lasted until 1980. For some years the factory generated its own electricity using coal brought in by rail. However, from 1932 electricity was drawn from the grid and thus coal imports by rail ceased.

Control of the passenger, and particularly freight, movements at Semley was undertaken originally from a classic LSWR style signal box on the east end of the up platform. This was replaced on the same site from 29th January 1961 by a new brick built BR design box.

Apart from the milk traffic general goods traffic ceased at Semley in April 1965; just under a year later passenger services were withdrawn. The main line was singled through the site in 1967, only the down line remains in use. Both platforms and the down side waiting shelter have been demolished, but the principal station buildings are still in place, now named 'Railway House'. The signal box is a house, 'The Signal Box'. The goods shed also survives, in an agricultural equipment scrapyard. The building from which the milk pipeline emerged is now 'Dairy Antiques'.

SOUTH MARSTON PLATFORM

OPENED: 29th June 1941 (on the branch serving the Vickers Armstrong Factory).
CLOSED: Late 1944.
REOPENED: 17th December 1956.
CLOSED: 30th June 1957.

A short branch line was constructed in the early 1940s east from the Swindon to Highworth branch, leaving the branch between the stations at Stratton and Stanton. Its primary purpose was to serve the Vickers Armstrong Factory east of the A361 Swindon to Highworth road. The factory was particularly important for the manufacture of aircraft, including Spitfires. From June 1941 until late 1944 a brick platform with a small booking office and waiting room served workers at the Vickers factory. It stood on the south side of the line, in a shallow cutting, immediately to the west of the A361. The only pedestrian access to the platform was by a private path to the factory, which ran, together with the line, underneath the main Swindon to Highworth road. A gate was situated under this bridge to keep out unauthorised visitors. A passing loop was provided opposite the platform. The halt was used again briefly during the the Suez crisis when petrol was rationed. The platform operated from 17th December 1956 until 30th June 1957. At no time in the 1940s or 1950s was the platform available for public use. The line itself was closed on 24th June 1965 and the cutting with the platform was filled in and thus no trace can now be seen.

STANLEY BRIDGE HALT

OPENED: 3rd April 1905 (on the GWR Calne branch originally opened through this site in 1863).
CLOSED: 20th September 1965.

Sited a quarter of a mile south west of the hamlet of Stanley and south east of a minor road over-bridge, the halt opened in April 1905. This coincided with

LEFT Stanley Bridge Halt. A view of the halt south east from the adjacent road bridge on 27th July 1961. The earlier timber milk shed stood beyond the GWR pagoda hut.

BELOW LEFT Stanton. Looking north from the Mill Lane level crossing during the late 1940s. The small goods yard was behind the station building.

the introduction of a steam rail-motor service on the Chippenham to Calne branch. The opening of new halts on lines at the same time as the introduction of the steam rail-motors was a common feature on the GWR network, another example in Wiltshire being on the Chippenham to Trowbridge line (eg Lacock, Beanacre and Broughton Gifford Halts). Sited on the west side of the single track, the platform was basically an earth bank held in place by a wall of sleepers and topped with a gravel surface. A typical GWR iron pagoda hut provided shelter.

Near the hut was, for many years, a timber milk shed called locally 'the shed with the hole at the back'; the hole was where churns were passed through to the platform after being unloaded. Behind the halt was a large space where milk carts queued up to unload. At times the milk traffic at Stanley Bridge was so great that a porter from Chippenham was sent to assist the guard load the churns on to the evening train. A further practice was the off-loading of milk whey in churns sent from the Wiltshire Farms factory at Chippenham for use as pig feed. The milk shed became redundant after the Second World War and was demolished in 1947/48.

The halt was unstaffed, being supervised by the Chippenham station master. Lamps on the platform and in the hut were, for a time, attended to by a porter from Chippenham but later they were turned on and off by train crew. A lad porter from Chippenham was apparently sent once a week to brush out the hut but not the milk shed! Passenger numbers were never great in this sparsely populated area; in 1929 2,075 tickets were issued but by 1935 this had reduced to only 440.

The halt closed in September 1965 with the withdrawal of passenger services on the Calne branch. The line north west from here towards Chippenham forms part of the National Cycle Network; isolated wooden and concrete posts mark the site of the former halt but all other structures have gone. The road bridge remains in place.

STANTON

OPENED: 9th May 1883 (with the opening of the Swindon & Highworth Light Railway).
CLOSED: Passengers and goods - 2nd March 1953.

Sited on Mill Lane that runs west from the village of Stanton Fitzwarren, the station opened in May 1883 with the commencement of services on the Swindon & Highworth Light Railway (see Highworth text). The small wooden building on the brick platform was on the east side of the single track line. As at other stations on the branch, a small wooden extension at the southern end of the building once housed a small ground frame. This frame controlled the points into the small goods yard on the line to the north of the station. Sited behind the station building, the yard had two sidings; a small shed stood beside the outer siding. In 1926 the siding behind the platform was removed, leaving only one siding to serve local goods traffic. Also behind the station was a small coal store and a lamp hut for oil lamps and their fuel. Oil lighting was replaced by gas at a late stage.

The branch crossed Mill Lane at a level crossing immediately south of the station; a station master's house, built in about 1928, faced onto Mill Lane to the east of the level crossing. Stanton was in fact the only station on the line, apart from Highworth, to have a station house. It was not, however, occupied by a station master, as by the time it was complete the post had been abolished; the first occupant was the porter, who by then was the sole member of staff. Neither passenger nor goods traffic was ever very high. In 1903 2,968 passenger tickets were issued, and in 1933 only 533.

There were however two periods of significant activity at Stanton. In 1916, during the First World War, the Government decided that, in order to boost wood supplies for the war effort, it was necessary to increase timber products. Stanton Big Wood was identified as a source and a temporary siding was laid about ¼ mile south of the station for the loading of timber. During the late 1930s and up to 1941 Stanton station was used in bringing supplies and personnel to the new Vickers Aircraft Factory at South Marston, though this traffic ceased with the opening of the new track to South Marston in the early 1940s. The supplies to three army camps in the area also came via Stanton station. More traffic at Stanton related to local agriculture, but milk traffic was less important than at other stations on the Highworth line.

Both passenger and goods services were withdrawn in March 1953; Stanton had been re-designated as a halt in March 1949, by which time it was unstaffed. The branch to Highworth remained open north of Stratton for goods trains until August 1962 and during these years workmen's trains continued to use the branch. The one remaining siding at Stanton was lifted in June 1958. Following complete closure the station building was soon demolished, though the platform survived until 1970. Today, some 50 years after closure, limited traces can still be seen of the former railway activity; in particular three former level crossing gate posts are still there on Mill Lane, together with sections of one crossing gate and a kissing gate on the south side. The former station house remains in residential use as 'Old Station House', with a major extension at its western end.

STAVERTON HALT

OPENED: 16th October 1905 (on the Thingley Junction - Westbury line originally opened through this site in 1848).

CLOSED: 18th April 1966.

Sited to the south of Staverton village and the Nestlé milk factory, Staverton was one of four halts built and opened by the GWR at, or shortly after, the commencement of a steam rail-motor service between Chippenham and Trowbridge via Melksham. Such services, designed to increase patronage on local trains had been introduced, some two years earlier by the GWR in the Stroud valley in Gloucestershire.

Staverton Halt opened in October 1905, a fortnight after the start of the rail-motor service. Initially the two wooden platforms were only 2 ft high, this being overcome by the use of retractable steps on the rail-motors. Just after the First World War the height was raised so that all trains could use the halt. None of the halts on this line seem to have been initially provided with GWR pagoda huts; this was unusual as at that time it was common practice

Staverton Halt. Looking north in 1963. The height of the platforms has been raised above their original low level. Small wooden huts provide shelter for passengers.

Stratton. Looking north east through the station on 3rd May 1959. A GWR pagoda hut used as a store and extra waiting room is beyond the wooden main building. A galvanised iron goods shed (left) stands opposite the platform on a brick platform.

at GWR halts. In the case of Staverton small wooden huts were provided, and pagoda huts were never installed (in contrast to Lacock). Access to the halt was via two sloping paths down from an adjacent road bridge to the south.

Patronage at the halt was by local residents and also workers at the large Nestlé factory (see Holt text). The halt closed with the withdrawal of local passenger services on the line in April 1966. Today very little remains at track side though a pile of rubble suggests the probable site of the up (towards Melksham) platform. The line of the path to the up platform can be traced; a new gate is in place but the old posts remain. An old post and a piece of old track are also in place on the approximate line of the path to the down platform.

STRATTON

OPENED: 9th May 1883 (with the opening of the Swindon & Highworth Light Railway)
CLOSED: Passengers - 2nd March 1953.
Goods - 4th October 1965 (coal depot only from 19th May 1964).

When the Swindon & Highworth Light Railway (S&HLR) was proposed during the 1870s (see Highworth text), Stratton St Margaret was a rural community quite separate from the town of Swindon to the west. Stratton station, some 1¼ miles north of the branch's junction with the GWR, and adjacent to the old line of the A419, opened when services commenced on the S&HLR in May 1883.

Sited on the south east side of the line opposite a goods loop on the otherwise single track line, the main timber building, with a chimney but no canopy, stood on a brick platform. Double doors from the rear led to a booking office on the left and a ladies' waiting room and toilet to the right. The gent's toilet was situated alongside the ladies' at the rear of the building, divided by a partition but sharing the same window! As with other stations on the branch, a small wooden extension housed a ground frame for a number of years. After this use ceased in June 1909, the extension was used first as the station master's office and then as a store.

A number of GWR corrugated iron structures provided supplementary facilities at Stratton. In particular beside the main building to the north east was a pagoda hut of a style often found at halts on the GWR network. Installed around the time of the First World War, it was used as a parcels office and general waiting room. At the other end of the building beyond the extension was a small corrugated iron lock up used for parcels storage. At the south west end of the platform was a galvanised hut used for lamp storage. Finally, opposite the station building, on the outside of the goods loop was a galvanised iron goods shed on a brick platform which was slightly longer than the shed itself. The shed, like the pagoda shelter, was erected around the time of the First World War. Behind this shed was the goods yard served by two sidings one of which was added in 1909. Yard facilities included a 3 ton capacity crane, the largest on the branch. The original Stratton signal box closed in June 1909, being replaced by a ground frame.

Passenger traffic was relatively high compared

with many Wiltshire stations in the early years of the twentieth century: in 1903 28,042 tickets were issued. There was eventually a dramatic fall to 2,521 in 1933; by that time there was competition from buses serving the Swindon residential areas by now beginning to incorporate Stratton St Margaret.

Sited originally in rich dairy farming country, major quantities of milk were handled at Stratton, particularly in its early life when up to a hundred churns were handled per day. In the 1920s churns were loaded onto special milk trains and taken to Swindon where they were transferred to London bound trains. This large scale milk traffic was reflected in there being, at one time, fifteen platform trolleys at Stratton. By the early 1930s the traffic was insufficient to warrant special trains and the Stratton station lorry collected the churns from the stations on the Highworth line and took them to Swindon. The nearby Arkell's brewery also generated considerable freight traffic – imports of hops, malt, sugar and coal were balanced by the limited export of beer. The volume of freight was second only to Highworth on the branch. Other freight included cattle cake and potatoes. Traffic related to the Vickers Aircraft Factory at South Marston was also important at Stratton before the South Marston branch opened in the early 1940s. To handle the varied traffic, four staff were based at Stratton for most of the 1920s, three in the 1930s and four in the 1940s. For the period 1932-1942 the Stratton station master had responsibility for all stations on the Highworth branch, all other station master posts having been abolished. From 1942 responsibilities for Highworth and Hannington ceased, a separate station master for these two stations having been reinstated. Finally, from 1950, the Stratton post was not filled, the station coming under the control of the Highworth station master.

Passenger services ceased at Stratton with the withdrawal of these services on the Highworth branch in March 1953. However goods traffic continued on this southern section of the branch for another twelve years. Stratton closed for general goods services in May 1964 but continued as a coal depot until October 1965.

Following complete closure, all the station buildings were swept away. The former station site is now developed as the Europa Industrial Park, and the whole area has been completely absorbed within the large Swindon urban area – such a contrast from the rural setting when Stratton station opened in 1883.

LEFT Stratton Park Halt. The Castle Class 4-6-0 No. 5090 Neath Abbey passes the up platform on 3rd May 1959 with a Weston-super-Mare to Paddington train.

STRATTON PARK HALT

OPENED: 20th November 1933 (on the Didcot - Swindon section of the GWR originally opened through this site in 1840).

CLOSED: 7th December 1964.

With the eastward expansion of the Swindon residential area in the 1930s, the GWR decided to provide a new halt on the main Didcot to Swindon line. Sited immediately to the east of the old alignment of the A419 (Ermine Street) that ran north west to south east through the expanding town, the halt opened in November 1933. Originally intended to be called Stratton Green Halt, and costing an estimated £457, it comprised two platforms on each of which stood a corrugated iron shelter. Paths led up from the platform to the A419 road bridge. Originally lit by oil stored in a specially provided hut, electric lighting was later installed.

Despite the growth in the local population in the 1930s, passenger figures were low. In 1934 1,727 tickets were issued and in 1935 only 450. By the last year the competition from the Swindon bus network was strong particularly for local journeys into and out of Swindon town centre (see also Stratton). After 1935 no separate figures were issued for the halt, they were included in the figures for Swindon GWR.

Closure of the halt came in early December 1964 with the withdrawal of local passenger services between Didcot and Swindon. Today there is no trace of the halt at line side. Modern concrete steps lead down to the track on the down side on the alignment of the former access path to the Swindon bound platform.

SWINDON GWR

OPENED: 14th July 1842 (on the section of the GWR originally opened through this site in December 1840).

CLOSED: Passengers - remains open for services on the London (Paddington) - Bristol/South Wales/West of England/Cheltenham lines).
Goods - 1980s.

The broad gauge GWR from London (Paddington) to Bristol opened as far as Faringdon Road, 13 miles east of Swindon, on 20th July 1840. Sections of the GWR from Paddington had opened east of this point over the previous two years. Bad weather conditions during the autumn of 1840 delayed work on the next section in the Chippenham area and the GWR decided to open the line as far as Hay Lane, three miles west of Swindon in December 1840. Passengers then continued their journey to Chippenham and Bath by road, where they connected with the already opened line from Bath to Bristol. The complete through route to Bristol was opened on 30th June 1841 following the completion of the Hay Lane to Chippenham section (31st May 1841) and the line through Box Tunnel.

The section of the Cheltenham & Great Western Union Railway from Swindon GWR to Kemble and the branch to Cirencester opened on the same day as the line to Chippenham. A third rail laid on the London to Bristol route came into use in 1872 to allow the passage of both broad and standard gauge trains; the broad gauge was abolished as from 21st May 1892.

At an early stage in the development of the Paddington to Bristol line, the GWR Directors, acting on the advice of Brunel and the Company's locomotive superintendent Daniel Gooch, resolved that 'the principal locomotive station and repair shops be established at or near a junction with the Cheltenham & Great Western Union Railway at Swindon'. A Swindon station was considered desirable for three reasons: a branch to Gloucester had been authorised; a station at this point would, with Reading, divide the London to Bristol line into three operating sections; and the North Wilts Canal running north-south at Swindon could, through its links with other canal systems including the Wilts and Berks Canal, supply both coal and building materials. It was also felt that Swindon would be a good site for the change of locomotives running on the entire London to Bristol route. Despite these early plans a station was not provided at Swindon when the Faringdon Road to Hay Lane section opened in December 1840; it is thought that some form of exchange platform was provided once the line to Kemble and the branch to Cirencester was opened in May 1841.

In the early 1840s Swindon, with a population of some 2500, was a small market town on a hill, centred on what later became known as 'Old Town' (see text on Swindon Town Station). The GWR line ran east-west to the north of the town, and indeed for some years the station stood in an isolated position surrounded by fields and linked to the 'Old Town' by a track. The coming of the railway, and particularly the locomotive works in January 1843, changed the character and life of Swindon for ever. Originally the works undertook only repair and maintenance of locomotives but, as from 1846, locomotive construction began and the world famous Swindon Works developed with at one time over 12,000 being employed. Further development came in 1868 with the establishment of the GWR Carriage and Wagon Works. A new community grew between the station and Works and the Old Town, including the famous GWR Railway Village. Many books and accounts have been published setting out the history and development of the Works and the Village and readers should refer to these as set out in Further Reading. The following text refers principally to the station itself.

In view of its anticipated major role on the GWR system, the Directors regarded it as important that a fine station should be provided at Swindon. However, the overall cost of developing the whole London to Bristol line was becoming a problem. In an attempt to reduce capital costs the GWR entered into an agreement with J. & C. Rigby, a firm of London contractors who were involved in building other GWR stations. The agreement was that Rigbys were to bear the cost of the station's construction in return for a lease of the station's refreshment rooms and hotel accommodation for one penny a year. A further clause in the agreement was that all passenger trains in either direction would stop at Swindon 'for a reasonable period of about 10 minutes'. Furthermore the GWR also agreed not to provide any other refreshment facilities on the line between London and Bristol; the idea was that Messrs Rigby would recoup their costs from catering profits. Under this agreement the station was completed and opened on 14th July 1842, some 19 months after the line opened through the site.

The original station, designed by Brunel,

Swindon GWR. Looking down in about 1890. Note the small engine shed over the line into bay platform 6 and the train from Gloucester on the outer platform 8 (right). See also the mixed gauge track on the through lines (left).

comprised two island platforms on each of which stood a three storey stone building (see the engraving on the 'Contents' page). The two inner platform faces were used by trains on the main line between London and Bristol and the outer by Gloucester line trains. Two further tracks ran through the station between the platform tracks. The station was designed in this way to facilitate interchange between the main line and Gloucester line trains (for many years it was called Swindon Junction).

The two buildings were basically similar with offices and kitchens in the basement (below platform level), first and second class waiting and refreshment rooms on the ground floor (no facilities were provided for third class passengers) and hotel accommodation on the upper storeys. This latter comprised mainly bedrooms in the north side building and sitting/coffee rooms in the south. The two buildings were connected by a covered footbridge used by both hotel guests and passengers until a subway was added in 1870. A fire in March 1898 destroyed much of the upper storey of the north island building; this was never rebuilt and the hotel facility was abandoned. All platforms were, from the outset, covered by canopies supported by decorative pillars. A separate Brunel design booking office stood on the down side south of the Gloucester down loop and at the point closest to the town. The down island platform was reached via a short subway and steps; to reach the up island passengers originally used the covered footbridge and subsequently the 1870 subway.

The refreshment rooms at Swindon were the subject of comment for many years. Elaborately decorated, each room was divided into two sections by columns and an oval counter at which refreshments were sold. The columns and counter served also to separate first and second class passengers! In the early days business was brisk, generated by the enforced 10 minute stop and the lack of other facilities on the line. By all accounts however, the standard of service and food was not great, the excuse usually given being that the 10 minute stop was insufficient. The name 'Swindlem' was coined by some for the refreshment facilities. The lease of the facilities changed hands a number of times, indeed the Rigbys sub-let it within a week of the agreement! As speeds increased the required stop became an increasing burden, particularly as the GWR wished to run some trains non-stop through Swindon. After a number of failed legal actions to over-turn the '10 minute rule' the GWR purchased the refreshment rooms lease for what was then the large sum of £100,000 and, as from the 1st October 1895, the enforced stop was abolished. Now under

ABOVE Swindon GWR. A 1913 view looking west. Note that the upper storey of the up side building (right) is now cut back following the 1898 fire.

BELOW Swindon GWR. Looking up in about 1900. An engine is being examined at the down bay platform 2. A horse box stands at the west end of the main down platform.

BELOW Swindon GWR. A view of the main up platform in 1946. A carriage shed covers three sidings behind the west end of the platform.

GWR control, the rooms flourished for some years: the Prince of Wales, later King Edward VII, on occasions hired a special train to bring friends to dine at the station in what became known as the Queen's Royal Hotel. Fresh produce was apparently brought from London for these and other special occasions.

With the increased services on the main line, and the opening of new branch lines, pressures grew on Swindon station. By 1880 new tracks had been laid serving bay platforms on both islands. Extra sidings terminated at the remaining ends of the islands including a carriage shed served by three sidings at the west end of the up. The bay platform of the down island was used by trains on the Trowbridge and Swindon Town lines and that on the up island by local trains to the east, including the Highworth branch. The original four platforms had now expanded to eight; from south to north: No 1 (Down loop trains to Gloucester); nos 2 and 3 (Down bays); no 4 (Down main line to Bristol); no 5 (Up main line to London); nos 6 and 7 (Up bays); no 8 (Up loop trains from Gloucester). No.7 was designated for use by the Highworth branch trains. For a period a small engine shed stood over the line into bay platform 6. Late in 1904 the down island platform was extended at both ends; seven years later extensions were made to the up island. Both were then over 500 ft long. By this time Swindon was the hub of GWR services to the west with over 140 through services per day. In 1903 260,276 passenger tickets were issued; following a peak of 335,629 in 1925 the figure fell to 226,110 in 1933.

In parallel with these developments a large number of sidings were laid. This was particularly associated with major developments at Swindon Works. A goods depot was constructed three quarters of a mile east of the station, a large structure of brick and corrugated iron with three roads under cover. Complex signalling was needed at Swindon GWR and in the early years a number of boxes controlled movements all around the station and works. The signalling was consolidated in 1910 and 1913 into the major Swindon East and West boxes, both on the down side at each end of the station, the West box being close to the junction with the Gloucester line. These two boxes were eventually replaced by the new Swindon MAS Panel on the down side east of the station, which came into operation on 3rd March 1968.

The introduction of the new MAS box was linked to major changes at the station itself, which had

Swindon GWR. A splendid photograph of the Brunel design booking office on the down side with the 1872/1873 extension at the far end. Note the early GWR bus and the horse drawn carriage.

largely remained unaltered since the changes introduced around 1880. The covered footbridge had been demolished in 1962, but the withdrawal of virtually all local services by the mid 1960s meant that less platform space was required. As from 3rd March 1968 all through services were concentrated on the former up island platform, the northern face being principally allocated for use by up trains towards London and the southern face for down trains to Bristol, South Wales and through trains to Gloucester and Cheltenham. A new bay platform was created at the west end of the island for use by local trains to Gloucester. The original platform 8 changed to platform 1, the original platform 5 to platform 3 and the new bay platform was no 2. The southern side booking office, main down side building and the west end of the down platform were demolished being largely replaced by a 12 storey office block now, in 2004, named Signal Point, and occupied by Threadneedle Investments. The east end of the down platform was retained however for use as a parcels and mail platform; it was also used on occasions for football supporter specials. The site of the west end of the platform is now used for a slip road into a car park that has been developed on former sidings. Passenger access to and from the station is now via the original but now refurbished subway; a new travel centre opening in 1975 on the ground floor of the office block.

On the remaining island platform a buffet and bar was developed at the west end whilst toilets, a waiting room and a bookstall were sited towards the centre close to the steps to and from the subway. The canopies continue to be supported by the original decorative pillars but these are now protected at the bottom by concrete set in old oil drums. Although the upper storey of the building is still of a Bath stone finish, at platform level it is cement rendered. Passenger numbers remained good during and after this period of change: in 1976 236,506 tickets were issued; by 1980 this had risen to 304,520. Over the same period the number of season tickets rose from 3,651 to 7,098. In complete contrast to the continued success of the station, the Swindon locomotive works closed in June 1987, the carriage and wagon works had closed back in 1962.

The 1968 reorganisation of the track layout and the station remodelling did however bring problems, in particular for the operation of down trains stopping at Swindon. All such trains needed to cross over the through up line that carried London bound trains not stopping at Swindon and extensive freight services. These crossing movements often led to delays. The decision was taken to reinstate a down platform on the site of the original north side of the

Swindon GWR. A 1967 view of the station building from the south shortly before its demolition.

southern island platform; a part of this had been retained, as noted above. This retained section was now demolished and a completely new concrete component platform 4 reopened for passenger services on 2nd June 2003. The formal opening by Richard Bowker, the Chairman of the Strategic Rail Authority, took place in July, the ceremony also being attended by John Armitt, the Chief Executive of Network Rail. Three platforms are now available for use by through trains stopping at Swindon: platforms 1 and 3 are both used by up trains towards Reading and London whilst down trains call at the new platform 4. The bay platform 2 is used by terminating local services from Gloucester, and also from Southampton Central and Trowbridge.

A number of facilities, including a waiting room, toilets and a buffet, have been provided on the new platform 4; the facilities as originally provided in the 1968 changes continue to serve passengers on platforms 1,2 and 3 though these have recently been renovated and extended. A covered bridge from the island platform across tracks on its northern side is for use by employees and visitors to the Research Council offices. The former goods depot east of the station has now gone.

Finally, to the west of the station 'Steam', the excellent Museum of the Great Western Railway , has been developed in a well-restored building originally at the heart of the Swindon Works.

Swindon Town. Looking east from the Devizes Road bridge. A 4-4-0 locomotive hauls a northbound train out of the station around the time of the First World War.

SWINDON TOWN

OPENED: 27th July 1881 (with the opening of the Swindon Town - Marlborough section of the Swindon, Marlborough & Andover Railway).

CLOSED: Passengers - 11th September 1961.
Goods - 19th May 1964 (except coal and private sidings since closed).

The original proposed route for the Swindon, Marlborough & Andover Railway (SMAR), as authorised under an Act of July 1873, did not pass through what was later to become the site of Swindon Town station. The alignment envisaged took the railway north from a little to the east of the future site, through a 700 yard tunnel, to join the GWR London to Bristol line just to the east of Swindon GWR. Although work commenced in 1875 at the northern end of the tunnel, it was short-lived because of financial problems largely brought about by the costs of excavation.

Four years later, after re-examination of the proposals, a new Act was passed authorising a realignment of this northern section. This time the railway was to swing west south of the Old Town hill and then, passing through Rushey Platt, join the GWR main line west of Swindon GWR. From this junction trains would travel east for some 1¼ miles to the 1842 station. Swindon Town station was included in the revised proposal, in the then commercial centre of the Old Town.

The single track standard gauge line between Swindon and Marlborough opened to the public on 27th July 1881. As the turning of the first sod for this line took place in Marlborough, it was agreed that the opening would be principally celebrated in Swindon. Thus, on the day prior to its public opening, a special train travelled from Marlborough. It was greeted on arrival at Swindon Town and, led

Swindon Town. A general view west of the main building on the down platform. The station master's house with a tall chimney is closest to the camera. The impressive offices of the Midland & South Western Junction Railway are in the far distance over the main building canopy; part of the building survives today.

by the Swindon Town band, the guests made their way to a banquet at the Corn Exchange. A few days later on August Bank Holiday the normal advertised service was replaced by trains at 1½ hour intervals taking trippers south to the Savernake Forest for picnics.

The short northern section of the SMAR from Swindon Town west and north to the junction with the GWR opened in February 1882, a shuttle service being introduced between the two Swindon stations. This shuttle only ran for just over three years, being abandoned as from February 1885 because of the high costs charged by the GWR to the SMAR for use of the 1¼ mile of track into Swindon GWR. Through services south from Marlborough to Andover commenced in February 1883 (see Marlborough introductory text).

The Swindon and Cheltenham Extension Railway amalgamated with the SMAR in 1884 to form the Midland & South Western Junction Railway, the name referring to the titles of the two major railway systems the new Company linked, the Midland and the London & South Western. It opened to passengers from Rushey Platt (Swindon) to Cirencester in December 1883 and on to Cheltenham in August 1891. Swindon Town was now at the mid point of this long line that provided a through route between the Midlands and the south coast.

This important role at the heart of the system resulted in the development of the most impressive, spacious and well laid out station on the M&SWJR. At some 440 ft above sea level, Swindon Town was close to the heart of Swindon Old Town at a point where the M&SWJR ran west-east on the southern slope of the hill. It was thus well placed for both passenger and freight business, adjacent to the cattle market in Newport Street, so long as the Old Town continued to be the town's commercial focus. This gradually changed as major developments took place in what became known as New Town, north of the hill and towards the GWR station and railway works.

The principal brick building, incorporating the main offices, toilets, a refreshment room and accommodation for the station master stood on the down (north) side of the line accessed from Station Approach. A large fretted canopy, supported by pillars, provided shelter, as did a small canopy over the station entrance on the road side forecourt. A metal waiting shelter, also with a small canopy, stood on the up platform behind which ran sidings. As well as the up and down platform lines, a third central line through the station was used for the run-round of locomotives; from this there was a link across the up line to a two road locomotive shed at the south east end of the station site on the up side. In the early days passengers crossed between the platforms by rail level wooden boards. During 1885 an open steel footbridge with wooden planks was erected west of the main building; later the sides were enclosed and lamps installed but no roof was ever provided.

Water columns stood at the platform ends and also close to the corrugated iron locomotive shed; outside the shed was a small turntable. A goods shed served by a trailing siding stood to the east of the station on the down side adjacent to Marlborough Road. Two signal cabins constructed by the Gloucester Railway Carriage and Wagon Company controlled train movements. One stood on the down platform at the west end and the other beyond the east end close to the goods shed also on the down side. The M&SWJR offices were established in 1881 in a large house overlooking the station site from the north west. It was accessed from Station Approach which led off Newport Street close to the latter's junction with Devizes Road.

During 1904 and 1905 major redevelopment was undertaken at Swindon Town to handle the greatly increased traffic following the opening of the line to Cheltenham in 1891 – and thus the completion of the through Midlands to south coast route. The down platform was extended to an overall length of 510 ft. The up platform was lengthened to 528 ft and widened. It became a true island platform, two up tracks being laid on the outside, one alongside the platform itself. These extra lines compensated for the removal of the old central line, there being no room for this following the platform widening. The outside up loop line provided a link to a new large turntable; its siting was unusual being some distance from a new locomotive shed south east of the station. Adjacent to the turntable was a large water tank supplying pumps on the station site.

A new general waiting room and a ladies' waiting room were constructed on the enlarged up island platform, the original waiting shelter being demolished. Two separate brick buildings were linked by a overall roof surrounded by wide canopies. The outside (south) face of this platform was used by shuttle trains to Swindon GWR station when these were re-introduced in 1924 following the take over of the M&SWJR by the GWR. With these major developments the original 1880s main station building was apparently judged to be adequate, few changes being made in 1904/5. Two ticket windows were introduced in 1912 as was a boiler for heating foot -warmers in 1908. The revised track layout required the demolition of the 1885 engine shed on the up side, its retention would have restricted the length of the new up loop lines.

A new two road brick shed was constructed a quarter of a mile south east of the station on the down side. This shed had a comparatively short life as a loco shed being closed on 21st January 1924 when the new owner, the GWR, decided to concentrate the maintenance of locomotives at its major facilities near Swindon GWR station. The former Swindon Town shed, after initial use as a bus depot, served as an oil depot for some years until its demolition in the 1970s. Further developments soon after 1904/5 saw the construction of a new large goods shed on the site of the original; at its west end was a small goods office. It incorporated a 5 ton capacity crane. As the station stood close to the cattle market, cattle pens were also provided. All the track changes and extensions necessitated the provision of two new signal boxes, replacing the originals. The 'A' box stood at the west end of the down platform ramp and the 'B' box at the east end of the station on the up side just beyond the Evelyn Street bridge. Both boxes were of the then London & South Western Railway style, 'A' being of brick and 'B' of wood; the latter being lighter due to its standing on an embankment.

As with most stations in Wiltshire business was good in the 1920s but began to fall in the 1930s with growing competition from buses. Sales of passenger tickets at Swindon Town fell from 65,000 in 1923 to 28,000 in 1938. During the Second World War further amendments were made to the track layout to give extra capacity for movements on what was a crucial through north-south link for military traffic.

The usual post war decline set in during the late 1950s and passenger services were withdrawn at Swindon Town as from September 1961; the station refreshment room remained open until January 1965, it had become a local facility for non-rail users. The buildings and platforms remained for some while but were eventually demolished, some materials being acquired by the Swindon & Cricklade Railway, which was by then developing its preservation scheme at Blunsdon, north east of the town. The goods shed continued to handle general freight until this traffic ceased in May 1964. Traffic continued to use a coal yard to the east of the station until late 1968. By this time most of the sidings had been lifted. A short revival came in 1970: the former up main line was re-laid at the station site and, for a short period, became the rail head for the receipt of trains carrying stone from the Mendip quarries used in the construction of the M4 south of Swindon.

Today virtually the whole of the former station site has been redeveloped as the Central Trading Estate. Within the estate the main road line approximately follows that of former principal rail lines. The alignment west of the site under the Devizes Road bridge is laid out as part of the 'Old Town Rail Path'. A mural beside the path close to the road bridge depicts scenes from Swindon's railway history. The mural is immediately below the only significant remnant from the railway history of this part of Swindon, the impressive 1881 M&SWJR offices. Out of railway use since 1924 and now minus its south west section, the house has been well restored and is now used by a firm of chartered accountants. Nearby on Newport Street a public house, the 'Steam Railway Company' also provides a reminder of the earlier era.

Tidworth. Looking north in about 1913. A four coach local train stands at the platform. The goods shed can be seen in the distance beneath the canopy and beyond the train.

TIDWORTH

OPENED: Military traffic - 8th July 1901, goods - 1st July 1902, passengers - 1st October 1902 (with the successive openings of the Tidworth branch from Ludgershall).

CLOSED: Passengers - 19th September 1955.
Goods - 25th November 1955 (general goods), 31st July 1963 (military).

At the end of the nineteenth century the Government decided to develop large military barracks at Tidworth, initially to meet the demands arising from the Boer War. Some fifteen years earlier in 1882 the Grafton to Andover section of the Swindon, Marlborough & Andover Railway (SMAR) had opened through Ludgershall some two miles north east of Tidworth. The SMAR was absorbed into the newly formed Midland & South Western Junction Railway (M&SWJR) in 1884, and when its directors learnt of the plans to develop at Tidworth they approached the War Department with a proposal to open a branch line from Ludgershall. Agreement was reached in November 1900 and construction soon followed. The branch left the M&SWJR west of Ludgershall station and climbed to a summit at Tidworth Down, where a steep sided cutting was opened up through the chalkland. The line then descended steeply to the then small town of Tidworth. The whole of the branch was built on War Department land. A line west into the barracks area itself left the branch to the north of the station. The barracks eventually incorporated, at its peak activity, some 2½ miles of track, but none of this was available for public use. Bricks for the construction of the barracks came by rail to Tidworth from a mineral line connecting with the M&SWJR at Grafton (see Grafton text).

The Tidworth branch opened for military manoeuvre traffic in July 1901 and to War Department traffic in May 1902; the War Department then agreed that the branch could become a public railway. It was leased to, and operated by, the M&SWJR and its successor Companies, opening for public goods traffic in July 1902 and to passengers in October 1902. The line terminated at Tidworth station, which developed into the third most important station on the M&SWJR system, after Ludgershall and Swindon Town. The station stood astride the Hampshire/ Wiltshire border and it is said that when a passenger booked a ticket he or she stood in Hampshire whilst the booking clerk was in Wiltshire! (In recent years the county boundary has moved south to bring all of Tidworth into Wiltshire.)

The main station building with four chimneys and a horizontal fretted canopy stood on the down (west) side platform (400 ft). Alongside to the south was a smaller building used as a porters' room and coal store. Opposite the main building and platform was a wide very long (835 ft) troop platform.

To the north of the station on the down (west) side was a goods loading platform and a goods shed with a small office beneath. Adjoining the platform and shed was a 5 ton capacity crane. Separate goods offices also stood nearby to the west. The original Tidworth engine shed was sited again to the north of the station on the down side; however this was dismantled and re-erected in 1915 at the terminal end of new sidings behind the main station building. The additional sidings were laid in response to increasing traffic during the First World War. The engine shed was for the use of War Department locomotives, as the Tidworth branch was worked by locomotives based at Ludgershall. Other war time development included an extension of the station canopy in 1916 and the provision of a checker's cabin in 1917. At its maximum the Tidworth goods facilities could accommodate 290 wagons or ten trains of twelve coaches each. Traffic movements at Tidworth were controlled from a 26 lever signal box at the north end of the troop platform.

During the 1930s the number of staff at Tidworth averaged about 13; some 15,000-20,000 passengers were despatched per year, the majority being servicemen. A major peak was on the occasion of the annual Tidworth Tattoo when excursion trains arrived from all over the country. In some years the total receipts at Tidworth exceeded those of all the other M&SWJR stations in total. This reflected, in particular, major freight activity. Daily traffic was considerable, with coal and ordnance supplies forming the bulk of incoming traffic in roughly equal proportions. Coal was sent from Tidworth station to eight separate coal yards within the garrison. There were weekly deliveries of flour – three van loads from Spillers Mills at Avonmouth. Every other week a meat train brought thirty insulated containers on flat trucks. Outgoing traffic mainly comprised military 'products'; these apparently included 'dog droppings' transported in old barrels to tanneries in the Midlands and horse manure to Swanwick in Hampshire where it was used on the extensive strawberry beds. The scale of both passenger and freight traffic at Tidworth was such that the post of station master was graded higher than at any other M&SWJR station. Houses were provided for the station master and the chief shunter; there were also six other railway cottages.

After the Second World War traffic dwindled and by 1952 there were only three passenger trains per day from Tidworth to Ludgershall. The only train on a Sunday was an evening service from Ludgershall to Tidworth conveying troops back from weekend leave. The line into the barracks and garrison area closed in 1953 and passenger services on the Tidworth branch ceased in mid September 1955; the public goods service ceased some two months later. The signal box closed when passenger services were withdrawn, being replaced by a ground frame. The branch line reverted to solely military use until its closure on 31st July 1963; in its last years the line was operated by the No 1 Railway Group of the Royal Engineers Southern Division. The branch line was lifted in early 1964.

Today virtually nothing can be seen on the former station site that lies to the north of Station Road. It is now covered by landscaping associated with recent housing development. Shops align Station Road; to the east of one of these, 'Fun and Fantasy', stands an old blue brick post with a sign 'No parking in front of gates'. This appears to be one of the former gate posts at the original station entrance.

TISBURY

OPENED: Passengers - 2nd May 1859 (with the opening of the Salisbury - Gillingham section of the Salisbury & Yeovil Railway to passenger traffic) goods - 1st September 1860.

CLOSED: Passengers - remains open for services on the London (Waterloo) - Salisbury - Exeter line.
Goods - 18th April 1966 (except for private sidings since closed).

Sited on the southern edge of the small town, the station opened for passenger traffic in May 1859 with the commencement of services on the Salisbury to Gillingham section of the Salisbury & Yeovil Railway. Goods services started just over a year later in September 1860.

Tisbury. A Yeovil bound train passes in 1964. Note the small shelter on the down platform (far right) and the long canopy extending east.

The principal station buildings, including the slate hung station master's house, were on the up side (towards Salisbury); a waiting shelter stood on the down platform. A feature of Tisbury station was the long canopies on pillars which stretched east along the platforms away from the main building and shelter. A footbridge connected the two platforms at the eastern end beyond the canopies; originally covered and glazed, the roof was later removed. In 1928 15,257 passenger tickets were issued, by 1936 only 6,591. The 1932 weekday service comprised eight down and nine up passenger trains.

As with other stations on this line, freight traffic was of equal, if not greater, importance than passenger movements. Sidings were laid to the west of the station on both sides of the main line; the goods shed, feed store and coal bunkers being on the up side and a traders' store, cattle pens, weighbridge and a 5 ton capacity crane on the down. The gas works, on the down side, south east of the station were also served by a siding at one stage. At Tisbury, as at Semley, the next station to the west, milk and milk products were a major source of traffic. The scale can be seen from the fact that in 1936 93,379 gallons were forwarded. In 1932 three up and three down milk trains called at Tisbury per weekday, the latter being empty workings.

Train movements at Tisbury were controlled originally by a LSWR box standing at the west end of the up platform. It was replaced by a BR design box in October 1958, sited off the west end of the platform and adjacent to the old box.

Goods facilities were withdrawn from the station in April 1966; the down line and sidings were lifted in 1967 and the signal box closed in February 1967. The down platform and shelter and the footbridge were demolished following the singling of the line and the land sold off right to the former edge of the platform. It is now occupied by Parmiters, suppliers of agricultural equipment. The former up siding and yard have now gone; the site is now Station Yard Industrial Estate.

The main station buildings and canopy remain today on the up platform, the facilities were subject to an improvement scheme completed in 1995. The buildings are in various uses but the 1958 signal box, though being classed as a store on a plan displayed at the station, appears to be unused. Behind the station stands the 'South Western Hotel'.

Tisbury. A view of the up platform. The buildings include the main offices and the slate hung station master's house. Note the long canopy stretching east beyond the house and also the original pre 1958 signal box.

The station is served by virtually all trains on the London-Salisbury-Exeter line, the weekday service 2003/2004 was 20 down and 21 one up trains. Not all are through trains to London or Exeter but commence or terminate at Salisbury, Gillingham or Yeovil. This scale of traffic movements brings operational problems on the single line and in a number of places loop lines have been installed. One was deemed necessary in the Tisbury area because of a lack of a passing place in the 19 miles between Wilton and Gillingham, but could not be placed at the station because so much land had been sold off! Thus the Tisbury loop, opened in March 1986, is sited a little to the east. It cost £435,000!

TROWBRIDGE

OPENED: 5th September 1848 (with the opening of the Thingley Junction - Westbury section of the Wilts, Somerset & Weymouth Railway).

CLOSED: Passengers - remains open for services on the Cardiff/Bristol - Westbury - Southampton/ Weymouth lines.
Goods - 10th July 1967.

The railway came to Trowbridge with the opening of the Wilts, Somerset & Weymouth Railway from Thingley Junction, west of Chippenham on the GWR, to Westbury in September 1848. Three days prior to the opening of the line to passenger and freight traffic, directors of the Railway travelled through the town on route to Westbury. What was described as 'a great assemblage of people' greeted the train at the new station, with a salute being fired from cannons at a nearby iron foundry.

The station, sited to the west of the town centre, took on the role of a junction with the opening in 1857 of the line from Bradford Junction, to the north of Trowbridge, to Bathampton on the main GWR London to Bath and Bristol route. From that time, Trowbridge was served by passenger and freight trains travelling north-west to south-east from Bristol and Bath to Salisbury, Southampton and Portsmouth, and also services from London via Chippenham to Yeovil and Weymouth.

Trowbridge station, built to the plans of Geddeth and Nolloth at Brunel's office in London, served a town with an 1861 population of some 10,000. The principal building, with an extensive canopy and incorporating the main offices, was on the town side of the station. A large waiting shelter, also with an extensive canopy, stood on the up side (towards Bath) behind which was the up bay used by local trains running to and from destinations such as Devizes and Chippenham. The passenger access to the station was only on the town side from a large forecourt. Passenger numbers were relatively high with 159,848 tickets being issued in 1903 and 120,519 in 1933.

Before the major changes in the 1980s a number of additions and amendments were made to both the platforms and the buildings. The original 1882 footbridge was relocated in the early 1900s from the southern end to a position immediately north of the main building. When the road bridge to the south of the station was rebuilt in 1931/32, the opportunity was taken to extend the platforms under it.

Not only is Trowbridge the county town of Wiltshire but it was, and continues to be, an

Trowbridge. Looking south in 1963. The main building is on the down platform (left), the footbridge is in its revised post 1900s position. A truck stands at a dock siding behind the down platform.

Trowbridge. The extensive station forecourt in the early years of the twentieth century. Horse drawn carriages and wagons are drawn up in front of the building.

important small industrial town. For many years it was a manufacturing centre for broadcloth, whilst bacon and milk factories stood close to the station. These activities generated considerable goods traffic. The export of local stone was, for some years, another important source of traffic.

An extensive goods yard with a large goods shed (unusually with a double track doorway) served the town north of the station on the down side. An 8 ton crane was provided, as were a cattle dock and pens, the latter being sited close to the northern end of the platform. Sidings were laid on the up side to the north of, and behind, the up bay and also a siding leading to an engine turntable. Trowbridge signal box, controlling movements both on the main lines and in the goods yard and sidings, stood on the up side north of the station.

An engine shed was provided for some years at Trowbridge on the up side some way north of the station towards Bradford Junction. Built in 1875 it contained three 100 ft long 'roads'. By 1901 26 locomotives were based at the shed; its importance

Trowbridge. A GWR diesel car in the station in 1936, a year after it came into service on the Bristol - Weymouth line.

Trowbridge. Looking north on 6th June 1960 at the extensive buildings and canopies on both platforms, the covered footbridge is towards the north end.

declined however, after the opening of a large shed at Westbury in 1915. Closure came in June 1923, after which the building was used for some years for carriage and wagon repairs.

During the Second World War Trowbridge, like many stations in Wiltshire, was particularly busy because of the major military presence in the county. However, soon after the War, and certainly by the early 1960s, decline had set in. The signal box closed in 1968 and platform shortening took place in 1983. Other small demolitions had started two years earlier, but in 1984 the attractive historic buildings were declared unsafe and demolished. Replacement buildings were in situ by 1988 with the principal facility now serving passengers travelling towards Bath. With the sidings removed and replaced by a car park an access was also introduced on that side of the station. A small waiting shelter was built to serve Westbury bound passengers. A new footbridge was erected; the old covered bridge was dismantled and is now awaiting re-erection by the West Somerset Railway at Williton.

The goods yard closed in 1967, the goods shed remained in place for some years, but it has now gone and the whole of the former goods yard is a private car park. A railway related car park is provided in the extensive station forecourt at the entrance to which stands a small red brick building, a small remnant of the former extensive railway buildings. The signal box closed in September 1968.

Today Trowbridge station is served by trains on the South Wales/Bristol to Southampton/Weymouth services. It is particularly used by commuters and shoppers travelling to and from Bath. Two signs illustrating features of Trowbridge were erected by the pupils of John o' Gaunts School in 1999.

WARMINSTER

OPENED: 9th September 1851 (with the opening of the Westbury - Warminster section of the GWR Westbury - Salisbury line).

CLOSED: Passengers - remains open for services on the Cardiff/Bristol - Salisbury - Southampton/ Portsmouth line.
Goods - 2nd April 1973.

Warminster opened in September 1851 as the terminus of the first section of the broad gauge GWR line from Westbury to Salisbury. Its terminus role lasted just under five years until the opening of the line on to Salisbury in June 1856. Sited north-east of the town centre, the original Brunel style structure, with an overall roof, was typical of that era and was similar to that which still remains today at Frome in Somerset. Warminster station was the work of J.H. Bertram, one of Brunel's chief assistants and engineer of the GWR for eight months after Brunel's death.

The principal wooden buildings, incorporating the main booking and waiting facilities, were on the south (town) side of the station. Passengers travelling towards Salisbury on the down line were provided with a wooden waiting room, originally heated by an open fire whose chimney protruded behind galvanised iron rear walls. The overall station roof

Warminster. Looking east in the 1900s with staff posing for the camera on both platforms. Note the very ornate footbridge and the wooden train shed beyond. Churns on the down platform (left) serve as a reminder of the importance of milk traffic at the station.

was still in place in 1928 but by the mid 1930s it had been replaced by individual steel canopies attached to the original buildings. Attractive valences often found on canopies of an earlier era were not provided on these later Warminster examples. Inter platform connection was originally provided by an early standard GWR style footbridge with ornate lattice sides, decorative valences and a galvanised iron roof. In later years the roof was removed but the original bridge was retained.

Freight operations were important at Warminster, sidings being sited both north and south-east of the station. The latter served a goods shed with a nearby crane. South of the goods shed sidings led to cattle pens and also Warminster cattle market. A gated siding led to a series of users, including the West Country Creamery and a Warminster U.D.C. depot. Milk traffic was important for many years. To the north of the station the Geest Ltd. banana packaging plant was served by trains of insulated vans from Southampton and Bristol Docks. The plant ceased to be rail linked in the mid 1970s and the siding was lifted in 1979. The Air Ministry used three sidings north of the station between 1942 and 1949.

Warminster. An engraving of the principal wooden buildings shortly after the station opened in 1851.

Controlling movements of passenger and freight trains, Warminster signal box was sited at the east end of the up platform (towards Westbury); opening on 19th June 1904, it closed seventy five years later on 3rd June 1979 when it became a ground frame controlling one of the two remaining cross-overs and the one siding still in use.

Both passenger and goods traffic were at a good level early in the twentieth century. In 1903 47,769 passenger tickets were issued, but by 1933 the figure had dropped dramatically to 24,338. During and immediately after both World Wars passenger and freight traffic was particularly busy associated with the movements of military personnel and equipment. Eight sidings, two loops and tank loading platforms were added during the Second World War at Beechgrove on the down side, one mile east of the station. The R.E.M.E. and the School of Infantry were established at Warminster in 1945, generating considerable extra traffic. General goods services were withdrawn from Warminster in April 1973.

Today the station itself is little changed with the original buildings still in use. The up side principal building incorporates a booking office, toilets and an office used by a vehicle hire firm. When visited in December 2003 the building was in some need of repair and repainting. The shelter on the down side

Warminster. A view west on 2nd June 1963. Canopies have replaced the overall roof removed some thirty years earlier. The footbridge has also lost its roof. Note the waiting room with chimney protruding behind the down side shelter (right).

was also still in place though unfortunately the waiting room was locked. The original footbridge, though now without a roof, still provides the link between the platforms. All sidings have been lifted, the former goods yard on the up side east of the station is in various industrial and storage uses, the goods shed itself gone. On the north side behind the shelter, the land is now used as a car park. The site of the large Geest factory north-west of the station is now occupied by a modern housing development.

WESTBURY

OPENED: 5th September 1848 (with the opening of the Thingley Junction - Westbury section of the Wilts, Somerset & Weymouth Railway).

CLOSED: Passengers - remains open for services on the London (Paddington) - West Country and Cardiff/Bristol - Southampton/Weymouth lines. Goods - 1st November 1966 (except private sidings some of which remain in use today for mineral traffic).

Westbury station opened in 1848 as the terminus of the first section of the Wilts, Somerset & Weymouth Railway from Thingley Junction, on the GWR west of Chippenham. Sited about a half mile to the west of the town, this original station was a typical Brunel type wooden building designed by J. Geddes, one of the engineer's principal assistants. An overall roof covered the two platforms and tracks. The photographic record of this station is limited but *GWR Architecture* contains a cross section diagram based on 1847 plans. This source also suggests that an additional platform was probably added between the existing platforms (24 ft 6 inches apart) between 1852 and 1855. A footbridge linking the main platforms stood beyond the south end of the covered train shed. What is clear is that this first Westbury station, which served passengers for some fifty years, was similar to that which survives today at Frome, the next station south on the Yeovil line.

In 1895 the GWR decided that a new shorter route was required from London to Taunton and the South West. This new route was to include two new sections of line known as cut off routes, first from Patney & Chirton (on the Berks & Hants Extension line from Hungerford to Devizes) to Westbury and the second west from Castle Cary (on the Westbury, Yeovil & Weymouth line) to Langport and Athelney linking with the existing Bristol to Taunton line. The first line, known as the Stert Valley line, some 14½ miles long, opened in 1900, and the second in 1906. With the completion of the latter, through express trains from London to Taunton and Exeter ran through Westbury, many stopping at the station. Westbury had now become a major rail junction at the crossing point of services from London to the South West and also South Wales/Bristol to the south coast at Southampton, Portsmouth and Weymouth.

With such a major increase in traffic, the original 1848 station was clearly inadequate. In 1899 it was demolished and replaced by a much enlarged station. The new structure comprised two 600 ft long island

Westbury. A rare undated photograph which shows, on the left, a section of the original 1848 station with its overall roof.

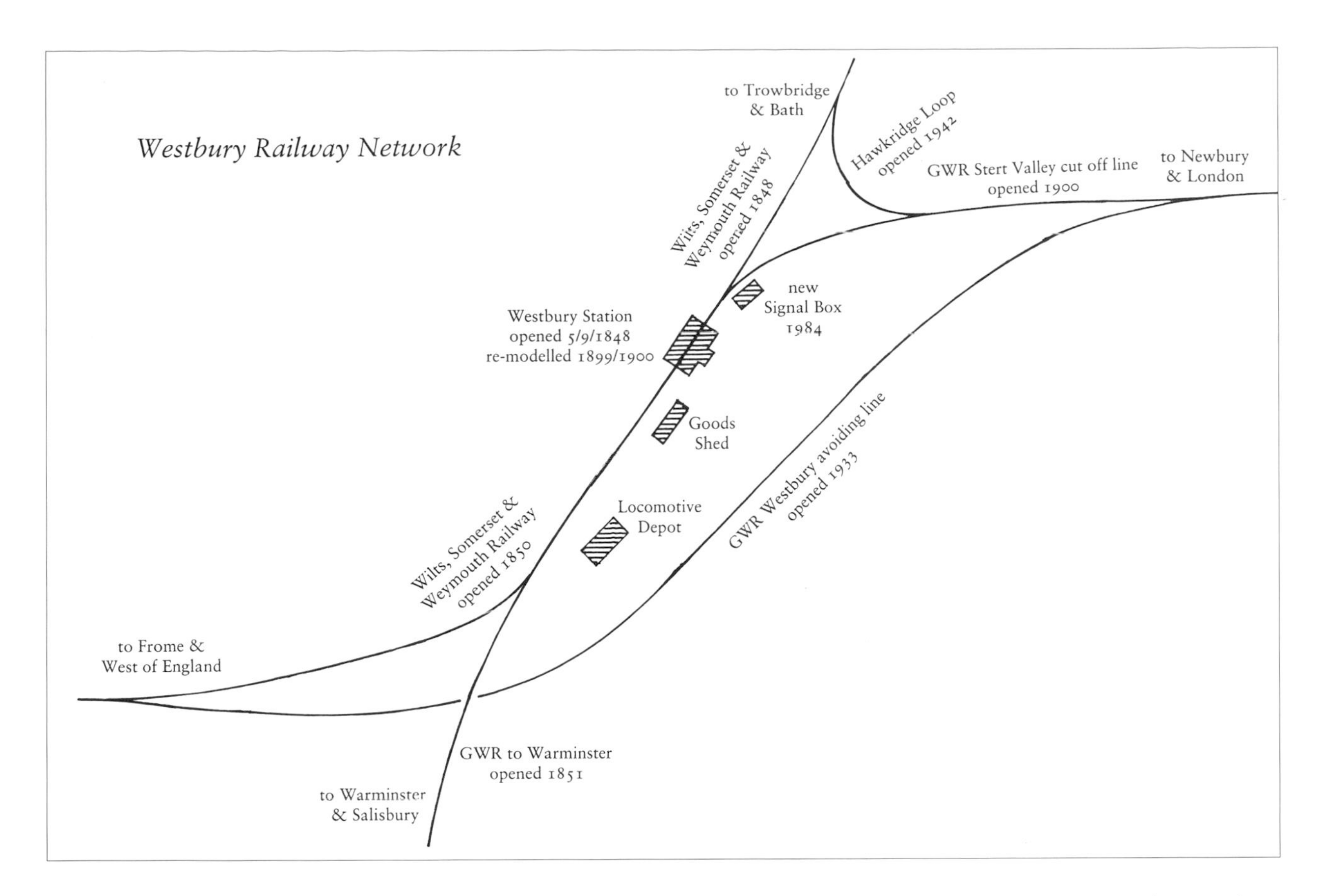

platforms, accessed by a subway from the main station building with a canopy, incorporating booking facilities and a parcels office at a lower level on the east (town) side of the station. Luggage lifts were provided as were long fretted canopies over both platforms. Two brick buildings on the up (towards Trowbridge) island platform incorporated gent's toilets, a porters' office, a general waiting room, ladies' waiting room, ladies' toilets and an office. On the down platform five brick buildings housed the gent's toilets, the telegrams office, station master's office, inspector's office, third class ladies' waiting room, first class ladies' waiting room, ladies' toilets, third class general waiting room, first class general waiting room and the refreshment room. The station master's house stood north-east of the station across the station approach road from the booking office. Staff numbers based at the station increased from 45 in 1903 to 130 in 1923, largely because of the opening of the Westbury locomotive shed in 1915.

As an important junction, Westbury also developed as a major centre for freight traffic with a large complex of sidings being laid out, particularly to the south of the station. To relieve congestion and conflict with passenger trains, two goods avoiding lines were laid either side of the station between signal boxes to the north and south. In 1907 an avoiding line was opened on the down side and eight years later an even longer line was provided on the up side. To the south of the station on the down side goods traffic was catered for in a goods shed with a loading platform. A 30 cwt crane was also provided. Cattle pens were sited at the southern end of the down island platform.

For many years freight traffic was enhanced by operations associated with the large Westbury Iron Works sited to the west of the station. A dedicated siding served the works from 1870 to 1941. Within the works complex a 2 ft gauge line connected various buildings and also linked to nearby iron ore mines. The works ceased iron production in 1908 and ore extraction stopped in 1923. Following closure of the works various engineering companies occupied the site.

To the south of the station, and accessed off the Salisbury line, was a large locomotive shed, opened in 1915. The shed contained four straight roads; a well equipped workshop was attached and nearby was a large water tank and a turntable. The shed

Westbury. A fine overall view looking south at the extensive facilities in the late 1950s. Trains stand at the two island platforms and on the far right is the large Westbury North signal box.

which, in 1947, was the base for 71 steam locomotives closed in September 1965. A diesel depot to the south-west of the station served the new diesel fleet for some years from 1959 until it too closed in 1993.

The extensive and varied nature of the passenger and freight traffic required complex signalling arrangements. The original two 19th century boxes were replaced during the 1899 reconstruction by three boxes. The North Box south of, and close to, the intersection of the Trowbridge and Newbury lines continued to operate until a major revamp of the track layout at Westbury in 1984. By then it had taken over the operations of the Middle Box, sited at the south end of the down platform, and the South Box, originally built close to the intersection of the Salisbury and West of England lines.

The layout and functions of Westbury station itself remained largely unchanged from 1900 until the mid 1980s. In 1933 however, pressure created by the through station workings was eased with the opening of the Westbury avoiding line, east of the station. This line linked the Newbury line north-east of the station to the West of England line south-west of the station, passing under the Salisbury line (see diagram). This allowed express trains not stopping at Westbury to avoid the curved nature of the tracks, both in the station itself and on the approaches.

Westbury saw heavy traffic during the Second World War both for passengers and freight, in particular it was a base for ambulance trains. A significant addition to the layout was the construction in 1942 of a new north-east link between the Trowbridge and Newbury lines north of the station (the Hawkridge loop) thus allowing through movements between the two without reversal in Westbury station. Although passenger traffic remained reasonably steady after the War, general goods movements declined and facilities were withdrawn from November 1966. Against this trend was the maintenance and increase in traffic associated with operations at the Mendip stone quarries.

Although limited alterations were undertaken in 1978, the mid 1980s saw a major remodelling of operations at Westbury, in particular linked with the introduction of modern electronic signalling. The station itself closed briefly in the spring of 1984 to allow extensive changes to the track work at the northern end of the station and the revamp of signalling. A large new signal box was commissioned in May north-east of the station and adjacent to the Newbury line, the 1899 North Box by then having closed. At the station itself the track was removed from the outer face of the down island (the original platform 1) and the three remaining tracks (re-numbered 1 – 3) were signalled for bi-directional use.

Today the station retains much of its 1899 form, modified by the 1984 changes. All the brick buildings on the two island platforms remain: those on the down platform are largely occupied by Wessex Trains staff though a waiting room is provided for the limited number of services using this platform. The section in the middle block with attractive wooden windows is now no longer used, although it was for many years a refreshment room.

Westbury. A print from an Edwardian postcard shows many of the large number of staff then based at the station (plus a few children). The canopies were introduced with the 1899 rebuild of Westbury. Note the symbolic large milk churn in the foreground!

The up platform buildings are used by both staff and the public, for whom a waiting room and toilets are provided. The Westbury Buffet, a kiosk between the buildings is open for long hours throughout the week and provided the author with a cup of hot Bovril on a chilly December day! On both platforms the canopies remain in good condition. The subway leading to the entrance building remains with the booking office in use.

Across the station approach road the former station master's house, re-named 'Ingleside', is used as a training centre for Wessex Trains staff; it is also the offices for the manager of the Wessex Trains Cardiff to Portsmouth/Brighton/Weymouth services. The former station yard north-east of the station is occupied by the Westbury permanent way depot, operated by Carillion Rail. West of the station much of the former large site of the Westbury Iron Works is now occupied by Westbury Motor Auctions. Many of the sidings to the south are extensively used by trains associated with the Mendip Rail quarry operations.

Mounted on the bridge crossing the line north of the station are two small plaques indicating that it was constructed in 1899 by F. Finch & Co. Engineers and Iron Founders of Chepstow, the year of the station's major reconstruction.

WILTON GWR

OPENED: 30th June 1856 (with the opening of the GWR Warminster - Salisbury (Fisherton) line).
CLOSED: Passengers - 19th September 1955.
Goods - 6th September 1965 (except for private sidings since closed).

Wilton GWR opened with the commencement of services on the broad gauge single track line from Westbury to Salisbury in 1856. Sited on the northern edge of the town it was one of six intermediate stations opened through the Wylye valley. The others were Heytesbury, Codford, Wylye, Langford and Wishford. Conversion to standard gauge came in 1874. The suffix 'North' was added in September 1949. The line south to Salisbury was doubled as from 1896 and north to Wishford in 1901. Close by to the south was Wilton (South) LSWR station, which opened in 1859 on the Salisbury to Yeovil line.

The principal building on the up side (towards Westbury) was, like others on the Wylye line, of a

ABOVE Wilton GWR. Looking north west in about 1960 at the up platform (left) and the down island platform. The impressive covered footbridge links the platforms.

BELOW Wilton GWR. A Salisbury bound train stands at the down island platform erected in 1896 some forty years after the station opened.

Wilton LSWR. The main building on the up has survived in residential use; the signal box has been re-erected at Medstead & Four Marks on the Mid Hants Railway.

typical early GWR country station chalet style built of local stone with a tall chimney and small canopy. A small waiting shelter served passengers on the down island platform, behind which ran a loop line. The island platform and loop were introduced at the time of the 1896 line doubling. A large covered footbridge linked the platforms at the north west end; unusually the roof remained throughout the station's life. A goods yard with a large goods shed was sited to the north west of the station on the up side. Movements at the station and in sidings were controlled from a signal box on the down side, north-west of the down platform. A small lamp hut stood close to the footbridge on the down platform but this had gone by the mid 1950s.

Passenger numbers were relatively high in the early part of the twentieth century but then dropped dramatically. Such traffic was generated not only by local residents, travelling particularly to Salisbury, but also by visitors to the town itself and Wilton House. In 1903 22,994 passenger tickets were issued, a figure which had collapsed to 865 by 1933. As with Wilton LSWR (later South) this decline was partly attributed to competition of the local bus service to Salisbury, 3 miles to the east. Freight services at the station served the local wool trades, particularly the Wilton carpet factory, whilst the gas works and workhouse generated demands for coal supplies, brought in to Wilton through the two stations.

Passenger services ceased in September 1955 but general goods services continued for a further ten years. The main buildings and platforms were demolished soon after. Today the former station site and goods yard are in various industrial uses; the basic structure of the goods shed remains but with extensive alterations. It is occupied by Equishop, a saddlery and county clothing shop.

WILTON LSWR

OPENED: Passengers - 2nd May 1859 (with the opening of the Salisbury - Gillingham section of the Salisbury & Yeovil Railway to passenger traffic) goods - 1st September 1860.

CLOSED: Passengers - 7th March 1966.
Goods - 6th July 1964.

Sited in the north of the town, the station opened for passenger traffic in May 1859 with the commencement of services on the Salisbury to Gillingham section of the Salisbury & Yeovil Railway. Goods services started just over a year later. The suffix 'South' was added in September 1949. Close by, and to the north, was the Wilton GWR (later 'North') station on the Westbury to Salisbury line.

The main station building, incorporating the slate hung station master's house, was on the up (north) side of the curved line. Passengers on the down platform were served by a brick waiting shelter. Inter

Wilton LSWR. A view the 1960s. The footbridge roof over the main lines has gone. Note the small shelter on the down island platform. The 'Devon Belle' loop line is to the left.

platform connection was via an impressive covered footbridge immediately to the west of the main building; this extended south without a roof beyond the down platform over what was known as the down loop line. In later years the main footbridge lost its roof and glazed sides. To the east of the station, on the up side, was the goods yard with goods shed, dock and 2 ton capacity crane; cattle pens on the down side, also to the east of the station, were served by sidings linked to the down loop. Traffic movements were controlled from a typical early style LSWR signal box on the east end of the up platform, adjacent to the main building.

Both local residents of the historic capital town of Wessex and tourists visiting Wilton House generated passenger traffic at the station. The importance of visitors arriving by train was reflected in the comparative totals of passenger tickets issued and collected. In 1928 2,480 tickets were issued but by 1936 this had dropped to 917. In the same years 3,051 and 1,687 tickets were collected from arrivals at Wilton. The lower figures for 1936 were, without doubt, a result of the opening of local bus services to Salisbury only three miles to the east. Local industries generated considerable freight traffic, in particular the Wilton carpet factory and other wool trades. The local gas works and nearby work-house for a long period also brought rail borne coal supplies through the station. Wilton South closed to general goods traffic in July 1964 and to passengers just under two years later.

For a brief period in the late 1940s and early 1950s Wilton played an important role as the engine change point for the 'Devon Belle' express. This prestige Southern Railway train was first scheduled to stop at Sidmouth Junction but because of the lack of water troughs on the Southern Railway it was necessary on such a long journey either to stop and take on water or change engines. A stop at Salisbury was considered but rejected because of the potential for delay at such a busy station. Instead Wilton was selected, with the relief engine waiting in the down loop line; only six minutes was allowed for the engine change! The practice commenced in 1947 but only lasted until 1954 when the 'Devon Belle' service was withdrawn.

Today the line through Wilton retains its double track, the next passing point to the west being just east of Tisbury. The down platform, loop line and sidings have all gone, the land on that side being fenced off. The former up building (and platform) remain in place, but when visited in December 2003 a number of windows were boarded up and most of the building seemed unused and derelict. The signal box, which continued in use until 1981, was dismantled and re-erected at Medstead and Four Marks station on the Mid Hants (Watercress) Railway in Hampshire. The signalling and track control is now operated by the Panel at Salisbury.

Wishford. An early photograph soon after the line was doubled in 1901 at which time the up platform (left) and footbridge were added. The station master poses on the down platform as a train approaches from the Warminster direction.

WISHFORD

OPENED: 30th June 1856 (with the opening of the GWR Warminster - Salisbury (Fisherton) line).
CLOSED: Passengers and goods - 19th September 1955.

Wishford was one of six intermediate stations opened in the Wylye valley when services commenced on the broad gauge single track line between Warminster and Salisbury in 1856. The others were Heytesbury, Codford, Wylye, Langford and Wilton GWR. Conversion to standard gauge came in 1874, and the line here was doubled in 1901.

Sited on the south-west edge of Great Wishford where the Wylye valley turns south towards Wilton, the principal building on the down platform was, like others on the Wylye line, of a typical early GWR country station chalet style built of local stone with a tall chimney and small canopy. It was a design used on many parts of the GWR at that time and similar to that which is preserved today on the West Somerset Railway at Bishops Lydeard. A smaller building with a chimney and small canopy served passengers on the up platform (towards Westbury), installed after the line was doubled. A covered footbridge constructed in about 1901 linked the two platforms at the northern end.

Freight traffic at Wishford was catered for in a goods yard to the south of the station on the down side. Cattle pens, and a dock were served by sidings on the up side south of the station. A 1901 GWR style brick and wooden signal box on the down side between the station and goods shed remained in use until about 1968, but the sidings were lifted in 1961. The station master's house, an impressive structure, stood north of the station on the down side.

As with other stations on the Wylye valley line passenger numbers fell greatly between 1903 and 1933. In 1903 12,340 tickets were issued, and by 1933 only 3,944. Over the period the local population declined and there was growing competition from buses which ran through the valley villages. Both passenger and freight services ceased at Wishford in September 1955. Today no trace can be seen of former railway activity at line-side; however the former station master's house is still in residential use as 'Station House', and a mural of a railway scene adorns the front wall.

Woodborough. An early photograph looking west of staff and passengers on both platforms. A small cube shaped store is to the west of the main building and a wooden shelter serves passengers travelling towards Newbury (right). Note the large goods shed.

WOODBOROUGH

OPENED: 11th November 1862 (with the opening of the Berks & Hants Extension Railway from Hungerford to Devizes).

CLOSED: Passengers - 18th April 1966.
Goods - 15th August 1966 (coal depot only from 19th May 1964).

In the heart of the Vale of Pewsey, Woodborough station, which opened in November 1862 with the commencement of services on the Berks & Hants Extension Railway (B&HER), was well placed to serve a number of villages and hamlets in this rich agricultural area. During the planning of the Railway a number of settlements sought to have a station, one example being Patney (see Patney text). The B&HER decided however that Woodborough could by itself serve this central part of the Vale. Sited to the south of Woodborough village, the station was, in the mid 1860s, provided with a passing loop on the otherwise single track broad gauge line. The line was converted to standard gauge at the end of June 1874 and was doubled through Woodborough in 1899.

The principal building, standing on the down platform, was of a typical Berks & Hants 'Elizabethan' style; it was similar to other stations on the line but smaller, for instance, than that at Pewsey. Two tall chimney stacks rose above the slate roof. At various times further small structures were erected on the platform, including a wooden building used primarily as a store. In the early days a small cube-shaped building stood on the platform; this was later replaced by a brick structure. Passengers on the up platform were served by a wooden shelter with a roof sloping back. No footbridge was ever provided at Woodborough. A rail level board crossing provided an inter platform link at the west end of the platforms. Inter platform movement was also possible via the approach road to each platform and the road bridge at the east end of the station.

The sidings and associated freight facilities evolved gradually over the years. Initially in the broad gauge era the principal siding was on the down side west of the station; this ran through a large goods shed. The width of the shed doors indicated its design for use by broad gauge trucks. The shed incorporated a 30 cwt capacity wooden crane. Subsequently a small siding was added running back to a dock at the west end of the down platform. In 1903 a further siding was added south of the goods shed. Two sidings were also provided west of the station on the up side; beside the outer one was a 5 ton capacity crane. By the early years of the twentieth century the siding layout was virtually complete.

Freight exports from Woodborough were almost entirely related to local agriculture, including hay, straw, sacked grain and milk in churns. The last was

Woodborough. A slightly later photograph, looking east, with staff posing for the camera on both platforms. An extra wooden store has been erected beyond the main building on the down platform (right).

particularly important between the two World Wars with milk churns being taken to the London area from Woodborough, either on special milk trains calling at the station or on passenger trains. Livestock movements were never high and no special facilities, such as cattle pens, were installed at the station. Considerable quantities of wood from a local saw mill were handled at Woodborough; initially this was not possible because of the lack of a large capacity crane. At that time traffic continued to use the Kennet and Avon Canal, some two miles to the north, and of great importance for the handling of all goods in the Vale of Pewsey prior to the coming of the railway. Coal and agricultural fertilisers were the principal goods imported through the station yard. A number of local firms collected and delivered goods to the station, originally by horse and cart and then by lorry. At one time a GWR delivery lorry was based at the station.

Incoming traffic was boosted during the First World War by aircraft sections from the aero factory at Bristol. A training school for the Royal Flying Corps, as it was then known, was established at

Woodborough. A much later view west on 4th September 1965. All the principal buildings on both platforms remain as does the large goods shed.

Upavon, five miles away, and aircraft in a dismantled form were delivered to the station and then taken by steam lorry to Upavon for re-assembly.

This variety of goods traffic, not only in the yard, but also at the station itself, was reflected in the relatively high figures for the number of parcels handled at Woodborough. This rose from 28,456 in 1903 to 116,250 in 1933. In contrast passenger traffic dropped over the same period: 16,124 tickets were issued in 1903, and 6,694 in 1933.

During the Second World War a new long down loop line was constructed west of the goods yard. The long former up siding was also lengthened and converted to a loop. Both loops came into operation in 1944 and were designed to improve capacity on the otherwise two track line to ease the movements of increased war-time traffic. Both these loops were extended further in April 1979, the down loop extension being back through the former goods yard to the station site. A short trailing siding was also added. Finally during the 1970s two further parallel sidings were added west of Woodborough, primarily for use by engineers working in the area.

Traffic movements at the station, in the sidings and later on the loops, were controlled from a signal box at the west end of the up platform. The first box was replaced by a larger box virtually on the same site and operative as from September 1944, coinciding with the coming into operation of the two loops west of the station. The base of the old box was retained for use as a store for coal used on fires in the signal box and in the station offices.

Passenger trains ceased to call at Woodborough in April 1966 with the withdrawal of services on the Devizes line; goods facilities were withdrawn four months later. The goods yard had only operated as a coal depot since May 1964. From November 1965 the station was unstaffed, a contrast to the 1903-1938 period when an average of seven to eight staff were employed at the station.

Today although virtually all trace of the former station and goods yard has gone, the site is still a focus for much railway activity with loops and sidings still in operation. On both sides of the main West Country lines the former station site is used by railway engineers. A small brick building and a telecommunications mast occupy the site of the former down platform and main building. The only traces of the earlier era are small sections of the former up side retaining wall near to the road bridge and a small length of old railway fencing close to this old wall.

WOOTTON BASSETT

OPENED: 30th July 1841 (on the Hay Lane - Chippenham section of the GWR opened through this site two months earlier on 31st May 1841).

CLOSED: Passengers - 4th January 1965.
Goods - 4th October 1965 (coal depot only from 19th May 1964).

A section of the broad gauge GWR from London (Paddington) opened from Faringdon Road (Oxon) to Hay Lane, some 2½ miles east of Wootton Bassett, in December 1840. The line west from Hay Lane opened as far as Chippenham in May 1841 and through Box Tunnel to Bath in June 1841, thus completing the through route to Bristol. Hay Lane (or Wootton Bassett Road as it was also known) continued to serve Wootton Bassett and the surrounding rural area until 30th July 1841, on which date Wootton Bassett station opened on the south edge of the small market town.

This 1841 structure was a small station with up and down platforms, on each of which stood one of Brunel's 'chalet style' buildings built of local stone. It is likely that the architects was one of Brunel's pupils. A small goods yard was provided west of the station on the up (towards Swindon) side; the yard included a goods shed and a head shunt siding leading to a loading dock. On the opposite down side of the line was a single trailing siding, the up and down main lines being connected by a trailing cross-over at the west end of the station. In about 1873 a small brick signal box was erected on the west end of

Wootton Bassett. A rare but poor quality view east towards Swindon of the original station buildings, including the Brunel chalet style structure on the up platform and the large goods shed (left).

ABOVE Wootton Bassett. Staff pose in this view east in about 1919. The main building is on the up platform (left). Note the integral roof and canopy, a contrast to other stations on the Badminton cut off line where separate canopies were the norm.

BELOW Wootton Bassett. A fine view looking west of the station just before the opening in 1903 of the cut off line from just west of the station through Badminton to the Bristol - South Wales line at Patchway. Note the impressive covered footbridge.

Wootton Bassett. No 5369, a Churchward 2-6-0 passing through in a westward direction on 28th April 1961. The nameboard is in need of repair.

the down platform; this was enlarged at the end of 1887, by which time amendments had been made to the original sidings and points layout.

These relatively small scale facilities continued until the early 1900s. The catalyst for major changes was the construction and opening in 1903 of the Bristol & South Wales Direct Railway from a junction immediately to the west of Wootton Bassett station to Patchway, north of Bristol on the Bristol to South Wales line. Often known as the Badminton line (one of the stations on the new line), this was one of the GWR's cut off routes, in this case giving a shorter more direct route from Swindon to the Severn Tunnel and South Wales rather than via Chippenham, Bath and Bristol. A tender of £4,409 was awarded to Eli Hadley & Sons of Stafford, the work involving not only the construction of a new station but also the demolition of the old and the provision of temporary facilities during the construction period. The work by Hadleys only related to the buildings, as the major modifications to the track at the station and the junction were undertaken by the GWR itself.

Renamed 'Wootton Bassett Junction' as from 1st July 1903 (when passenger services commenced on the Badminton Line), the up and down platforms were surmounted by red brick buildings with large integral roofs and fretted canopies and each topped by two chimneys. The principal facilities, including a ladies' waiting room, general waiting room, booking office, parcels office, station master's office and toilets, were incorporated in the up side building. The down platform building incorporated a general waiting room, a ladies' waiting room and toilets. The main station approach road led from the north end of a road bridge east of the station behind the up platform to a goods yard west of the station. A minor approach road led to the rear of the down platform. The platforms were linked by an impressive covered footbridge east of the station buildings, the cover being constructed by Hadleys and the main structure being provided by the GWR in the Company's then standard design. A footbridge had been originally provided in 1880 and it is not certain whether this original bridge was re-used in the 1902/1903 reconstruction of Wootton Bassett.

The goods yard incorporated a small goods shed and loading platform, cattle pens and a 1 ton capacity crane. A head shunt led east from a goods loop line to a loading ramp behind the west end of the up platform. Located at the heart of an important agricultural area, a considerable volume of goods traffic was handled including fertiliser, grain, livestock and coal. Timber generated considerable trade and an open stacking area was provided at the Chippenham end of the station on the down side.

Movements at the enlarged new station and at the junction were controlled by two signalboxes, Wootton Bassett East and West. The West Box, immediately to the west of the Badminton line junction, came into use on in November 1901; the slightly larger East Box on the down line west of the station and east of the junction opened in July 1902, at which time the original 1873 box closed. The 1901/1902 boxes closed on 24th March 1968. A 22,500 gallon water tower was also erected on the up side soon after 1903 providing water for both the station and locomotives.

Levels of passenger traffic were comparatively high at Wootton Bassett: in 1903 55,263 tickets were issued, and in 1933 32,112.

In charge of this busy station was a station master who originally supervised some twenty other employees, including ten signalmen at boxes in the Wootton Bassett area. The remaining staff included two general clerks, two goods shunters, three porters, one goods checker and one van man. The van man is of interest as, by 1930, the GWR had established Wootton Bassett as a centre for one of its country lorry services, with a lorry based at the station operating over a wide country area; the concept was to provide an integrated rail and road service. Also at about this time a new warehouse was provided in the goods yard. A new road to the warehouse, additional gates and revamped fencing were also installed.

After the Second World War traffic at Wootton Bassett continued at a reasonable level. An article, published in 1955, indicated that by that time a corrugated iron building had been erected on the site of the former cattle pens, a late addition for the storage of grain and animal feedstuffs. The article also indicated that in the mid 1950s about 200 trains passed through the station every day, over 500 passengers from the local area used the station per week and over the same period 300 parcels and 100 tons of freight were handled. The principal traffic at that time was, however, milk with nearly 15,500 gallons sent to London from the adjacent factory every week. A private siding had served this United Dairies Creamery as from 1931.

Passenger services ceased at Wootton Bassett in early January 1965 with the withdrawal of local Bristol to Swindon trains. General goods services had ceased in May 1964 but a coal depot remained rail-linked until October 1965. Today sidings west of Wootton Bassett, close to the junction, continue in use associated with movement of stone aggregates by Mendip Rail to Johnson Aggregates. All trace of the station buildings has gone, demolition taking place soon after closure in the mid 1960s. Much of the station site on the up side is used as a rail maintenance depot by Carillion Rail.

WOOTTON RIVERS HALT

OPENED: 24th September 1928 (on the Newbury - Patney & Chirton line originally opened by the Berks & Hants Extension Railway through this site in 1862).

CLOSED: 18th April 1966.

The halt, opening in September 1928 on the original Berks & Hants Extension Railway, was sited at the southern edge of Wootton Rivers close to the south bank of the Kennet and Avon Canal. By its opening this section of line had, for over 30 years, served as part of the GWR London (Paddington) to West Country route via Newbury and Westbury. The halt stood between the stations of Savernake Low Level to the east and Pewsey to the west, and initially comprised two 200 ft long wooden platforms each with a corrugated iron shelter. Subsequently the wooden platforms were replaced in part by concrete components.

The platforms were slightly staggered in position, the up platform being closer to the road bridge, east of the halt, that carried a minor road from Wootton Rivers to Milton Lilbourne and Pewsey. The stagger

Wootton Rivers Halt. The entrance to the down side platform behind the metal shelter. The notice indicates that tickets can be obtained from the agent at 8 Wootton Rivers.

Wootton Rivers Halt. Looking east at the slightly staggered platforms. The entrance to the down platform (right) was on the photographer's side of the metal shelter whilst that to the up was close to the road bridge. Both entrances can be identified today as can the site of the down platform.

was required to allow level access to both platforms, that to the up side leading to the east end of the platform and that to the down leading to the centre of the platform behind the shelter. Lighting on the platforms was by two pressurised oil lamps on tall posts. The estimated cost of the halt's original construction was £740. In June 1934 a 6 lever signal box was opened some fifty yards west of the up platform; the box was provided in order to increase the capacity of the line and was in operation only at busy times. It was closed from 1939 to 1949 and ceased operation as from 6th October 1963.

Passenger traffic peaked in 1930 when 2,865 tickets were issued, giving receipts of £227. A local agent at 8 Wootton Rivers issued the tickets, a fact revealed on notice boards at the entrances to the halt. Photographs suggest that milk churns were also loaded onto trains at the halt but no records of such traffic are known. Passenger services ceased in April 1966 with the withdrawal of local stopping services on the line. Today the access points to both platforms are clearly to be seen, as is the site of the down side platform; at the down side entrance a post is probably a survivor of the old gate into the site.

WYLYE

OPENED: 30th June 1856 (with the opening of the GWR Warminster - Salisbury (Fisherton) line).
CLOSED: Passengers - 19th September 1955.
Goods - 2nd October 1961.

Wylye (Wiley until August 1874) was one of six intermediate stations opened in the valley of the same name when services commenced on the single track broad gauge line between Warminster and Salisbury in 1856. The other stations in the valley were Heytesbury, Codford, Wishford, Langford and Wilton GWR. Conversion to standard gauge came in 1874. The line was doubled west towards Codford in 1900 and east towards Wishford in the following

Wylye. A close up of the buildings on the down platform including the cast iron gent's urinal to the left of the main building.

Wylye. Looking east, the main building with a very tall chimney is on the down side serving passengers travelling towards Salisbury. Beyond is the broad gauge era goods shed. The tall water tower stands at the west end of the up platform.

year. The station was on the southern edge of Wylye village, immediately west of a level crossing carrying a minor road south to Dinton.

The principal station building, on the down platform (towards Salisbury) was, like others on the Wylye valley line, of a typical early GWR chalet style built of local stone with a tall chimney and small canopy. It was a design used on many parts of the GWR at that time and similar to that which is preserved on the West Somerset Railway at Bishops Lydeard. Also on the down platform, west of the building, was a small metal shed and a cast iron gentlemen's urinal. A small shelter served passengers on the up platform, installed after the line was doubled; this platform was enhanced for some years by elegant topiary. A tall water tank stood at the west end.

Catering for freight traffic generated largely by the local agriculture, a goods yard with a large goods shed was sited east of the station on the down side. The wide arch of the goods shed rail entrance indicated its origin in the broad gauge era. A typical GWR brick and timber signal box also stood east of the station but on the up side adjacent to a level crossing The original box dated from 1877 but this was replaced in 1943 when a larger frame was required to control three sidings that were laid parallel to the up refuge siding east of the station and level crossing. These sidings served the RAF Grovely Wood Depot and were in use until about 1951. The box closed in April 1982 when the 1973 level crossing barriers were automated. The down refuge siding ran parallel to the main line, a little to the west of the station.

The pattern of passenger traffic at Wylye was similar to that at other stations in the valley: from a total of 11,483 tickets issued in 1903, the number fell to 5,314 in 1933. The fall in the 1930s is attributed to competition from bus services on the parallel main road. Passenger services ceased in September 1955 but goods facilities continued at Wylye for a further six years until October 1961. Today there is virtually no trace of former railway activity at Wylye station as trains pass through between Warminster and Salisbury. A small section of the signal box brick base can be seen adjacent to the level crossing on the up side; the former station site and approach road are in private ownership and not accessible.

FURTHER READING

Bartholomew D., *Midland & South Western Junction Railway*, Volume 1, Wild Swan, 1982

Bray N.S.M., *The Devizes Branch*, Picton Publishing, 1984

Bryan T., *Return to Swindon*, Avon Anglia 1990

Butt R.V.J., *Directory of Railway Stations*, Patrick Stephens, 1995

Christiansen R., *A Regional History of the Railways of Great Britain, Volume 13 Thames and Severn*, David & Charles, 1981

Clark R.H., *An Historical Survey of Selected Great Western Railway Stations, Layouts and Illustrations*, Oxford Publishing Co, *Volume 1* 1976, *Volume 2* 1979, *Volume 3* 1981

Clinker C.R., *Register of Closed Passenger Stations and Goods Depots 1830-1977*, Avon Anglia, 1978

Dale P., *Wiltshire's Lost Railways*, Stenlake Publishing, 2002

Fenton D.M., *The Malmesbury Railway*, Oakwood Press, 1977

Hale M., *'Twixt London and Bristol*, Oxford Publishing Company, 1985

Leigh C., *GWR Country Stations*, Ian Allan, Volume 1 1981/1985, Volume 2 1984

Maggs C.G.,
Branch Lines of Wiltshire, Alan Sutton, 1992
Railways of the Cotswolds, Peter Nicholson, 1981
Rail Centres: Swindon, Ian Allan, 1983
The Calne Branch, Wild Swan Publications, 1990
The GWR Swindon to Bath Line, Sutton Publishing Ltd, 2003
The Midland & South Western Junction Railway, David and Charles, 1967
The Swindon to Gloucester Line, Alan Sutton, 1991

Maggs C.G. and Beale G., *The Camerton Branch*, Wild Swan Publications, 1985

Measom G., *The Illustrated Guide to the Great Western Railway*, W. Marshall & Sons, 1852 and Berkshire County Library, 1983

Mitchell V. and Smith K., *Basingstoke to Salisbury*, Middleton Press, 1991
Branch Lines around Wimborne, Middleton Press, 1992
Branch Lines of West Wiltshire, Middleton Press, 2003
Cheltenham to Andover, Middleton Press, 2000
Didcot to Swindon, Middleton Press, 2002
Fareham to Salisbury via Eastleigh, Middleton Press, 1989
Salisbury to Westbury, Middleton Press, 1994
Salisbury to Yeovil, Middleton Press, 1992
Swindon to Bristol via Bath Spa, Middleton Press, 2002
Swindon to Newport, Middleton Press, 2004
Westbury to Bath, Middleton Press, 1995
Westbury to Taunton, Middleton Press, 2002

Mitchell V. and Smith K., in association with Robertson K., *Newbury to Westbury*, Middleton Press, 2001

Phillips D., *Westbury to Weymouth Line*, Oxford Publishing Co., 1994

Phillips D. and Pryer G., *Salisbury to Exeter Line*, Oxford Publishing Co., 1997

Potts C., *An Historical Survey of Selected Great Western Railway Stations*, Oxford Publishing Co, Volume 4 1985

Priddle R. and Hyde D., *GWR to Devizes*, Millstream Books, 1996

Robertson K., *Great Western Railway Halts, Volume 1* Irwell Press, 1990, *Volume 2* KRB Publications 2002
Wiltshire Railways in Old Photographs, Alan Sutton, 1988

Robertson K and Abbott D., *GWR The Badminton Line*, Alan Sutton, 1988
The Marlborough Branch, Irwell Press, 1990

Roose G. and Ballantyne H., *British Railways Past & Present No 22 Wiltshire*, Past & Present Publishing Ltd, 1994

Sands T.B., *The Midland & South Western Junction Railway*, Oakwood Press, 1959

Smith T.M. and Heathcliffe G.S., *The Highworth Branch*, Wild Swan, 1979
Stretton J., *The Swindon & Cricklade Railway*, Past & Present Publishing Ltd, 2003
Strong P., *Woodborough,* Backtrack, Volume 17 No. 3, March 2003
Tanner G., *The Calne Branch*, Oxford Publishing Co., 1972
Thomas D.St.J., *Regional History of the Railways of Great Britain, Volume 1 The West Country*, David & Charles, 1981
Waters L., *GWR Then & Now*, Ian Allan Publishing, *Vol 1* 1994, *Vol* 2 2002
Wikeley N. and Middleton J., *Railway Stations, Southern Region*, Peco Publications, 1971
Vaughan A., *Great Western Architecture: A Pictorial Record*, Oxford Publishing Co, 1977

ACKNOWLEDGEMENTS

The author is very grateful for the permission to use photographs from the following collections: Lens of Sutton (inc photographs taken by J. L. Smith, the owner of Lens of Sutton); pages 25 (top), 27 (bottom), 41 (top), 41 (bottom), 45 (top), 45 (bottom), 48, 50 (top), 51, 55 (top), 56, 58, 60, 61, 64 (bottom), 65, 68, 69 (top), 72 (top), 72 (bottom), 74, 75 (top), 76, 79, 80, 81 (top), 81 (bottom), 84, 90 (bottom), 100 (middle), 104, 110 (middle), 112 (top), 122 (middle), 128 (middle), 130 (bottom), 131, 133, 137 (top), 143, 144 (top), 145, 146, 147, 154 (bottom), 155: National Railway Museum/ LGRP; pages 13, 18 (top left), 47, 59, 100 (top), 105 (top right), 105 (middle right), 128 (bottom): Michael Hale; pages 12, 16, 21, 22 (top), 23, 29, 34, 49 (top), 66, 71, 78, 93 (bottom), 94, 97 (top), 115, 116, 122 (top), 124, 125, 138, 152: Colin Caddy; pages 20, 35, 40, 50 (bottom), 55 (bottom), 57, 85, 99, 112 (bottom), 120 (bottom), 123, 136, 140 (top), 149 (bottom): Colin Maggs; pages 26, 28, 33, 46, 96, 127: R. K. Blencowe; pages 15, 52, 83, 102, 118: P. J. Garland (via Roger Carpenter); page 53: E. T. Gill (via R. K. Blencowe); page 135 (top): J.Moss (via Roger Carpenter); pages 67 (top right), 69 (bottom), 73, 105 (top left): H. F. Wheeler (via Roger Carpenter); page 43: Roger Carpenter; page 119: M. Tozer; pages 36, 139 (top): Stations UK (Douglas Thompson); pages 39, 89, 97 (bottom), 108 (top), 114, 154 (top).

The remaining photographs were taken by the author or are from his collection where the copyright owner is unknown or unclear.